C000283181

Secrets

of

Planet Earth

Secrets
of
Planet Earth

H-A

channelled by

Tony Neate

Eye of Gaza Press

Secrets of Planet Earth

This edition was first published in Great Britain in 2009

Copyright © 2008   Tony Neate

Cover design copyright © 2008   Alan Hancock

IBSN number 978-1-873545 058

Compiled and arranged by Greg Branson

Edited by Ann Neate

Published by
Eye of Gaza Press,
BCM - New Age, London, WC1N 3XX
heliosc@dialstart.net   0207 713 7159

CONTENTS

TONY NEATE

Tony Neate is the well-known and respected channeller of H-A. He has brought this wisdom from the higher levels of consciousness since the 1950's. The teachings have been published in a number of books, including *New Dimensions in Healing* and *The Guide Book*.

He co-founded the Atlantean Society in 1957 with Murry Hope. In the 1970's he ran a health food business with his wife, Ann. In 1975 he became interested in the complementary treatment of cancer when his mother died of stomach cancer. He had the good fortune to tour Europe with Dr Alec Forbes, a retired consultant physician and first Medical Director of the Bristol Cancer Centre, visiting Dr Hans Moolenburgh in Holland and Dr Hans Nieper in German, both specialists in the field.

In 1979 he co-founded the Nature's Own/Cytoplan group producing nutritional supplements to the highest ethical standards. In the early 1980's Tony directed a Cancer Help Centre in Cheltenham with his wife and Dr John Cosh. He later became Chair of the Holistic Council for Cancer, and succeeded the late Sir George Trevelyan as Chair of the Wrekin Trust. He was also chair of the Council of a Rudolf Steiner school for 6 years.

In 1981, Tony co-founded Runnings Park Centre for Healing and Self-development in Malvern, which ran for 21 years, and also the College of Healing which continues to provide a highly accredited Healing Course. He also co-founded the Confederation of Healing Organisations.

In 1990, he started the School for Channelling, and is now its patron. Tony was then commissioned by Piatkus Books to write *Channelling for Everyone*. Currently, Tony acts as Spiritual Advisor to the Helios Foundation in London and he is the Chair of the Spirit Release Foundation.

INTRODUCTION

I met Tony Neate three years ago at a conference organised by the Spirit Release Foundation of which he is the chair. There was instant recognition. I had read some of his books when I came to London in the early 70's but they dealt with spiritual concepts that did not, at the time, resonate with me. I thought, "What on earth has 6th plane consciousness and Atlantis to do with the issues I am facing in my life today?" And so I went towards another respected trance medium, Maisie Besant who channelled Akhenaten, a much more practical spirit communicator. Together, we started the Helios Community in a single room in London and I was privileged to work closely with her until she retired in 2004, aged 96.

The Helios initiative had continued to grow and was now situated in rather more impressive premises in Kings Cross. As the Centre had always been inspired by spirit, we needed a replacement for Maisie's spiritual advice. Tony was clearly the man for this. I dug out my old H-A books and, in revisiting them, began to see the teachings in a new light. It became clear that I was required to compile this book and so promptly set about probing H-A to fill in the gaps and to bring the teachings fully up to date.

It is a synthesis of 52 years of trance transmissions, hundreds of them, first of all for 'The Atlanteans' and then for the Runnings Park Community. There is a deep vein of wisdom underpinning the teaching, truths that are vital for humanity to hear as we move towards 2012 and then open up to the Aquarian age of individual illumination and empowerment. I wanted the book to be comprehensive and fully integrated so that, by the end, the reader would have a thorough understanding of where humanity came from, why we are facing such severe upheavals today, and what we can do to extricate ourselves from the unbalanced Piscean age ways of control and divisiveness, so that we can move forward strongly and peacefully in the decades to come. I trust I have succeeded.

Over the years many other people have channelled H-A, and I would like to thank Gilly Wilmot, David Furlong and Frida Siton for the extracts from their transmissions that I have included. There are also two large sections from Akhenaten channelled through Maisie Besant. Thanks also to Alan Hancock for his delightful cover and to Tony's wife, Ann, whose stringent editing was invaluable.

Greg Branson

Chapter 1

IN THE BEGINNING

Defining God

Throughout these teachings, I will frequently allude to God, the Ultimate, the creative force from which all originates. I would like to offer you a concept of this state of beingness which can be comprehended by the human mind in its present stage of evolution. I use the term 'Ultimate' because, as you understand these things, it stands for a certain stage of evolution. When reaching a level of thought which can be regarded as the Ultimate, one enters into a completely unlimited understanding of all things, for the Ultimate is a creative, infinite thought force through which all cause and effect takes place.

I could describe it as being a state of thought perfection. However, this can be misleading if one chooses to accept the last two words literally, as I mean perfection of evolution in the sense that one's whole thought in itself reaches a stage of perfect infinity. In other words, it can progress unlimited by barriers. As a creative, timeless and limitless thought it has no beginning and no end, so progress at its level goes on and on into infinity. Hence your biblical reference to 'eternal life'.

One must realise that in this state of ultimate thought, the individuality is retained and, in addition to this state of unlimited perfection, there is also complete harmony and at-one-ment with the whole. This state is neither male nor female but a perfect blending of both principles, the positive and negative, the Father/Mother God. It is extremely difficult to further develop this in Earth terms, to explain how the spirit continues to evolve in this state, for the forms of experience encountered are completely beyond the comprehension of the physical brain. I can only put it to you thus:

1

The universe is infinite and everything in the universe is also infinite; and, by that, I mean that the Ultimate Being is infinite, all the planes are infinite and there are an infinite number of spirits, each one unique. Therefore, in that Ultimate state, thought stretches into the greatness of that infinite universe to understand and encounter every experience that has been, is, and will be. It is a state of unified comprehension of all planes and levels of thought.

In order to deepen your understanding I would advise you to read this several times, then close your eyes and meditate. Try to uplift your mind and broaden your concepts so that the inspiration behind such a profound state of Ultimate Beingness can penetrate your consciousness and help you to translate its magnitude into that which your mind can cope with.

The Significance of the Sun
I have no doubt that all of you know that pleasant feeling of wellbeing which comes to you on a sunny day. It makes you feel energetic and full of the joy of life; but have you considered whether it is purely its physical effect that makes the Sun so warm and comforting? If you go back to earlier civilisations you will find that a great many people have worshipped the Sun. To you today this may seem rather strange, indeed, rather eccentric behaviour, but many of those people of old knew what they were doing.

That does not mean that I am suggesting that you rush out of your homes tomorrow morning with your meditation mat and kneel under the rays of the morning Sun — though there is a very effective yoga practice that does just that; for theirs is a tradition that stretches back to those early times when people realised the Sun's esoteric significance. They had a far greater instinctive understanding of the universe than you have today. They knew that the Sun was the fountain source of their own particular solar system and in their way they were acknowledging that fact.

The Sun is the giver of life to your planetary group. From that strange gaseous mass has emanated each planet in the solar system. I say that with some reservation, as there are other masses within the solar system which are not regarded by your astronomers as planets because they are too small. If one is going to be absolutely factual, one

2

must take into account that many of these other masses have not emanated from the Sun but have been attracted and captured by the magnetic forces surrounding your solar system.

Since each of the planets in your solar system has emanated from the Sun you will appreciate that everything which happens to each of them affects the Sun; and, as a natural sequence, all that takes place within the precincts of the Sun affects each one of these planets. Everything you think and do, as an individual, has an effect, however small, on your entire planet and on the Sun itself. You can see how your whole solar system is a compact unit in itself, somewhat similar in structure to the atom.

The Planes of Existence
So that you can expand your understanding on these matters it is necessary for me to detail the various levels of frequency that exist beyond what you perceive as physical reality.

7ᵗʰ **Plane.** As I see it, this is the Plane of Supreme Wisdom, the ultimate reality, which means, the final evolutionary state in *this* universe. While being at one with God, each spirit retains a certain amount of individuality and yet is in complete harmony with all other thought. The Godhead is an expanding force and each spirit, having reached that stage of fineness, of breadth of thought and understanding, adds to the infinity of experience within the Godhead. The spirit itself continues to expand in complete harmony and oneness, until it is merged to such greatness that there are no words to describe it. God is neither male nor female, but a balanced blending of both qualities - the perfect androgynous state – the Father/Mother complete.

6ᵗʰ **Plane.** This Plane of Light is where a spirit will eventually experience its last contact with the physical vibration before facing the overwhelming experience that accompanies surrender to the liberated nature of the Godhead where dark and light are in precise alignment, in perfect balance. It is the realm of the Christ presence, and the other great archetypal energies. It is a plane of collective thought from whence all significant teachings emanate. It requires being intimately in touch with the essence of mind and also the vastness of creation, where the true expression of the spirit enables both an absolute devotion to the Creator as well as a willingness to take full responsibility for the advancement of some significant part of creation.

5th Plane.　This, I call the Plane of Illumination, where the spirit receives profound spiritual understanding and is uplifted by the beauty and the wonder, the knowledge and the wisdom of spiritual advancement. On its more subtle levels, you will find the archangels and those of advanced human evolution. Some developing spirits choose to go on towards the divine Source, while others turn back to help those coming along behind. All the truly great teachers come from this plane, Jesus, Buddha, Mohammed, Krishna and so on. They are inspired by sixth plane collective thought and so are able, while living in a human position of simplicity, to command great forces and channel inspiration that ranges far and influences many. As a motivating force they may be found behind any large grouping of Earth people, coming always from a position of balance.

Other master souls on their own level may be influencing religious sects such as the Sufis, or the Theosophical Society, and they will always be there to provide a unifying presence behind political activity on Earth. They are especially needed now to establish harmonious world order.

On this plane, a spirit will experience things not known before: states of quite exquisite beauty and sublime peace that exist only in the embrace of the divine. It will realise that all things are possible with God, and that understanding will lead it into a state of deep reflection as a preparation for the great leap of faith that is needed to progress further.

4th Plane.　This is the Plane of Teaching and Learning, a plane of finding new inspiration and new levels of understanding that can be unlocked. It is where the creative gifts develop and find expansion. Here, the mental body encases the spirit which exists now in a quite different kind of environment. There are not the bounds and limitations of the kind experienced on Earth, nor the emotional restrictions found in the astral. There is a much greater freedom to be and do exactly what you wish, but still, the creative purpose of existence tends to have a practical edge. This is the plane where cause and effect begin to become one. All sorts of refined experience is available. The spirit will encounter new vibrant colours, transcendental sounds and there will be contact with the beings of light that have been but figments of the imagination until now. There is much greater definition while, at the same time, the universal nature of thought can start to be experienced and understood. Because of this, altruism begins to arise for all are one and no one can truly progress on their own.

3rd **Plane.** This is the Plane of Transition, where you go when you leave the physical body. It is the 'Summerland' of the spiritualists and, as such, a plane of expectation where desires and fears and misconceptions become manifest. In many ways, it is a world of illusion where many of the structures of Earth are replicated by the mind. If you expect to be in heaven when you pass over, then you will be. If you do not believe you have died, you will continue to live, to an extent, as you lived before. It is the world experienced by the astral body, which is what remains active when the physical and etheric bodies have fallen away.

You meet up with spirits whom you have already known and, you will spend time assessing your life on Earth. You may decide to stay in this transitional state for a long period, thousands of years even, or you may move on very quickly – and I am speaking here of a spirit that is going through its normal evolutionary pattern. There are other spirits on its higher frequencies carrying out special missions for the further development of this particular plane.

Some spirits who were taught on Earth that they can expect to spend the rest of eternity in 'heaven' may be reluctant to leave; others are caught up with members of their own kind in a 'hell' of their own making; but eventually the impulse to progress will be felt. It is entirely the individual's choice. A spirit will remain there until it feels that it is possible to go ahead and experience further and will then choose where it wants to be. Some return into further Earth incarnation without first ascending into higher planes, but for those of mature spiritual development this is not usual or, in most cases, advisable. If it is decided to ascend then the rate of vibration becomes finer and the thought state moves at a faster speed and you transfer into a body of a higher frequency.

5

2nd Plane.   The Plane of Physical Existence, which encompasses both physical and etheric frequencies. I am not restricting this to human experience because it includes all other forms of physical evolution on your planet. The range of your physical senses is limited so that you can concentrate on the experiences to be had and lessons to be learnt within the human form. But there is another, more subtle, range of vibrational experience that enables your spirit to oversee your physical experience by providing an additional body that is a subtle counterpart of the physical. And so, whatever happens to your physical body, this finer etheric body will continue to provide the impetus for its proper alignment and functioning according to the karmic direction that you came into life to effect.

1st Plane.   The Plane of Pre-physical Existence or it could be called the Plane of Decision. When an individual spirit first comes into being it has no awareness of physical experience. It resides within patterns of intention that will, in due course, include the physical plane; but much experience has to be completed in other dimensions before this can occur. The spirit needs to embark on a stream of individualised experience enabling it to prepare for living on a planet such as your Earth.

When first created by the Godhead, each unique spirit is granted free will and choice. If it is wise it will go through a long period of prephysical experience where it will learn about the universe, and it will also learn much about itself. It may send probes into the physical plane within electricity, say, or into some form of the elements of fire, water, air and earth, into a wellspring, perhaps, or into an individual cell. These experiences will prepare the way for incarnation in physical form which will be necessary in order to take the next step forward. It may choose to experience life as a dolphin. It may choose to be a tree. It may choose a human body. That is its choice. And, although most spirits will follow through a particular kingdom, if they have, for example, chosen *homo sapiens*, there will always be the choice available to incarnate into a different form of experience later on.

There are many forms of evolution co-existing, the human, the animal, the plant life, the elemental life and so on, and each stream relates to the earth and the heavens in a quite specific way. In order to confirm the form of evolution that an individual spirit will evolve through, it will decide on this pre-physical plane which planet will become its home, perhaps over many lives. It will choose the life form that will best suit its development and purpose. In this cauldron of creative possibility, the evolutionary momentum is set up that will sustain the directional impulse behind whatever choice is made. Everything that enables parallel streams of evolution to progress and integrate is developed here, for the stuff of material existence has to be drawn out of the earth to support any spiritual manifestation.

So, this realm not only differentiates between the various life forms, it sets the scene for the spirit's progression into physical experience and there it will move forward on its spiritual journey. This could include incarnating into different racial forms to those that have been experienced previously, or a different gender, thereby gaining understanding of the complementary nature of physical evolution. All these continuing developmental patterns have their roots in a collective realm of decision.

8th **Plane.** Now, in order to extend this still further I would like to introduce another concept, the 'Absolute', a word which I have tended not to use in the past because I find it is generally used on your planet to define something that denotes a very specific perfection. On the Ultimate plane, the seventh, there are no absolutes because it is an evolving level of consciousness. But there are actually eight planes or levels, as in an octave, and the eighth is the Absolute, the God of all universes, beyond which nothing exists. It is perfect, unlimited and, I will add, unknowable.

Entering the 5th Plane

There is much that I would like to add concerning a spirit's entry onto the fifth plane. At this stage you will have passed through many initiations and will reach, in all humility, the earlier part of the fifth plane. By then, you will be a very beautiful and privileged spirit who is capable of reaching up and absorbing an energy from the sixth plane in a way that can be gently and lovingly passed on.

This is sometimes called the Plane of Colour and one of the first lessons for any spirit at this stage of evolution is to understand these indescribable hues. It will find itself amidst a blending of colours which would make your Earth shades seem small and unimportant. They are shades completely beyond your comprehension for they are of another dimension.

These colours are a result of the fusion of spirit and experience at different levels of thought. Similarly, every action and thought that you undertake, as a human being, can be allied to a colour. Within the fifth plane, the spirit will start its experience in the lower or darker octaves of colour and finish in the lighter or higher octaves.

Upon entering the first colour, it will find a rich and varied experience awaiting it. It will become engulfed in a dimension of music which is again beyond human comprehension. The music you hear on Earth is limited, but music from the fifth plane has no limitations; perhaps subtle sound would be a better description than music. On the waves of this multi-dimensional sound the spirit will be guided to various planets and celestial bodies where it has undertaken physical experience at a much earlier period in its evolution. Possibly its function at this stage would be to help an incarnate person in a special task, or it might become one of a group of spirits that are helping and teaching other spirits from the third and fourth planes.

Spirits on the fifth plane are not concerned with the control of celestial bodies in your Earth sense, although they do assist groups of individuals. When a fifth plane spirit follows the left-hand path it can be very treacherous, because it is still near enough to the Earth plane to exert an influence which can result in a material effect. Many fallen spirits functioning from the fifth plane control those who practise the black arts. However, these spirits should not be confused with the powerful spirits from the sixth plane that control whole groups of 'evil' spirits. Those from the shadow hierarchy seldom give all their attention to any one person or group of people, unless they are of the same evolutionary standing as themselves.

One of the most magnificent facets of the wisdom of the Godhead is that, in its all-powerful love, it does not condemn. It has given all spirits free will to choose by which path they wish to evolve and, in this evolutionary experience, whether they will elect to follow it. God did not create a 'downstairs' spirit complete with furnace and pitchfork upon which to ensnare you if you do not toe the line. It is only humankind and all kingdoms on Earth that can heal an evil influence by their individual and collective acceptance of true love, wisdom and understanding.

Now, let us return to the spirit that is experiencing in the lower levels of the fifth plane. It progresses through the understanding of inter-dimensional colour and music and, at the same time, reviews its past physical experiences and considers its inadequacies. Before it can progress further it must dispel any thoughts of an earthly nature which could cloud its true judgment and hold it down to the material. Having achieved all this, and summed up its evolutionary needs, a realisation will gradually come to it that it can no longer assist those around it, for it will find difficulty in maintaining the necessary density of thought to do so.

As the wisdom and experience of the spirit grows, its density decreases and its vibration becomes finer. Thus it ascends, metaphorically speaking, and it enters an entirely different vibration where the colour is lighter and of a new brilliance, and the intensity of the sound increases beyond description. This would be accompanied by a form of 'evolutionary meditation'. Certain schools of esoteric teaching have loosely referred to this experience as 'The Entrance to the Halls of Learning', a title which may have an impressive sound to the Earth ear but which is quite inaccurate. It is not truly a meditation, nor is it a spiritual classroom. It is a level of thought where the spirit negotiates a spiritual transition by gradually assimilating an awareness of higher thought around it.

At this stage of its experience the spirit will find itself subjected to very heavy attack from those that wish to impede its progress. One of the forms this attack will take is a sort of spiritual 'sound' which is aimed to 'blind' the spirit by penetrating into its very core. This tends to make it so intent upon that which it is experiencing within this sound that it ceases to become aware of other more important aspects of its experience. If the spirit is able to overcome this attack, gradually the realisation of a higher level of thought will dawn and, with it, the natural evolutionary desire to look upward again. It will then pass through a further series of 'spheres' or 'impressions', each one a little lighter in vibration than the previous one, until by this natural process of becoming finer and wiser it enters mastership, the world of pure spirit, and learns that it is an infinity unto itself.

Here I must make one point very clear. These spirit spheres beyond the fifth plane are not doubles, replicas or affinities of physical manifestations; nor are they in any way concerned with physical planets, solar systems, galaxies or celestial bodies of any shape, size or form in the material sense. The nearest description I can give you is that they are spheres of spirit existence and their form is so fine as to be imperceptible, even to the psychic senses. An advanced occultist or medium projecting to these planes could only gain a vague impression of their nature and immensity. It would be extremely difficult to translate such an impression into Earth terms.

When considering the planes above yours you are inclined to use the word 'higher'. As most of you realise, this is purely figurative and, indeed, it is essential that you do not visualise these planes as being above in the sense of a great height. Many people think that the various spirit planes stretch between themselves and that high point which they consider to be God, but this is not so. All spirit spheres interweave, so that within your room all are present, from the densest to the Godhead itself. It would be much more accurate to think in terms of spiritual filters, for as a spirit advances it becomes finer and naturally filters through to a finer vibration. The Godhead, being the finest, pervades all.

Finally, I would like to stress that, although in these teachings I speak of various planes of existence within your universe, these are only broad divisions to help you to visualise spirit existence beyond the physical. One could equally well divide these experiences into twelve, twenty-four or, indeed, an infinite number of planes, each plane providing an infinity of experience in itself. Such is the diversity of experience on all levels in this infinite universe.

The Transcended Sun
The Sun is a giver of light on all levels. However, the energy behind the physical Sun emanates from the fifth spirit plane and carries with it a certain form of vibration. Many of your scientists have tried to assess the nature of the Sun and, in the main, they have not been able to do so because there are elements there which are on a vibration quite beyond the scope of the instruments man possesses.

The guiding manifestation of the Godhead behind the Sun is the Solar Logos. It is responsible for this particular solar system, and represents a portal of the seventh plane. So, when your ancestors worshipped the Sun, they obeyed a deep instinctive understanding.

In actual fact, the Sun is a great deal larger in my estimation than it would be in yours. Indeed, on its highest level, the Sun is all embracing, because around that which is visible to you there are other planes of existence or, shall we say, other planes of vibration beyond your frequency. If you could observe this with your inner eye, you would see that these planes extend around your entire solar system and you on this Earth planet exist within those planes. In fact, you are all a part of the Sun. What you see when you look through your sunglasses is merely the core of the Sun, and I personally would not regard it as being separate from your own Earth planet. The energy behind this more all embracing aspect of the Sun emanates from the sixth plane.

When a spirit passes on from the sixth plane to the seventh plane, it enters an infinity of planes of existence, for the Godhead itself is an infinity and exists on various levels within itself. I would like to describe it to you as being an Infinite Thought, and every lower plane of existence is a part of it. Yet, the Godhead in its infinity is progressive for it is continually evolving within itself. That which is all wise is becoming wiser.

I do understand that this will be exceptionally difficult for those of you who believe in God as a personal being to appreciate. However, there is nothing wrong in considering God as being personal because, of course, God is personal to you, for you are a part of God, everything in your reality is a part of God.

The Ever-expanding Universe
The universe is ever changing. It always was and it always will be. The supreme intelligence behind the universe keeps a constant flow to and from itself. The stars, galaxies and solar systems you see will have an ending insofar as the physical matter of which they are composed will cease to exist in that state. But they will not truly end, for the atoms they are composed of will increase in speed or vibration and commence a new chain of existence in another reality. The

universe, you see, will cease to exist as you see it but it will nevertheless be there, functioning in a different dimension.

From the interchange of atoms from one dimension to another, a friction is set up, in turn bringing into being a new set of atoms of a denser nature. I am using very basic language in order to create a picture that can be comprehended by all, but those of you who are more scientifically minded will translate it into your own particular phraseology. These newly formed atomic structures are of a similar, but not identical, pattern and weight to those composing the parts of the universe that had broken up. Thus another galaxy is born, another set of suns and stars comes into being for future generations of intelligences to survey with what instruments they may possess. Although the vibration of this new set of physical expressions is of a material nature in its atomic structure it differs by the slightest fraction from the old one. Thus the experiences gained within its confines differ by only that much from those of its predecessors, for no evolutionary progression is identically repetitive.

To put it as concisely as possible: each time a segment of the material universe disintegrates, changes its vibration by evolving on to a higher, faster and less perceptible atomic scale, its act of disintegration sets up this re-creative cosmic friction. I will endeavour to elaborate on this by taking the example of your own solar system and considering its beginning.

Firstly, let me say that the universe did not start with a colossal 'bang'; nor is it constantly spreading out to leave a hole in the centre. There is, to put it into the nearest terms that your language will allow, one central atom constantly expanding from the central core. As it expands it fuses with other elements in the cosmos and, from this continual central fusion, universes, collections of galaxies, are born. As the universes break up in the manner I have described, the atoms raise their vibrations, and they inevitably reach a speed where they are reabsorbed into the central core and continue to contribute, in yet another method of evolution, to the constant flow of creation. Thus nothing is ever lost and the universe is forever expanding in a dimension beyond that of time, space and breadth. Gradually, man as he evolves will comprehend more of this picture, for his mind will be able to grasp it without rejecting it out of fear.

Another point to emphasise is that all levels of evolution exist within each other, so that within the room in which you are sitting there are levels of intelligence present from the lowest to the highest. This applies both scientifically and ethically and therefore shows that orthodox teachings are not wrong when they tell you that God is everywhere. The levels of consciousness you are able to tune in to will depend solely upon your own spiritual development.

Now, let us look at the creation and subsequent evolution of the galaxy of which your own solar system is a part. This galaxy was formed from the fusion of certain unstable elements in the cosmos which, strange as it may seem, is quite a natural and usual stage of evolutionary development. In fact, new galaxies are in the process of being formed in the universe all the time.

Each galaxy is moving within itself and these movements are orderly and conform to a definite orbital pattern. Life never stands still, although it may appear to do so when looked at from the viewpoint of a few Earth years. At its commencement, a galaxy is composed of millions of astral bodies. It then passes through a period of fusion during which these bodies split themselves into certain orthodox patterns that, to put it into simple language, are similar configuratively to the structure and field of the universal atom. These bodies eventually form what you might term 'asteroid belts' and these in turn are gradually broken down by their own natural process of evolution into a formation such as your own solar system. I find this interesting because, contrary to what many people believe, a solar system is something that is post and not pre-asteroid, the one being the product of the other.

Most astronomers know about the asteroid belts within your own galaxy and that there is one that is considerably nearer than the rest. Your solar system is part of this asteroid belt, atomically speaking. The Earth planet, like the other planets, was once part of the central core, the Sun, formed by these evolutionary progressions within the structure of the asteroid belt.

As the Sun proceeded upon its evolution it began to cool and certain portions of its outer crust were discharged into space, where they were held and pulled into an orbit around their parent body by its magnetic force. The Sun itself is also rotating and the speed of

13

these rotations creates the gravitational pull that holds the planets within the solar system. You are not aware of this movement on Earth, because your planet is part of this spinning.

Now, it took a considerable length of time for each of the planets ejected by the Sun to find its natural orbital balance within the solar system. Your Earth also had to find its balance and assume its present size, workable both from the point of view of the magnetic balance and also in respect of its role as an experiencing ground for plants, animals and *homo sapiens.*

The physical body of man has developed from the material constituents of the planet. It has continually adapted itself to the physical conditions prevalent during each stage of the planet's development. Therefore, contrary to what many people believe, *homo sapiens* is a natural denizen of this sphere and his growth is as much a natural part of the process of Earth's evolution as Earth is part of the evolution of the solar system and the solar system of the asteroid belt, and so on. All these events are very directly concerned with the many forms of spirit life that rely upon the numerous densities of physical matter as vehicles for their evolutionary paths. Here, I would especially like to emphasise the naturalness of this whole process of creation, re-creation and evolution and I hope that the picture I have given will enable you to visualize more clearly the constant flow of this ever-changing infinite universe.

Back to the Beginning
Let us go back to the way in which life came to your planet. Certain spirits — some esoteric philosophers call them archons — move through the cosmos in mysterious ways. Each time a new part of it is created, the matter is formed by the archons who build the atomic structure. These archons have the ability to move matter of a specialised kind such as that found in what you call asteroids. They create — and now I am looking for words — a cosmic dust storm of energy, tiny particles of matter and various other forms of existence the nature of which does not matter for the purpose of this teaching. Now, these particles blow, as it were, around the asteroids and the asteroids form into streams and start to spin and rotate. The tiny particles in this cosmic storm begin to adhere to these asteroids rather like iron filings around a magnet.

The process takes millions and millions of years but, in time, this partly physical, partly etheric stream of matter, gases and particles begins to solidify. As it rotates, it spirals inwards, causing atomic reactions as the matter forces itself closer and closer together. This is a very broad outline, as you must appreciate, but in time there is what you would understand as nuclear fusion and a sun begins to come into being. As this body spins, all the time becoming more and more dense, particles of it break away and rotate around it.

The rest is much as your scientists describe. The sun has many explosions upon its surface. One of these ejections was of greater proportions and began to revolve around its parent in a newly created magnetic field. Chemical reaction commenced, and planet Earth started its evolutionary cycle.

To put it scientifically, your universe is composed of electrons, neutrons etc, which move at different speeds and at different vibrations. It is through these varying speeds and vibrations that different substances come into being.

In time, the particles which break off form into planets, but each solar system must have as part of its structure a new belt of asteroids so that, from them, another solar system may be formed, because these asteroids absorb, as it were, the evolution of that solar system in which they were formed. When the solar system has completed its evolution they pass on to form another with the knowledge, the evolution, the understanding of the previous system recorded in them. The asteroids are, in a sense, the tape recorder of a solar system and they are also the seed from which another grows. They are not the remains of a planet that has exploded and been forgotten.

In time, various masses that have been cast off from the mother Sun, cool down and become the planets which encircle it. The Sun also attracts other bodies within its orbit and thus a solar system with all its attendant bodies is formed. Positive and negative forces are needed to bring a solar system to life. It is created by positive forces and seeded by negative forces, the opposite to your sexual form of creation. If you look through the various planes of evolution you will find that these polarising forces are reversed as they descend to each level below: negative, positive, negative and so on. Some very wise person saw this and represented it as two serpents twining round a rod!

All physical life is preceded by life in the world of spirit. It must first manifest in that world before it can manifest in matter. Those spirits which guide the evolution of your solar system have been given many names throughout history. They are the 'old ones' that watch over the destiny of universes. When the archons have fulfilled their task of creating a new solar system, then the 'old ones' come to guide it and bring it up as a child is brought up. But this is not a haphazard affair. The great beings who fulfil these tasks come from other stars in groups; and so, a group of such beings came to this solar system when it was new.

The Primitive Earth
Although I have presented a picture of the beginning of this planet which may sound somewhat scientific, it is, in fact, equally spiritual. Now, let us return to the gaseous mass which has left its parent and commenced an independent existence in an orbit of its own. As it cooled, so it gradually hardened, and condensation formed the oceans that are so essential to life. In due course, certain chemical reactions began to set in, and as these took place so did life begin.

How did life begin on your planet? It was a combination of many things. There are certain basic chemicals on the planet that can be affected by cosmic radiation. I am not merely referring to the rays coming from the Sun, but something on a far greater scale. These radiations may come from another sphere, another galaxy or, in fact, any part of your infinite universe. Scientists have said that there are certain parts of the universe or 'space' which are considered to be a vacuum. I would not agree, for there are many forms of life which your instruments can not measure. Many forms of cosmic life are drawn upon to help create a planet and gradually, slowly, the first type of planetary life comes into being.

The Elementals
A physical planet has an esoteric vibration, certainly, but what is it that gives a planet its particular archetypal character? All physical manifestation has a form of spirit life which guides or controls it. In the case of the human species, the spirit expresses itself through the

physical body, directing it and experiencing through it. Each person will also be helped and guided by another spirit, sometimes called a guardian angel, although most people are unaware of this.

The universe is composed of energy which manifests at different frequencies. The spirit is a very fine thought, a very fine substance, so fine that you would not see it with your physical eyes; but for those who have etheric sight, the planes can appear to vibrating within the same range. Achieve this, and then you can truly walk beside those evolved ones who have chosen to work with you.

Very few people today give much thought to what may appear to be mere processes of nature, for they neither see nor hear the beings or intelligences expressing themselves through these forms of evolution. I shall use orthodox terminology here and refer to them as the spirits of air, fire, earth and water. These are collectively known as 'the spirits of the elements' and individually as 'elementals'. These elemental spirits originate from the Godhead in exactly the same way as yourselves, but at an early stage they elect to experience through a different form of expression.

The spirits of the elements mould the form and express themselves through the physical matter and gases of which the planet is composed. Although they assist the planet as a whole, they are rather more concerned with the structure of the sphere itself than the forms of evolution experiencing thereon. The overall guiding influence of the planet comes from those advanced fifth-plane beings, or planetary devas as they are called, which have, in fact, evolved from the elemental kingdoms.

The orthodox names given to the spirits of the elements by the ancients were: 'salamanders' for the spirits of fire, 'sylphs' for the spirits of air, 'ondines' or 'nymphs' for the water spirits and 'gnomes' for the earth spirits. I consider these names to be very appropriate because the forms of experience which elementals undergo can be roughly classified under these four headings and aligned to the four expressions behind these terms.

Some people, either by training in the art of perception or by a natural gift, are able to see these spirits and observe the part they play. The beauty and innocence of children often attract them from their own kind to make friends, so do not scold any child who claims to have seen some 'little people', for it may be true. People see earth elementals as gnomes of varying size and appearance, while air elementals sometimes appear as fairies with wings. It must be understood, however, that it was man who created these images of his elemental brothers, not the elementals themselves. They merely adopt a guise by which they will be recognised. A child would not connect a gnome with a lump of quartz or a sylph with a beam of light. The thought forms which they adopt for recognition will change as man's concept of them changes.

Elemental spirits do not evolve in the same manner as *homo sapiens* spirits. They begin their evolutionary journey as a single element or as part of the group spirit of a particular element; and as they advance they become more and more individualised.

Normally, the group spirit of an element stays together and does not individualise unless for some special purpose or job of work. When an elemental has learnt all that it can of its own element it begins to seek experience within the spheres of the other three elements. These it will master one at a time; so while many elementals are of a single nature, some have a two-fold or three-fold nature. Once an elemental masters all four elements it is said to have won its four-fold nature, which means that it has ascended to the planes of the devas and will assist in the guidance of planets.

The Deva Kingdoms

The word 'deva' comes from the Sanskrit meaning 'shining one' and was originally bestowed upon those beings who, in Christianity, are known as angels. Deva evolution is a form of experience quite apart from *homo sapiens*.

When the devas first come, they create an etheric existence around a planet. Then the vibration is channelled downwards until it becomes moulded into the substance from which physical life stems. When a planet comes into being, which has to support many forms of life, such as animals, plants, fish and mankind, the whole creation is framed in the ether making, as it were, a blueprint.

The guiding entities responsible for the evolution of a planet, attract groups of spirits of varying kinds from within the universe that have chosen a certain life form through which to experience. The deva has a difficult task; it has to fashion matter rather in the way that you cook your cakes: the heat must be just right or they will burn, the mixture must be just right or they will not rise. In the same way, the clay bodies which the deva creates must allow those varied types of spirits to express themselves. Some spirits that come from throughout the universe are young in wisdom, some older, and it is the duty of the devas, the 'old ones', to see that the bodies are fashioned as suitable vehicles for each of them.

There are many types of devas and the early Christian fathers gave them names and divided them into nine 'choirs'. To place such labels on them is limiting and misleading for there is much overlap, but the early fathers were trying to say that certain types of angel or deva evolution were responsible for certain natural happenings in the evolutionary scheme of things. A planet is usually guided by a group of devas with one presiding deva. This group will consist of devas from all the many choirs of angels.

The presiding deva of each planet is progressing along its own evolutionary path. They are in differing stages of evolution and they influence the planets they guide according to their stage of wisdom, affecting not only their own sphere of rulership but also the other planets in the solar system. Thus the devic retinue of a planet such as Earth will include devas that help man, those that watch over the animal kingdoms, devas of plant and insect life, atomic devas and those that rule the seasons and elements generally. Cherubim, for example, are responsible for the growth and ascendancy of *homo sapiens*; archons work with the atoms, whilst seraphim are the cleansers or fiery ones. All these various forms of evolution intertwine and are complementary. This is a lesson to be learnt by man who has lost the art of acknowledging the part played by other intelligences in the everyday running of his planet.

As a planet evolves so also does its deva; thus both the guide and those growing up under its guidance will, in fact, assist each other's evolutionary progress. Similarly, the influence of one planet will affect the evolution and growth of another according to their relative positions and characters. It is the overall emanations from these devic influences, blending with the physical vibrations of the planets themselves, that have been observed and have given birth to the science you know as astrology, which is an interpretation of all the influences they give forth, beneficent or otherwise, according to their physical relationship to each other and to planet Earth at any given moment in time.

I would like to emphasise that each of the planets is guided, not controlled, by its respective Deva because a deva that is functioning on the right-hand path will never force its charges to follow its way. Indeed, every sphere of evolution on a planet has its free will as to how much it accepts or rejects of the Deva's guiding influence; although, on the other hand, one has to accept the fact that, regardless of this, the guidance from the Deva is of a powerful nature and will undoubtedly affect the overall character of the planet.

You may ask, "Is the Deva using the planet to expedite its own evolution or does it progress with the planet?" My answer is that it can be either or both. If the Deva is wise enough to progress with the planet so much the better; but this is not so in every case. It is possible for a planetary deva to misguide the planet within its care; in which case, assisting spirits from the same sphere of evolution may elect to leave their own world of spirit and incarnate into physical bodies to help put right the evolutionary retrogression caused by unwise guidance?

I must point out that though the highest elemental energies stem from the sixth plane, the individuality that you place on the devic kingdom emanates from very close to it on the fifth plane. So, the planetary Deva, Archangel Mikaal, is an advanced fifth plane presence. Remember, every spirit is vulnerable until it reaches the Ultimate and it may emphasise the shadow at any time before it arrives at that state of perfection, and this is exactly what happened with Lucifer.

Chapter 2

PLANETARY CONSCIOUSNESS

Early Life Forms
During the early stages of a planet's evolution, life is very primitive. In such times, the matter is mostly looked after and brought on by the spirits of the elements that form the cells into certain shapes. These primitive shapes in turn become primitive creatures. Such early life forms serve to give expression to equally primitive forms of spirit life which help to take them on to the next stage of their development. When this stage is reached, and these bodies are ready, the next group of spirits takes over. These are rudimentary spirits, young souls, with no chosen life form such as you would recognise. They influence the bodies into which they enter and the bodies, in turn, influence them.

All this time, these forms are being conditioned by the rays of the deity and the devas that work for the deity. When a radiation belt passes through a solar system, mutations are caused which can be utilised by the planetary deva to effect the changes in matter which are due and necessary to take the evolutionary streams forward - and so they each begin to progress, to assume a form which will lead the physical matter of their bodies into the exact nature required in the planet's overall design.

It is with the next grade of spirits that the split occurs, and the various branches of the tree diverge. The young spirits were rough and ready; knowing no form, they simply held the matter together, so that a shape could evolve from it, and those spirits that would ultimately find expression on the planet could take over from them and mould the matter into the true pattern.

Let us say that you have two very primitive type bodies which are neither man nor beast, for such beings did exist on your planet at one time. Into one, you bring a spirit which wishes to experience through an animal stream of incarnation and, into the other, you bring a spirit which wishes to experience as *homo sapiens*. Each of the spirits will live a series of lives in such bodies and by the end of that series the two types of body will look very different. One will have grown more fur, developed its instinct and so forth, while the other will have begun to stand erect, to fashion tools and to think constructively. Then, each strain will develop along its own line and attract to itself spirits of its own kind so that it perfects its species within its evolutionary bounds.

When the body has completed its growth in the evolutionary sense it will stop and stay like that. And so, each branch of evolution bears the hallmark of its creator, the type of spirit that takes it over. This is why your apes are still apes and have not become human, for their spirits are different. Your lions and tigers have not become human. The form of life these creatures have chosen has a limited brain capacity, a limited physical experience, but not a limited spiritual experience. Human bodies have a greater brain capacity, a greater intellectual and reasoning capacity but no greater spiritual capacity; in fact, the latter can be limited by the former. A spirit is only wise insofar as it uses the body it exists in to its full capacity, whether it is a furred one, a feathered one or one with a coat of skin. And so, your evolution proceeds in this way.

The 'old ones' take on many forms, and may have originated from within the orbit of a star existing far beyond your solar system, where life is in no way like your own; the people are not like humans, nor the animals like your animals and so, the relationship between people and animals is entirely different. They would have come from places which are more technically advanced than on your own planet and, in order that they may monitor or assist you on your own level, they left the star on which they functioned and travelled to take a look. So it was that those evolved souls came to this solar system in those early days. The first planet to be visited by these beings was the planet you call Venus; so Venus is strongly under the influence of that star.

Early Planetary Progress

Let us now return to those early days of planet Earth. Picture your planet as composed of rock, dust and water, but with no vegetation at all, no life as you would know it. A gradual transformation took place and Earth reached a stage where it was ready to receive new forms of life. Vegetation came, more chemical changes took place. Then came those early forms of life which your scientists have visualised, small creatures almost like embryos or fish bones; their impressions are still to be found in certain rock strata. They gradually developed and evolved until they became animated organisms. Each time a new form of evolution comes to a young planet, cosmic radiations are drawn upon to assist with this unfolding process.

Going forward millions of years again, these organisms progress-ed until they became mammals, fish and birds such as you would associate with prehistoric times. You would consider them monsters by your present-day concepts, but all aspects of physical manifest-ation, including the ground upon which you stand, are inhabited by various different forms of spirit life expressing themselves, evolving, and together creating the dynamics that are appropriate to each stage in the evolution of planet Earth.

There are spirits who inhabit the bodies of animals, of fishes, of plant life, of even the ground upon which you stand. These are all different forms of spirit life which together go to help complete the universe and eventually the Ultimate. Remember, all these things evolved from the tiny spark of life on the gaseous mass in the beginning.

Animal Evolution and the 'Missing Link'

There have been many theories regarding the place of animals in the scheme of things. Some people believe that the spirits of men inhabit the bodies of animals during an earlier stage of their evolution, while others reject such an idea. I should like to give you the picture of animal evolution as I see and understand it.

The evolutionary experiences undergone by animals are entirely different from those undergone by *homo sapiens* though they have undoubtedly evolved from the same life cells. The actual brain capacity of an animal is restricted compared with that of a human

23

being, and its form of experience is, on the whole, of a very much more disciplined nature. But when it comes to the question of spirit evolution, it is quite a different story.

The theory of somatic evolution as expounded by Darwin is correct as far as it goes, but he did not take into account the fact that, in all human expression, there is the fusion of two types of evolution: the spirit and the physical. Genetic evolution and spirit evolution are two entirely different things.

Now, there was a point in the evolutionary process when a human-type spirit incarnated into the bodies of certain apes accentuating the prowess that can be expressed through the brain – and so, the pattern of *homo sapiens* slowly emerged. On the spirit level, in other ways, the creative capability of the animal kingdom came into its own.

Man normally does not like to consider that animal evolution, from a spiritual point of view, is as great as his own, because this is a blow to his ego, but I assure you that a cat walking into a gathering of people could have a spirit of much greater evolution than the spirits of any of those present. And that is no insult to anyone.

Man must also understand that there are an infinite number of different forms of evolution throughout the universe, and although all spirits are as one in the sense that they are the 'children' or 'thoughts' of the Ultimate, the forms of evolutionary experiences they elect to undergo give them that definite individuality which distinguishes, say, the spirit of a cat from the spirit of a plant, or the spirit of a human being. They are like branches of a tree, each branch representing a different form of evolution and contributing its share to the whole, the main trunk.

In the pre-physical Plane of Decision, a spirit has the choice of entering the sphere of human evolution or one of the many other streams. With the exception of a few special cases, a spirit which chooses to experience life as an animal does not normally enter into the body of a man, but progresses through the animal kingdom to the higher spirit planes in exactly the same way that the spirit of man does. Spirits which have chosen animal incarnations and spirits which have chosen human experiences belong to two quite different streams of evolution, just as the spirits of the elements evolve into devic spirits, or angels, as you would call them, in their own way.

Now, there are many types of animals, birds and fish, but are some species more evolved than others? Yes, some forms are of a less evolved state, but I would prefer to use the expression, 'enjoy a lower state of consciousness'. The fish is an example of this, its genetic evolution being limited far more than that of a dolphin.

I would also like to say that the domestic animals, the cat and dog, are more or less at a similar stage of evolution though they express themselves quite differently. The cat represents the passive receptive instinct, and the dog, the active. Some animals within each group are more evolved than their fellows, just as men and women are. You cannot make set rules about the evolutionary status of your pets any more than you can about your human compatriots.

Animals do not change their type between incarnations. For example, a spirit which chooses to experience as a cat, would not return later as a horse or dog, but could experience in the many different branches of the cat family. Your little cat may have been a lion or tiger before, or even a panther. If you look closely you may be able to observe a likeness to one special branch of the cat family. The same applies to the domestic dog, whose spirit may have started as a wolf or jackal before becoming the docile pet who sleeps so peacefully by your fireside.

The number of incarnations an animal may have can no more be assessed than those which a human undergoes. There are no hard and fast rules, as each spirit advances at its own speed. And, "Do animals have free will?" is the next question which may have come into your mind. The free will of an animal is limited to the choices which its spirit makes when it is discarnate. As soon as it enters the body which it has chosen, it is subject to the natural conditions of that body and is obliged to accept them.

The spirits of animals can appear from the planes of spirit in exactly the same way as the spirits of men, and clairvoyants often 'see' them when they are looking on to the ether. Your deceased pet may stay with you for a long time, and may try to help you from the world of spirit. Some animals are excellent guards against the lower astral, especially cats, and the ancient civilisations of Earth knew of

25

these powers and used them. Animals who have become very attached to a human may even follow his or her evolution side by side, both in the world of spirit and the material world. You may have known your pet before on many occasions.

There is one thing you must bear in mind in relation to animals. Each animal is an individual, just as each of you are. They have their own little traits of personality or character, and will serve man in the way best suited. Treat your animals gently, yet firmly, and try to understand them. To feed them and turn them out occasionally, is not enough, for although they cannot answer you in the way you would like, or earn money for their keep, they can give you sympathy, and that certain harmony which you find so difficult to achieve with your fellow human beings.

There were times in the history of your planet when all animals were the friends of man and did not attack him; but in those days man knew how to communicate with his animal brothers in a way which has become lost over generations of cruelty. You can, however, look forward to a future when such times will return, and the spirits from all forms of expression on Earth will harmonise once again.

As Earth's evolution continued, many parts cooled and changed, and it was put under great evolutionary pressure until, at the time when the dinosaurs became extinct, the planet turned completely on its axis, causing an ice age. Since then, there have been two partial tilts that caused major disruption to the harmony of planet Earth and all forms of life on it, and now, in a less severe way, it is happening again. The great creatures that dwelt upon Earth during those early times lived vastly different lives from the wild animals you know today. If an animal survived the elements it did not survive its predators and most of those that were not appropriate for the new evolutionary phase perished during an axis tilt.

The Arrival of Man
So, the planet progressed from a hot, volcanic sphere, through its cooling and gradual change of face, a process that took millions of years during which the evolutionary cycles came and went, until the stage of prehistoric monsters gave way to the age of man. I have spoken of the Plane of Decision that focuses all forms of existence

collectively and, to that end, when an impulse descends from the Ultimate, it passes through a series of experiences until it reaches that stage of realisation where it decides whether to enter into the human evolutionary process, or a different branch of opportunity.

Clearly, this question of pre-human existence is tied up with the different evolutionary patterns experienced by the many distinct forms of planetary life but also, in a sense, with infinity. Whilst all these streams of life blend together in a planetary embrace, the types of experience which are part of an animal existence are quite different from those experienced by a human, except, to some extent, when their paths meet, for example, when cows are reared to give milk and be eaten by humans. It is seen, also, when the elementals work with humans in the healing process. Normally, each of these groups is going through a series of experiences quite independently, thus adding to the Ultimate in a different way.

Let us now consider the spirits which, in pre-historic times, entered into the bodies of early man. They were the 'cave men' eking out an existence in a hostile terrain, but they were still part of the evolutionary process that led directly into *homo sapiens*.

These early 'primitives' banded together into tribes, which rapidly increased in numbers. The tribes came together and gradually the first communities were formed. Their evolutionary progress was slow and it took many thousands of years for the necessary mutations to take real effect.

In answer to the question, "What was the missing link, and when did the transitional stage occur?", I can say that the true commencement of the existence of *homo sapiens* on Earth was when a different type of spirit began to enter these early bodies which allowed a more expansive kind of free will. These spirits influenced the physical brains and bodies they entered, causing them to gradually develop the ability to think and discern.

As the genetic development grew, so spirits of a slightly higher evolution were able to enter. It was the coming of these first truly 'human type' spirits, which gave rise to the first Adamic myth. The name Adam is taken from the letters A d m, which stand for 'first of man', or 'father of men'. In other translations it is said to stand for 'the ground'.

While it would not be useful for an evolved spirit to enter into a body of low genetic maturity, through which it could not express itself, if the gap in evolution between the spirit and the host body is not too wide, then this can speed up the evolutionary process over a number of generations.

Lemuria

The first land mass which 'man' inhabited we shall call 'Mu ', or 'The Motherland,' though it was given the name of 'Lemuria', by a British scientist, after the Lemurs. Mu occupied a large portion of the globe which stretched from the Middle East, notably Egypt, to China, and included other lands in the Southern hemisphere such as Australia and New Zealand, reaching right across what is now the Pacific Ocean to South America. China and Tibet were Mu-an.

Mu flourished for many thousands of years and, during this period, certain of the inhabitants, living in enclaves, advanced considerably more than others. These people built many edifices and cities, the remains can be seen in parts of South America today. Polynesian culture is yet another hallmark of the first 'civilisation' and the monolithic edifices on Easter Island, once part of Mu, stand like sentinels guarding the secrets of an age, lost and past, to which they belonged.

The evolution of the world was due to take a step forward, for it had been at a standstill for quite a while. Some time before the continent of Mu was due to be affected by cataclysms other more highly evolved spirits incarnated from other planets into Mu-an bodies. As these bodies grew to adulthood, the wisdom of their spirits began to manifest itself, and they found themselves to be considerably more advanced in understanding than those around them. The gulf between the more advanced and lesser evolved Mu-ans grew as time progressed. Many of the latter remained almost animal and led very bestial existences.

The advanced ones easily recognised each other and so, banded together. They saw that things were not as they should be, and set out to segregate themselves by setting up a community of their own on a peninsula of land which had, up to that time, been very sparsely populated.

It was shortly after these early Atlanteans under their leader had settled upon their newly found land that the giant catastrophe occurred which caused the face of the Earth to change. Another cosmic body passed near to your world, and upset its orbital balance causing the Earth's axis to tilt. The results were horrifying. A whole portion of a continent sank beneath what you now know as the Pacific Ocean. The remaining land masses became split into smaller continents. It was the most degenerate parts of Mu which were dashed beneath the foaming waves and boiling lava. This brought about the first ice age to occur during the planet's habitation by man, though there had been a number in the earlier history of the planet.

All cataclysmic happenings of the type that affect the structure of the planet and the rise and fall of continents are caused by magnetic adjustments between Earth and other planets in the solar system. It was a movement between the relationship of Earth and Saturn that brought about this particular upheaval that was to cause the Earth's axis to tilt and subsequently realign.

By ice age, I do not mean that the entire globe was covered with ice, but merely that the ice regions moved their positions. Due to the new position of planet Earth in relation to the Sun, climatic conditions throughout the world changed, and the first Atlanteans found that they had acquired a fine, warm land. Their peninsular had broken away from the main land mass and had become a close island grouping.

It occupied an area in what is now the Atlantic ocean, that includes existing islands such as the Azores, right down to the Canary Islands where many of the most evolved of the Atlantean people were situated. There they developed a civilisation the equal of which has not been known since. It was the area to the west of Madeira that became, in time, the most debased.

The Planets in the Solar System

There are twelve major cosmic bodies in your solar system other than your Sun that form a spiritual unit that relates gravitationally to your own planet; the eight major planets with which you are familiar - plus Pluto and one further out in space, that I have named Pan. (It is now officially known as Eris, after the Greek goddess of discord and strife). Pluto and Pan are classed as dwarf planets because they are too small. There are others still to be discovered and classified, but these are not as spiritually important to Earth.

There is one more planet that has an orbit between the Sun and Mercury and I have given this the name Orpheus. It has a finer form of physical vibration, not easily detected by your earth senses. I have named these planets after appropriate Greek deities for the natures of these two 'gods' are akin to the rays given off by Pan and Orpheus. And then there is your Moon.

As you probably realise, the type of evolution on each planet varies greatly. On some of them there is no form of life whatsoever as you would know it. On others there are life forms which are very much in advance of your own, and there are yet others where the life forms are purely those of the spirit as, for example, on Saturn and Mercury.

The solar system, as a whole, is required to function in a state of balance, just as all creation must be in balance in order to function properly. Therefore, if any of the planets behaves erratically, it has an effect on the other planets. Individually, each planet undergoes cycles of evolution in the same way as you yourselves do.

Your planet is by no means at the bottom of the evolutionary scale in this solar system, both Mars and Pan being younger spiritually. Venus has been very much concerned with the evolutionary pattern on Earth; so have Jupiter and Pluto to a lesser extent; their specific rays related to particular evolutionary epochs and the civilisations which arose during those epochs.

Each planet within your solar system has an esoteric vibration which relates to its specific role in the solar family of which it is a part. In addition, each planet has an astrological influence which relates broadly to its esoteric significance. These roles relate as follows:—

	ESOTERIC	ASTROLOGICAL
SATURN	Philosophic science	Limitation, structure, consolidation
PAN	Natural law	Growth
URANUS	Material science, technology	Sudden happenings, awakening, freedom
MERCURY	Mental receptivity, learning, knowledge	Communication, intellect
ORPHEUS	Art, creativity	Disciplined creativity
NEPTUNE	Psychic energy, inter-dimensional thought	Psychic communication, art, receptivity
EARTH	Music, healing	Music, healing
MOON	The mind	Response, fluctuation
JUPITER	Judgement	Expansion, preservation
PLUTO	Peace, the subconscious mind	Elimination, regeneration, transformation
MARS	Industriousness, energy	Assertion, activation, pioneering
VENUS	Love, harmony, beauty	Relationship on all levels
THE SUN	Light, life, the seed of the solar system	Essential character, striving.

You have much to learn yet concerning the planets in the solar system and even about your Moon. Although astronauts have landed there, there are many things they have not discovered and, if I might mention this, also some things which they have discovered and have not told you. But soon, man will not send his rockets to other planets, for this antiquated method of space travel will be rejected in favour of a new means of propulsion more in keeping with the laws of the universe.

Now, let us look in more detail at the planets within your own solar system, remembering that the number of solar systems outside this one is infinite. Firstly, let us take those which are inhabited by individual forms with a soul. The most evolved planet of this nature is Venus. The Venusians are considerably more advanced both materially and spiritually than any of the other planetary inhabitants. Next in order come the Jupiterians, then the people of the planet Pluto, followed by the Martians.

Extra-terrestrial reality

When I say that spirits have lived or incarnated on other planets in our solar system, and still do, clearly this contradicts the beliefs of your scientists and, they would say, common sense; but then, they have a very limited understanding of three dimensional reality. Needless to say, none of those planets is currently inhabited in the way you inhabit Earth.

Before proceeding, there is one point I must make clear: All life within the physical range of experience is governed by the conditions which surround it and from which it has evolved. Just as the physical body that you inhabit exists within a clearly defined band of frequency, so it is that there are other bands which allow bodies on other planets to 'firm up' in their own way. Everything about them is of a finer nature, a different chemical level of vibration. Yet, if you were to see them with inner sight, they might appear to have form that is not so unlike your own; but that would be a subjective interpretation of your mind, for their physical form would be outside the range of your Earth senses.

Similarly, when a human soul passes to the spirit world it carries the energy of that physical body, and this is why when you look at a spirit who has passed over you will see it as a person. You are not actually seeing them, they are a spirit.

There are many forms of evolution within your solar system in addition to physical life as you know it, and it would be impossible to measure these by the yardstick of your own human experience. If you were to land on a planet billions and billions of miles from here you might not see anything on the planet, yet it could be swarming with evolution on a different energetic level. And you can be sure that their planet is as real to them as your world is to you.

There are many spirits from other planets trying to make contact and help your planet, but they do not look like they are so often portrayed in your science fiction films for, by and large, they are coming from a completely different kind of experience. You can give full reign to your imagination on this one, for the possibilities and the probabilities are infinite.

The planet nearest Earth from the point of view of the structure of its inhabitants is Venus. Their shape, would depend on your imagination, to be truthful. A Venusian has reached the stage where there is very little physical manifestation, as you would understand it, so if you were to experience on Venus it would be on a subtle level, but your mind would interpret it with a distinct form. They have 'etheric sight', in other words they can see not only the encasing body but also the spirit which inhabits it. Thus, they are able to recognise those spirits who have had experiences on other planets but who are now incarnate in Earth bodies.

The Venusians have an outer composition that moves constantly in waves and you would be aware of very bright colours. Also, what passes for lungs are accustomed to breathing the different atmospheric components which they encounter. The energy of the Venusians is extremely beautiful, and you would relate to them in wonder. They are not ascended beings, however.

Venusians manifest on a subtle level of the same range of frequencies as you do on Earth. They are those of God's creatures who have progressed a little further along the road of evolution and must be viewed accordingly. They have much to teach the people of Earth, for they have passed through many evolutionary stages. They do not fight or war on Venus and they cannot understand why the people of Earth have a desire to kill each other. Their laws and system of government differ from anything you know and they are all trained in matters occult from an early age. They know of the future events to take place in the solar system which will affect Earth and they are particularly aware of the movements of the planet Uranus.

There is a very beautiful spiritual influence on Venus and it is one of the most important planets in the solar system for that reason. It is difficult to describe how they live because there are no suitable Earth terms, other than that colour plays a predominant part in everything that they do; and, of course, like any form of spiritual experience, the spirits tend to come together in group energies.

The Venusians have been closely observing the Earth for many years now. They come in peace and love and want to help planet Earth over the period that is upon you.

When a spirit passes from a physical body, it is not limited to the physical experience to be gained upon one planet only, and there are spirits who have had incarnations upon several planets. I have already established that Venus, Jupiter, Pluto and Mars are inhabited by beings comprehensible to you.

Overall, Mars is not quite as evolved as Earth even though the Martians are ahead of you in scientific matters, having learned much from the Venusians who visited there. They do not fight or war, but they are less wise in other aspects. Martians are certainly very energetic people.

Now, let us consider those which are essentially 'spirit' planets, or where spirits will congregate to learn from those wiser than themselves. The planet Saturn is one such spirit planet that encompasses both the second and third planes. It is an evolved planet. Mercury is also a 'home' for spirits and many of them will attend this planet for a period of rest before incarnating into a different galaxy. The most advanced spirit body is, of course, the Sun. Here, a spirit may experience its last contact with a 'physical' vibration before ascending to the realms of pure spirit.

The next group comprises those planets which have different forms of evolution from those which you know and recognise, and consists of the planets Neptune, Orpheus and Pan. These have organic life and animals but not in a form you would understand. Orpheus is the most evolved of this group, followed by Neptune, with Pan at the other end of the scale, having barely started its evolutionary cycle. The planet Uranus is the oldest planet in the solar system. It has almost completed its evolution, and will soon break up. At the time of Atlantis, Uranus was inhabited by people such as you would know on Earth, and many of these spirits came into Earth bodies following the destruction of Mu. Since those times, however, its population has dwindled down to nothing, and now it merely supports spirit life before its final spiral.

Jupiter is the Planet of the Judges, and Pluto, the Planet of Peace. The natives of the latter live mostly in sheltered places, for the conditions upon Pluto, flung way out at the borders of the solar system, are extremely severe. There are two main races upon this planet, which is very sparsely inhabited. The leading race are above ground dwellers who live on the warmest parts although, of course, due to its distance from the Sun, there is neither the light nor warmth of a kind that you would recognise.

A great many of the spirits who inhabited the bodies of the early Atlanteans came from Venus. That is why there is such a great connection between Venus and Atlantis, for the Venusians are advanced in matters psychic and they know of their past experiences upon the Earth planet. There were also some spirits from other planets incarnate upon Atlantis and many of these have now returned to Earth in bodies to assist with the world's future. Many of you who read these words may feel an affinity with the planetarians, and the urgency that they bring to Earth for change.

The story of Adam and Eve has caused much confusion amongst students of ancient works, for there are parallel myths in the ancient records of many countries and civilisations, and these are, in fact, describing shifts of consciousness. A shift into a higher level of consciousness occurred twice in the history of your world, firstly, as aforementioned in Mu, and secondly, when spiritual leaders from Venus established the great Atlantean civilisation.

Chapter 3

THE GARDEN OF EDEN

The Transformed Planet

Let us visit Atlantis at the height of its glory: a true Garden of Eden if ever there was one, a perfect state of existence for those in Earth bodies. How did they live? What sort of government did they have? These Atlantean people were more advanced than the people of today and knew many secrets of science and occultism that have been lost to man down the centuries.

The young island state grew gradually, steadily, drinking in the warm sunshine that blessed its fields and shores, appreciating the light and kindness shown by its benevolent supervisor, 'our Lord, the Sun'; as such it was known to the early Atlanteans, who were monotheistic. They recognised a supreme force that they believed was responsible for and ruled over the land upon which they dwelt and all other lands, seas and skies. This force was interpreted as a Father/Mother God and its physical manifestation was the great star, Sun. Only the priests could communicate with the spirit forms that emanated from this divine source, but the Sun was there for all.

There were many ceremonies connected with both the Father and Mother aspects of the Sun, the main one being the annual 'feast of the Sun'. The Sun emblem was worn to denote office in the priesthood and, when it appeared as a winged disc worn on the forehead, it indicated that the priest or priestess had the ability to travel in spirit to higher realms.

The high priest of early Atlantis was the ruler of the state as well as of temple matters. He carried the title 'Sun Chief', a position which was handed down from the earliest times. These chief high priests were chosen by the elders according to the state of evolution of their spirits, which could be ascertained by the use of etheric sight. Thus no one ever attained to such a rank without the wisdom to carry the responsibility it involved. Below him we find a priestly hierarchy, but nothing like the religious systems known today. Candidates for the priesthood were chosen at a very early age, under occult guidance, in accordance with their evolution. The higher priests could tell whether a child would be suitable for training as, say, a sensitive or healer. The priests were also scientists, astronomers, mathematicians, doctors and people of all other professions. Six administrators worked under the direct guidance of the high priest, dealing with civic problems such as waterways, agriculture, shipping, industry etc. and each was the expert in his own field. There was no army in Atlantis and no police force, as such things were not considered necessary. Miscreants could be detected by occult means and judgment and justice were fair and helpful.

Atlantis had areas that were extremely warm and temperate, that enjoyed the type of climate you would associate with the South Sea Islands of today and those that were somewhat cooler. These zones were given names that vibrated to the atmosphere and life lived in each of them. The northern zone was called Portea, the central zone Cintrala and the southern zone Usiqua. There were cities, towns and villages throughout that were mainly circular in shape, well irrigated and beautifully kept. Colour was used profusely in both dwellings and temples.

The areas to the north were mainly flat and inclined to be dry although it was by no means barren. Most of the mountain ranges lay to the south but the topmost peaks coincided with the islands of the Azores; although it would be difficult to equate any existing landmasses with specific parts of Atlantis, as the topography changed so drastically at the time of the axis tilt, this is roughly correct.

The capital of the southern province was Kudra, while the northern province was dominated by Keriophis. Menocea was a large city in the north-east, while the nearest city to the capital itself was Mentis, to the east. The Atlantean civilisation lasted for many thousands of years and many townships sprang up and crumbled away during that time. A person who has a memory of Atlantis from an incarnation in the latter days would doubtless bring back many facets of experience that would contrast strongly with the experiences of those who were incarnate much earlier; think how buildings, clothing and life generally has changed over the past few hundred years.

A Fabulous City

The capital of Atlantis lay on the eastern side of the central zone, some twenty-five miles from the sea. This was built on the great river Chalid and was called Chalidocean. It was sometimes known as "the city of the golden gates", a name which had an esoteric meaning. In the main square of Chalidocean were situated many great buildings such as art galleries, the houses of government and the great colleges where science and occultism were studied by the priests and student priests. There were four waterways running through this great city, three of which were canalised from the river Chalid. Outside the city itself were great storage houses for grain and other commodities.

The Atlanteans did not build closely as you do today, for they knew the benefit that could be obtained from leaving large spaces of ground free. The grass and plants that grew there purified the air and kept the people healthy and strong. In the centre of this fabulous city stood the great temple, complete with its blue tiled courtyard, fountains and stately pillars. Therein glistened precious and semi-precious stones of every type, some of which you would not recognise today for they were peculiar to Atlantis, such as the metal orichalcum.

Orichalcum was like a pink version of gold and was extremely beautiful. It was used much in external building, for it did not tarnish and needed little polishing. Much of the jewellery worn by the priests and people was fashioned from this lovely metal, as were such household things as drinking bowls and platters. Jewels and metals did not have the value for the Atlanteans that they have for people today, for their country abounded in them and there was no monetary system such as you know to inflate their value.

Each zone of the continent yielded certain natural products which the other zones lacked; for example, much metal working was done in the south, while the northern shores were rich in fruit. There was therefore a need for the exchange of such products and this was effected by means of barter. Also, certain portions of all things grown or manufactured, were handed in to the temple and these were duly distributed to other zones, or stored. By this system there was plenty for everyone and the local temple provided the essentials of life for all: food, clothing, accommodation, equipment and so on. The remainder of everything that was made, grown or manufactured by the people could be bartered by them privately or publicly. In the gaily coloured barter lanes one could exchange a sack of corn for a silk garment, a barrel of fish for a diamond bracelet, or household goods for sparkling jewels that the smiths set in metal over the heat of their small solar lamps.

Thus, people were able to obtain anything they wanted if they worked to produce the extra goods needed to make the exchange a satisfactory one. The people ate fish and bird meat, but they did not touch red meat of any type, nor did they slaughter such animals as pigs and sheep to make meals for themselves. There were no cows in Atlantis and the milk used was taken from goats. The temple authorities, through careful storage and planning, made sure that stocks of goods would be available for all throughout the season, come famine, flood or natural disaster. Many Atlanteans were vegetarians and, although it was not compulsory for the average man to abstain from fish or bird meat, it was found that the consumption of meat increased the density of the physical body and was therefore detrimental to psychic and spiritual work.

When a spirit passed from its physical body the body was neither buried nor cremated but disintegrated by the occultist priests by the use of certain cosmic forces. There was a ritual connected with this 'dematerialisation' and it is from this ancient ritual that the somewhat distorted phrases 'remember, man, that thou art dust and unto dust shalt thou return' or 'ashes to ashes and dust to dust', which appear in many modern burial ceremonies, originated. The original Atlantean invocation was that the spirits of the elements, air, fire, earth and water, come forth and claim that part of the anatomy that had originated from their domain. In the language of the physicist the atomic particles were reabsorbed into the cosmos, thus supporting the interchange of matter and energy. The secret of speeding this change at will was known to the old Atlantean priests who were able to bring about a temporary change in the atomic structure of any material object by altering its rate of vibration or density.

As the Sun rose in Atlantis the people from all walks of life proceeded about their daily duties: the healers to their patients either at the temple or, if necessary, at their homes; the students to study their own planet and the universe; the teachers to their charges and the high priests to their seats of hearing and judgment. But what of the person in the street, who did no esoteric work; did people carry out the ordinary pursuits as you do today? Of course they did, although the 'ordinary things' of those days differed somewhat from certain activities today. People did not work in factories although they did manufacture goods. There was far less manual work, although crops were sown and reaped in the fields as they are today. There were many trades that the individual could pursue if not destined to play a priestly role.

There were buildings where certain types of manufacture were carried out, the energy employed being of a solar nature. Clothing was woven, houses built, farms tended and animals reared for their wool and milk. Ornaments of all types were fashioned and the skilful hands of the artists made the temples throughout the land objects of great beauty and colour. Around the coastal areas the people fished and brought their wares inland to barter. The ships sent by merchants to foreign shores returned laden with rare prizes for barter and much knowledge was acquired of the lives of other peoples all over the planet.

There were no such things as telephones because they did not need them. Messages were sent telepathically from temple to temple and many of the more powerful priests could levitate and transport themselves from place to place. There were messengers who travelled on horseback, although the horses were not quite the same animals that you know. These horse-like animals were called tarsias. They had thick bodies and short legs and were ideally suited to a race of people who did not need to hurry through their existence.

All heavy work was done sonically; houses and villas were built by the use of sonic gongs tuned to the correct pitch of the substance being used. The gong was struck and, by prolonging the note and controlling the tone, huge blocks of stone could be raised or lowered without the aid of machinery or human labour.

Heat and power were supplied by solar means, for our early Atlantean friends had learned how to harness the power of the Sun to provide energy and warmth for their industries and homes. They were very taken with geometric shapes, for in those shapes they saw tremendous energy and potential power. They used crystals of various kinds, which they cut and shaped, in order to direct the specific rays of energy needed for the dispersal of a particular disease or illness.

The Atlanteans understood and accepted other forms of evolution such as the animal and elemental kingdoms and treated them with complete equality and understanding. There were other domestic animals in Atlantis in addition to the tarsia I have already mentioned. There were several types of hounds or dogs and a type of cat known as a 'chata' that was slightly larger than the domestic cat you know today. The tarsia also had a cousin somewhat similar to a donkey. Larger animals from the cat family, such as the lion, were often kept as pets by occultist priests and such was the understanding between animal and man that there was no wildness displayed by any of these creatures towards their masters. The cat family are especially suited to psychic work, and as a protection against the lower astral they are invaluable.

Atlantis was more a close group of islands than a single large land mass. There were many dialects, but the language on the whole was something of a cross between Latin and Spanish. Words and phrases from the old Atlantean language found their way into many of the known early languages of the Mediterranean.

There was a system of writing employed in Atlantis, portions of which were absorbed into Sanskrit and the early Hebrew letterings. Unlike the Mu-ans the Atlanteans did not employ a pictorial system of recording but rather a phonetic one. In other words, certain signs were used to depict certain sounds. Great importance was attached to such things as the vibration of a name and it was the sound of the name rather than how it appeared when written that interested these people. Names were simple in Atlantis, although a child was entitled to use the rank of its father until the time of its union.

The name Helio-Arcanophus was formed by Helio, which means 'of the Sun', and was given as a personal name to all those destined to become high priest, while the 'Arcanophus' was titular; 'arc' meant 'high' or 'advanced', when 'an' was added, making 'arcan', high priest of matters secret or occult; while the 'ophus' stood for 'head', 'leader', 'first' or 'chief'. I personally held that position of 'High Priest of the Sun', ruler of Atlantis, in the period about 8,000 years before the civilisation came to an end.

The garments worn by the Atlanteans were simple and somewhat like those you would associate with classical Greece. Children wore knee-length tunics with a belt or cord at the waist and older people tended to wear clothes of varying lengths. Clothing and colour meant a great deal to the Atlanteans and within the priesthood were indicative of rank. Blue was the occult colour associated with the priesthood. All senior priests wore white garments and gold was an indication of the higher ranks. Also, certain coloured sashes or belts denoted not only the rank of the priest but also the type of esoteric work upon which he was employed. Sandals were worn by all and golden sandals were the insignia of the priesthood. The ceremonial robes of the high priest, including the great cloak of office that could be worn by none but the chief high priest himself, were of great magnificence.

The length of adult garb was determined somewhat by the type of occupation in which people were employed: a farmer would not wear an ankle length robe although garments of such length were always worn by the priests and could be hitched up to just below the knee when walking for any distance. When people swam in the sea for pleasure, they did not wear bathing suits for they were not ashamed of their bodies as people are today. Clothing was ornamental and protective and in colder regions worn for warmth. Most people wore their hair long and in a single plait at the nape of the neck if they wished it to be out of the way. This custom is still found among the Chinese and North American Indians. Hair has much significance both for the physical body and the psychic powers; the story of Samson in the Bible has an occult meaning.

The Atlanteans were, on the whole, a fair race and certainly tall by present day standards. The people of the northern province were more red-skinned, like the early Egyptians or the North American Indians; those who dwelt in the southern provinces were fair. But the main characteristic of the Atlantean race was that their eyes were somewhat slanted. The combination of black hair with violet eyes was common especially in the province of Cintrala. The Atlanteans were a handsome race, even by modern standards.

Following the early days of the Atlantean civilisation many evolved spirits from other planets and solar systems incarnated into Atlantean bodies and, therefore, a great majority of those spirits incarnate on Atlantis were not native to your planet. This helped to raise the general level and diversity of evolution amongst *homo sapiens* on Earth.

Women enjoyed equality with men and all people were acknowledged for the evolution of their spirit rather than for their sex, wealth or status. The equivalent of what you know as 'marriage' was called 'union' in those days. One could union with the mate of one's choosing but, should this prove unfortunate, at a later date the couple could go to the temple and have their union dissolved. The Atlanteans believed that the Great Spirit did not wish people to live in unhappiness because they had made a mistake when young in Earth years or had grown apart. As everyone was kept by the state, the problem of children born out of union did not arise. Unwanted children could always be taken by foster mothers or fathers and the wisdom of the priests was such that they seldom erred in their occult judgments upon such matters.

The ceremony of 'union' was available for those men and women who wished to live together. They would go to the temple to receive the blessing of the priests and the bracelet of union. This bracelet was worn on the left arm of both parties, in the way that a wedding ring is worn on the finger today, for it was fashionable for everyone to wear heavy jewellery in those days. When a couple applied for the blessing of union it was the duty of the priest to advise them as to the suitability of their partnership. In many cases they were in love physically but the evolution of their spirits differed, which meant that as soon as the physical love had subsided they would have little in common. A trained priest could always detect this and would advise the lovers accordingly. If, following a spell of 'married life', they were unable to live in harmony they could return to the priest who would either reconcile them if it were possible, or strike off the bracelet of union if he could see no future for them together. This was, of course, the equivalent of your modern divorce and both parties were free to pursue their lives as individuals once again. In an economic system where money was non-existent, couples could take care of children other than their own without having to consider the cost; thus many older people whose own children had grown up and left them offered their services to the temple as foster parents to unwanted children.

Priests and priestesses usually unioned with each other. They could also union outside the priesthood, though this rarely happened. They had families who were brought up in the same way as all other children and it did not necessarily follow that the offspring of a priest and priestess were sufficiently evolved to follow in their parents' footsteps. In the priesthood and government women shared equal responsibility with men, qualifying as healers, sensitives, occultists, scientists or administrators as they were best suited.

The people of Atlantis lived in dwellings of varied size and shape, from the little white stone homes of the farm workers and shepherds to the stately villas of the high priests. Those who required the help of servants were served for generation after generation by one particular family who lived with them as equals. The children of the cook or gardener played freely with the children of the priest and priestess and they were at liberty to share their master's table. When a child was three years of age, no matter from what station of life it came, it was presented at the temple for occult judgment. If the wise priests saw that the spirit within that body was an evolved one, then that child would be brought up and trained for whichever branch of the priesthood it was most suited. Children were educated in the temples. It was necessary for those who entered the priesthood to be sensitive and evolved and to have sufficient wisdom to understand some of the great mysteries and teachings they had to learn. Many children were chosen to train as healer priests but, fortunately, at the zenith of the Atlantean civilisation there was not much illness and most of the healers' work was concerned with accident cases.

The ordinary people lived simple lives. They did not go to 'church' ritualistically as some people do today, but would often spend some time at the temple to rest and gain enlightenment. The Atlanteans worked during the day and at other times relaxed together in groups. They particularly liked to play games and gather round and sing. Certain days of the year were feast days to commemorate past events, such as the founding of the civilisation. These were great festivals with ritual dances that everyone joined in, for parents taught them to their children at an early age.

From this picture one may get the idea that the Atlanteans were an ideal race; but, of course, they were not. In many respects they were up in the clouds when they should have kept one foot firmly on the ground. They were a kindly people, but not very good at dealing with the aggressive attitudes adopted by lesser evolved people in other areas of the world. Their major fault was that they were inclined to be too philosophical. A person incarnate in an Earth body is there to experience the physical things that only the body can know. A perfect state of living for Earth man is fifty per cent spiritual and fifty per cent material.

In some ways, you see, they had reached stages of what they felt were perfection and this is something that your world needs to watch as it evolves. You have come round in a circle; you are beginning to realise that it is important not to pollute your food, nor to pollute the animals which you eat. But, as a civilisation starts to become more aware of these things, it comes up against other challenges and dangers. Rejecting God can mean that you are believing in yourself to the extent that you think you can handle your own power, drawing on those beneath you to sustain this. And this is what happened on Atlantis.

Any nation or community that becomes too extreme and idealistic in its way of life will come to grief. The Atlantean elite became so spiritual, so philosophically minded that by the time trouble came to their shores they had no idea how to cope with it and were overwhelmed by the lesser evolved infiltrators with their low practices. Those who undertake work of an occult or psychic nature undergo a series of initiatory experiences by which they learn to combat negative forces and protect themselves against undesirable influences. In such a way, they become immune to certain mental attacks, just as in modern medical practice the physical body is immunised against a disease by building a resistance to it. This, of course, applies on every level for if lessons are not learned in life and people are too sheltered they become vulnerable to attack, as they have no recognition of the enemy and therefore no defensive measures. Atlantis in the latter days was a perfect example of these practical deficiencies.

It is no use having an ideal if one is not prepared to see that it is honoured, for sooner or later both the idealist and the ideal will fall before the thoughts and determination of others who are less sympathetic. Yet man today has gone to the other extreme; the material world is his god and he enforces his beliefs on others. Man should aim for balance in all things, balance between the material and spiritual aspects of all sides of life.

As time progressed, the Atlantean priesthood became more and more philosophical and withdrawn. They began to abstain from normal living and practised celibacy. The gap between themselves and the ordinary people widened and gradually they became less and less aware of what was going on amongst their charges.

Immigrants came to Atlantis from lesser evolved lands and started to take an interest in the strange powers possessed by this handsome race. As the Atlanteans were not prepared for such happenings, because of their great trust they allowed many people to come to their country provided they abided by the rules of the state and were not belligerent. As the years went by many of the lesser evolved people from other lands intermarried with the evolved Atlanteans. The story of the 'sons of God and the daughters of men' recorded in the Bible actually originated in these happenings.

Chapter 4

THE FALL OF ATLANTIS

Thought Waves and the Solar System

It is now appropriate to go back in time and tell you of some cosmic events that happened far earlier than the Atlantean period. The universe is composed of various levels of thought or vibration. Bearing in mind that the universe is infinite, these waves or levels of thought are orderly, for they follow recognizable lines or patterns. If you were to send a thought to someone on the other side of your planet, that thought would travel direct to its goal, for thought is infinite and exists interdependently of time and space.

Every thought you think travels into the universe. The ether is full of thought-forms of varying types and intensity and there are also innumerable forms of evolution that have existed throughout time, both in this solar system and others. These thoughts create an orderly current and are channelled into what you might term 'waves'. For example, a 'wave' or current of thought travelling in a particular direction can provide a very powerful influence. So you can well imagine the type of thought-force that emanates from your planet at the time of, say, a major world war.

Millions of years ago your own solar system was caught up in a tremendously powerful thought-wave travelling from a galaxy some billions of light years away. As this thought-wave hit your solar system it brought with it a powerful influence of a baser or lower nature. When such a thought-force is large and powerful its effects can often be far-reaching, and it may momentarily engulf one planet or even a whole solar system, especially if there is a weakness there already. And there was one planet in a nearby solar system, that was affected more severely than all the others, the planet whose name meant, 'giver of light', for it shone with far more brilliance than most of its celestial comrades; yet, occultly, it had succumbed to weakness that had made it easy prey for these forces that had swept through the galaxy.

A number of planets in your solar system were affected although perhaps less intensely – particularly your own planet Earth and also Mars. This, unfortunately, has affected the influence that Mars as a planet bestows upon Earth. It is more often received as belligerence than industriousness; the latter being the natural positive vibration of Mars.

Now, this influx of disruptive energy was gradually dealt with by most of the planets affected and, over time, a reasonable balance was restored, except for that planet far away in the heavens where the mind of the ruling deva had become affected and one part of it sought to break away from the other. And, to an extent, this is what happened. It became possessed by the destructive purpose of the invading energies, and no intervention from the sixth plane was working. At the time of Atlantis it was becoming extremely unstable, and around 10,000 years ago this had begun to affect Earth which had now an imbalance between true and magnetic, North, as it has today, due to its own evolutionary pressures, and on the etheric level there was an even greater tilt, which if it were to burst through into the physical plane would cause havoc.

Every planet has a guiding spirit or planetary deva, who looks after its physical and spiritual evolution, and each is supported by a whole family of devic spirits, as are the archetypal presences that form the planetary family. When one of the planets is endangered, it is natural for there to be attempts to bring harmony back into the scheme of things. Earth is the Planet of Healing, and so it was that some of the imbalanced energy was particularly drawn to Earth, thus lessening the pressure on the 'planet of light'. Provided that the Atlanteans, who were custodians of the finest power on the planet, as well as the most dense, could resolve the shadow elements that had been invoked, then the physical dimension would have come through relatively unscathed.

As the overall evolutionary level in Atlantis fell, the lesser evolved began to learn the occult secrets that had assisted Atlantis towards the path of greatness; but they had neither the wisdom nor the evolution to control the forces they were tampering with. They learned to conjure up spirits, but those they called were not from the higher spheres as were those called by the priests, but from the realms of the lower astral. At the bidding of these spirits they did many terrible things and gradually the practice of a form of black magic spread across the country. Many young Atlanteans became entangled in its web and when they tried to struggle free they found themselves hopelessly caught.

The Shadow Energy
As the malign influence increased and penetrated more into the atmosphere of Earth, it found an enthusiastic welcome, an embracing of the energies by the less evolved members of Atlantean community, and so the gap widened. On one side was the high priest and his followers who pursued the paths of truth and light and, on the other, in the backwoods and secret places, the renegade priests practised foul ceremonies through which they could obtain power over the minds of the ordinary people. The true priests tried hard to disempower their 'black' aggressors but, as is often the case when the evolved come up against the unevolved, it is the unevolved who win, for the evolved are limited to clean methods of defence. Black magic encouraged degeneracy and debauchery. The ordinary people became afraid of these 'black' priests, afraid of what they would do to them if they did not obey their commands. Hideous orgies took place and human blood was drunk. Such was the nature of these terrible deeds. The highest and the lowest behaviour on the planet were there in Atlantis, existing side by side.

The great evolutionary happenings which affect the destiny of a planet are known to the higher spheres before that planet comes into existence for, outside the physical, there is no such thing as time and space, but sometimes things happen which were not in the original plan. So it was with Atlantis for, in order that this influx of negativity could be embraced, as it needed to be before it could be transformed, the loss of this great centre of high spiritual achievement was to come about. This was to cause the greatest retrogression of evolution this planet has experienced. The priests of Atlantis had made serious mistakes, and by this time around 8,000 years ago, the state had reached such a low that it could not now be reversed, and the highest of the priests knew it.

So, in order that the powers and abilities the priesthood held would not be further compromised by the declining situation, the presiding High Priest sent out small groups of his devoted assistants to many places around the globe, which were to become the focal points for a future spiritual renaissance, in a small, concentrated way initially, and in a mature, global way, when, at a time far beyond this, important events will occur on the cusp of a complete transformation into what one can call a full manifestation of divine love.

There was an old Atlantean legend which said, "Whosoever shall aspire to shine as bright as our Lord the Sun shall be cast from his orbit". The days and cycles passed and, to those who had psychic sight, strange signs began to appear in the heavens, signs that meant little to the 'black' practitioners, whose power was drawn from the material world, but much to the high priests of truth. They saw what was to come, and the wisest of them realised that it would be for the best in the long run.

On the etheric level, the planet was suffering a bout of 'the wobbles'. Physically, there were earthquakes where they had never before been experienced. Volcanoes emerged and the seasons became less and less defined. The evil which had set in amongst the Atlantean people grew and many of them worshipped any symbol and practised any form of ritual that had a magical meaning. Thus, they were an easy prey for the gradually strengthening influence of the approaching 'evil' energy from afar, for over-ritualistic methods are vulnerable and should never be used. Soon it was apparent that something was wrong. The planet that shone so brightly in the heavens no longer smiled on mankind but was shadowed by the aura of the incoming negative energy, which loomed ever more ominously in the sky. Panic started. What was happening?

Many people felt that the wrath of the Great Spirit had come because of their evil deeds. Fear spread its icy cloak around a strangely tense land. But the discarnate spirits of the great ones did not desert their charges in the hour of need. "You must leave your homes and familiar cities and villages, leave the good land which has been a home for you for so long and journey forth to the dark unknown. Build yourselves stout ships that will carry you to safe places," and because they knew and trusted their priests and leaders, they obeyed them. In small bands they set forth from the shores of their native land, eastward, westward, to the north and to the south, to join those small settlements of pioneers who had ventured out all those years before to establish, in embryo, a network of power places that could continue, for a time, some of the advanced practices of the Atlantean priesthood.

Only a few of the true priests remained, like the captains who stay as their ships go down, for they felt that their path of duty lay with their homeland. Yes, Atlantis had aspired high, but how many of its people remembered the old legend in those dark days?

Before the last days began, the reigning Arcanophus, or chief priest, called together all the powers that were used by the Priests of Light on the Atlantean occult vibration. By the use of a certain ritual he concealed and sealed these rays so that no one could call upon them until the time came when there would be people incarnate on Earth who would possess the right knowledge and wisdom to unseal them. The key to this seal he placed in a certain country in the world, the land you call England. Its symbol is the Sword of Mikaal, or the Excalibur of Arthur, and its withdrawal will signify the birth of a new Atlantean race.

The unbalanced, or 'shadow', energy from far off steadily approached Earth until it was drawn into its orbit, and part of this energy was to smash into Atlantis with such force, that the axis tilt in the etheric body of Earth, seeking to right itself, reverberated through the physical causing a cataclysm that carried both physical and occult consequences. Particles of matter were hurled through space followed by black rain that swamped the people it settled upon. The bowels of the Earth heaved in protest and the mountains spat back. These violent upheavals sent the great land of Atlantis, and those upon it, to the depths of the ocean.

Physically, Earth had withstood the impact, but it could not have dealt with all the negative energy at one time. The rest was absorbed by the Moon, to be dispensed gradually over the coming centuries of Earth time. And so, it was that one aspect of the high devic energy, which ruled planet Earth, was drawn towards this orb of negativity, a moon, to all appearances a pitted, gutted, dark sphere, fit only to influence the dreams of man, the tides of Earth and the deranged mind. Occultly, the picture was one of great disturbance for the whole planet that would continue even unto these times; an effective positioning that would give the fallen angel immense power and influence to turn people from the light. This influence over planet Earth and the wayward guidance that it represented, that was so malevolently bestowed upon many of the latter-day Atlanteans from afar, now assumed a close control.

In spiritual evolution, the Moon had been dragged to the bottom of the ladder. Yet, the Moon, there in the sky, still exerts a strange fascination for you Earth people, and little do most of you realise the real influence it exerts over you.

The Energy is Dispersed

Many of the Atlanteans who had left their land those years previously had already begun to build small thriving communities and, with the influx of many of their brethren, continued to evolve. In Khemu (Egypt) they had met with considerable success and some of the advanced Atlantean practices continued for quite a time there, as also in parts of Central and South America, Europe, the Middle East and other places. Many landed in the country you now know as Greece, which was larger in the coastal areas in those days. When the natives beheld these "tall fair strangers", for the Atlanteans were somewhat taller than the other peoples of those times, they fell upon their faces and worshipped them for they felt that with such beauty they must indeed be gods incarnate.

For many years, the Atlanteans kept to tightly knit communities and were able to maintain their way of life and keep up their spiritual practices. It was the immigrant Atlanteans who passed on their knowledge to the Egyptians who built the pyramids, using one of the sciences which has long since become lost to man, that of sonics. As time went on, outer pressures increased and the priests made a very serious error, and the ways of the natural inhabitants increasingly predominated. Stories of the deeds and teachings of these tall fair strangers have come down to you in legend form although much distorted by the physical surroundings of those times.

In returning to the mainland, the Atlanteans were actually returning to the descendants of the Mu-ans from whom they had fled centuries before. Because fewer and fewer of the more evolved souls chose to incarnate into their midst they were forced to inter-marry with lower evolved peoples until most of the Atlantean strains and influences became swallowed up, and by the time of dynastic Egypt, which began around 5,000 years ago, the higher understanding was diluted to the point where it was absorbed into the ritual, until it was eventually hidden entirely. Atlantis slipped gradually into obscurity, assuming mythical proportions as time crept by, remembered only through the pen of Plato and the teachings of mystics who have fought to keep her memory alive down the ages.

Chapter 5

THE RETURN OF THE GODS

The Gods awaken

During the early days of man's sojourn on this planet, when it was realised that all was not going well, the devas sought the aid of the Godhead and a spark from this divine source was projected down to Atlantis to try to help mankind fight against the retrograde pull of evil. To aid this spark in his work, certain devas attended it in retinue. Some came from the binary star you know as Sirius to join with other devas already within this solar system. They came because it was from Sirius that the wave of unbalanced thought, which permeated your solar system in its early days, originated. The Siriuns had overcome it themselves, but they felt a certain responsibility for the chaos it had caused in this solar system. These devic spirits became known to the Ancients as the 'gods'.

Man has given God many names over the centuries. The early Atlanteans understood the names of God in greater depth than successive civilisations. They also understood the archetypal principles which the devic spirits from Sirius represented. Archetypal forces are constant and can be represented as divine beings or angelic forces, known to past civilisations as gods or heroes. Names are a constant source of worry to Earth people; if someone calls God by one name and his brother calls God by another, this can cause strife between the two. This is childish, for none of you really know the vibrational name of the Ultimate; such a power would be beyond you in your present stage of Earth existence.

The early Egyptians decided to create structures of belief that would codify the Atlantean beliefs and abilities into a system that would, they hoped, protect them against abuse. So, they chose the names Isis and Osiris to embody the concepts of the Great Mother and the Eternal Father. These included the belief that the Christ spirit was symbolised by the Sun but, as time passed, things lost the purity of understanding and so, as the Sun was obscured from the eyes of the people at night, the legend arose that this spirit descended to hidden places during night time and thus began the legend of the God of the Dead which the Egyptians associated with Osiris. The Egyptian names have been chosen not because they are necessarily accurate, for the Atlantean names were nearer the true vibration, but because the Egypt civilisation is known to you and the Egyptian names are the nearest you have to the Atlantean.

Isis was originally Aset in the Egyptian tongue meaning 'a throne' - early pictures show her with a head-dress shaped like a throne - but this was translated to the name Isis by the Greeks so, in fact, the name bears both an Egyptian and a Greek influence. As both lands were colonised by the Atlanteans this makes the name doubly appropriate.

Nevertheless, it must be borne in mind that God is neither male nor female, neither masculine nor feminine; it is a perfect comple-ment of both. In its true state both aspects are perfectly blended in the androgyne. But when a spark descends from the Ultimate the two aspects become accentuated and take on individual personalities. And so we have the Isis or maternal aspect, the consort of Osiris the paternal aspect, the two polarities of the same spirit.

The Egyptians called the abstract concept of the Godhead, Ra, standing for the complete state of beingness not individualised in any form that man could comprehend. This equates with the 'Father' referred to by Jesus, meaning the whole spirit of which he was a manifested spark or aspect, here to undertake a specific task.

The retinue of devic spirits from Sirius who came to help this solar system and serve with Isis and Osiris were known affectionately as 'the family'. The Atlanteans and, later, the early Egyptians recog-nised these beings as representing archetypal forces and gave them names according to their individual characters. They interpreted the cosmic drama in story form, a story which has been handed down to you as legend and which is even now still unfolding. To members of the family they gave the names Horus, son of Isis and Osiris, Hathor, Nephthys, Thoth, and Anubis. The other spirit from this family, whom the Egyptians called Set, was unfortunately adversely affected by the evil vibrations of negative thought and chose to work against his brothers and sisters. This is the biblical Lucifer, originally a bright archangel but now a fallen deva. Set's influence upon the planet Earth and the solar system has almost finished its reign and is due to be expelled by Horus, with the aid of the Christ spirit.

There were, of course, many other gods in the Egyptian pantheon, deities of the sky, of the seas, of trees and of animals, but many of these were of Mu-an origin and were not amongst the gods or angels known and acknowledged in Atlantis.

Let us now examine each of the vibrations in turn which equate with the archetypes or archangels of Atlantis and Egypt and which are concerned with this battle for Light. First of all, our adversary, Set or Lucifer. This vibration manifests against cosmic law. In an individual it can make for cruelty, arrogance, pride, selfishness and so forth. On a planet it causes wars, dissension, disregard for other life forms, arrogance, mindlessness, a refusal to accept individual respon-sibility, closed mental attitudes. . . Need I go on? In the Egyptian legend, Horus defeats Set, and Set is, like the biblical Lucifer, bound over for a period in time during which his spirit will need to adjust once more to cosmic law and then go about the task of putting right the wrongs it has perpetrated. And yet Set was not evil when he was with his 'family' in the Siriun system. It was only when he was immersed in the wave of negative thought after it left Sirius that he became unbalanced and spiritually sick.

The 'planet of light', which so strongly influenced the Earth's Moon, was the most affected by Set's evil influence; after which it was used as a battering ram in the occult affray between Set and Earth's rightful deva. Some of the negative energy causing this, was captured by the gravitational pull of Earth. The Moon became involved in the latter Atlantean days when Set took control, and from such close proximity Set now wields his evil influence upon this planet. Earth was one of the planets worst affected because it was the Planet of Healing and attracted more sick souls than it could cope with!

Yet evil could not exist on your planet if men did not welcome it and sustain it. As the Set spirit has rejected the Godhead it has cut itself of from its natural supply of cosmic energy, so it needs to feed upon forms of life lower than itself. This it does by encouraging these life forms to indulge in activities which give off a certain type of power, such as the hatred and violence which comes from war, intolerance and greed and from the power generated by the abuse of sex. If men turned their backs on evil, the ray of Set would wither and die, so really man is as much to blame for the state of affairs on Earth as Set, for one could not exist without the co-operation of the other.

The Family

The family of Isis are not solar or planetary devas, they are the seraphim of your Bible, the fiery angels who are called into help when things go wrong. In the Egyptian pantheon the spirit Mikaal was shown in female form as Hathor or Sekhmet. The Egyptians 'married' Hathor to Horus, thus indicating that, in the affray which lies ahead when Horus will defeat Set to free mankind, he will need the help of Hathor (Mikaal) in her role as warrior goddess Sekhmet when she dons the mask of the lioness and takes control of the eye of Ra. Humankind will need to watch its step in the days which lie ahead for, as the legend tells, there will be much shedding of blood.

In the Egyptian story Horus, son of Isis and Osiris, returns to his father's kingdom to dethrone Set the usurper, but it is necessary for a certain awareness to develop in the nature of men before this state can be attained. The Egyptian version is slightly garbled but the battle cannot be won without the aid of the cosmic consciousness of the Christ, so Horus cannot dethrone Set until he receives the aid of the Ultimate, a manifestation of which will return to Earth as the third coming.

In the final battle Horus will ride forth on a white horse to meet Set, or so you are told in the Trismegistic teachings. The legend tells how Osiris gave his son the choice of a helper from the animal kingdoms and Horus chose the horse. Osiris asked him why he did not choose the lion, one of Osiris's own solar symbols, and Horus replied that the horse signified purified passion. The unicorn, or horned horse, is associated with Isis in her virginal aspect; hence the legend that only a virgin, or pure minded person, can control the power of the cornucopia represented by the horn of the unicorn. Incidentally, the white horse was the sacred animal in the latter days of Atlantis and Atlantean settlers engraved these animals on hillsides wherever they settled.

As well as being the deva who battles with Set, Horus also represents an archetypal principle of light and art, depicted later as the Greek Apollo. All forms of creativity come under this ray, as do music and beauty. But let me define music as the harmony of the spheres and not the disharmony which is so prevalent upon your planet today. Some of the noise which is called music is the sound of the 'formless ones', those spirits from the spheres of pre-human existence that have not yet found a harmony in form or chosen their branch of evolution. The problem lies in the fact that the evolutionary gap is rather wide on Earth. At one end of the scale are the older souls who are trying to help to right things, while at the other end are primitive spirits who are scarcely used to bodies at all.

When Horus takes on an incarnation, as he will in the future, he will be born in the normal physical way. He will understand manifested form and know how to cope with it, for all practical matters come under his rulership. This planet has only seen the shadow of Horus, the shadow of the falcon sweeping down from on high, and even that was impressive in Atlantis of old. When the time comes for the falcon to land, then the new golden age will be with you. The Horus ray is of the future, a ray yet to come. It embodies the male, the female and the elemental. It embodies the understanding of men and beasts. It is the ray of balance and, because it contains spiritual understanding, the symbol of the hawk is used.

Many people ask why sacred principles are often depicted by a creature of prey or a hunter or huntress. There is an answer to this; the archetype of the hunter or huntress has many meanings at different levels. It is a principle which stands for evolution and should not necessarily be interpreted as cruel simply because it appears so when taken at its face value. The hunter seeks out and destroys that which holds it back, thereby evolving through it. It is symbolically destroying the lesser evolved aspects of the self, surmounting and conquering them and yet gaining sustenance from them.

The Greeks signified the ray of the hunter in female form as Artemis, sister of Apollo; thus the Greek Apollo equates with Horus and Artemis with the huntress, Bast, the Egyptian cat goddess who represented the divinity of fecundity, pleasure and laughter. The hunter seeks out his own evolutionary path and strives to devour that which is less evolved than himself. Yet there is also an aspect of this archetype which seeks to devour that which is wiser, in order that by so doing it may gain the knowledge and wisdom of that which it devours. In primitive society, a man who hunted the lion and ate its heart, firmly believed that he would thereby partake of the strength and courage of that beast; a form of sympathetic magic, if you like. But in its higher octave the archetype of the hunter denotes the seeking of knowledge, wisdom and spiritual advancement which, by their light, cancel the lesser forms of darkness.

Now, let us turn to the Osiris figure, the king and ruler. Osiris represents the Sun god incarnate. He is the king/teacher archetype who teaches the esoteric truths of wisdom and philosophy. Like the Sun, he rises in great brilliance, sets and descends into the underworld only to rise again. The analogy is a good one. Once the Sun is unseen and darkness descends, man feels alone for he cannot see his god and he has to approach him without being truly aware of what he is praying to, and this is where Isis comes in. It is strangely interesting and not inappropriate that many schools of occultism associate Isis with the Moon. This confusion arose because many people believed that when the Sun went down, the light of the Moon took over.

And so the story continues. Osiris came to Earth and was destroyed because he recognised the evil forces of Set manifesting in men. Man destroyed him mercilessly and it is only the intervention of Isis on man's behalf which can evoke in Osiris the compassion which causes him to love his tormentors and aid mankind in spite of it all. Just as the Sun sets in the west only to rise again in the east, Osiris dies and is resurrected. Legend tells us that he returns in spirit because Isis speaks for man, acting as advocate, the role ascribed by Christianity to the Holy Ghost.

As Jesus foretold, the Holy Spirit has come to man, only it is not the abstract theological concept of the third person of the Christian trinity portrayed by the dove; it is Isis, the Mother of all, the advocate who mediates between man and the Ultimate. The dove was often used as a symbol of Venus and those earlier goddesses associated with the love principle. It is strange that those who acknowledge the dove symbology of the Holy Spirit should not realise that it is the symbol of a feminine principle.

At present you have an unbalanced concept of the Godhead; one aspect only, the male aspect, has become completely out of proportion in your minds and behaviour. To rescue humankind from this situation that began so strongly in Egypt, the feminine aspect, is now coming much closer to Earth.

It is important to understand that it would be just as misguided to have a planet which was dominated by the feminine aspect, for either concept alone would be a faulty translation of a higher principle. The balance will, however, be established in time, for this state of equilibrium is part and parcel of the Horus ray. Then and only then will humanity enter a golden age.

The ancient Egyptians could not abide a straightforward story. They had to embellish and embroider it, and if they could throw in a little sex, blood and intrigue then so much the better; as did the Greeks. The Atlanteans on the other hand were a more straight-forward people, so what has filtered through to you today is a mixture of the purer Atlantean interpretation of the cosmic drama with Egyptian embellishments. Some of the gods and goddesses of Egypt were early Mu-an deities on which the true Atlantean teachings were superimposed, while later deities were figures of convenience engineered by a crafty priesthood. If the archetype is pure then so also is the ray and the priesthood attached to it, but in later Egyptian times there was much spiritual pollution. So, if you allow for this duality of rays and accept the pure Atlantean strain you will gain much spiritually. But should you tread without due care there are pitfalls to be encountered through Egyptiana.

The Gods as Archetypes

It is up to you to sort the wheat from the chaff by seeing all these mythical characters in terms of principles or archetypes rather than as actual people. All these gods are part of your own consciousness. At the moment you think of them being 'there' and you being 'here', it becomes inaccurate. All is one. Another mistaken concept is to think of these 'forces' as being like the discarnate entities with which some mediums communicate. The intelligences behind them are discarnate, agreed, but not quite in the way you may think. The nearest analogy is to radio waves. It does not affect a radio wave how many receivers are switched in to it; you have millions and millions of receivers tuned in to a radio signal without the wave being in any way affected. In the case of the 'gods', these waves are personalised.

You may call on any of the archetypal principles to help you to resolve a problem by rebalancing the situation which has caused that problem. They will not, however, do your task for you. If your problem results from the fact that you are lazy and you ask for help with it, then a situation will be put your way wherein you will have to face up to your own laziness and do something about it. If your problem is that you are unable to stand on your own feet, the archetype will help you to stand up for yourself and accept the responsibilities which you are trying to shirk.

A part of your mind corresponds to the power within each archetype, so you will find yourselves more in harmony with one force, perhaps, than with another. Never hesitate to ask for help, for the very act of so doing will awaken that aspect of the archetype, the god or goddess, within your own mind. You are only, in fact, using your own power and switching on that part of your brain which was originally designed to give you access to the forces of the universe, those principles which are constant and infinite: the higher Self, in fact. Also, it helps the higher forces to bring through their powers of light if people ask for their aid. "Ask and ye shall receive," said the Master, for no higher spirit can help if that help is not requested; such is cosmic law.

Although you are individuals in one sense you are also a part of a whole, a cell in a cosmic body if you like. The link with the rest of that cosmic body is good and helpful both to you as the individual cell and to the cosmic body of which you are a part. As long as you carry out your individual task and responsibility as a unit cell and do not lean too heavily upon the units around you, then you may seek to remain in balance with the whole by communicating with other cells and other aspects of it.

No archetype is concerned with how it is called. Over the centuries they have been called by thousands of names each slightly different, each covering a different aspect of their vast range of activities. So, to specify Isis, Osiris or Horus is rather like picking up a teaspoonful of water and saying you have an ocean. It is well to bear in mind that you can onl · be helped in accordance with the stage of spiritual development you yourself are in. The divine beings cannot appear to you in all their glory for, since you are of flesh and blood, their splendour would devour you. How well the Greeks illustrated this with the story of Zeus and Semele!

Now let us glance at the remaining spirits who form the family of Isis. Nephthys is the revealer. She is the deity or archetype of mysticism and the psychic and receptivity and of all that is hidden or of other dimensions. In the myth she was originally joined in partnership with Set who represented the human intellect. When the split took place, intellect and intuition became separated in the minds of men. This was one of the significances of the fall from the outer or cosmic worlds of intuition to the lower or restricting worlds of matter. The Nephthyan bridge of mysticism and natural intuition had to be withdrawn as it constituted a weakness through which the powers of Set could penetrate the minds of men.

This was how man lost the faculty of long-memory, for in the early days of this planet he had a natural faculty of etheric sight which enabled him to communicate with animals, plants, elements and so on, and also be aware of his own karmic past. In those days one part of the mind was ruled by rational knowledge, the ray of Set, and the other by intuition, the ray of Nephthys; so early man, before the fall, possessed the qualities of reason *and* intuition in equal parts.

The story tells how Nephthys left Set and gave herself in the service of Isis to help restore the kingdom of their brother Osiris. It is a cosmic principle that if two forces unite, a third force results; thus you have your trinities of the early religions and the somewhat distorted version which later made an appearance in Christianity. Nephthys and Set had not united to create a third force and Nephthys was concerned both about this and the absence of Set's ray in the Osirian scheme of things. The principle of two forces uniting to produce a third can be evidenced at one level in chemistry and physics, at another in the procreation of physical species and at a cosmic level in the blending of rays to create a necessary principle. Seeking to correct the imbalance, caused by the malfunctioning of the Set ray, Nephthys sought the aid of Osiris himself, or we might say she turned to a higher power than herself for help. This part of the legend tells how a son, in the form of a dog, was born to Nephthys and Osiris which they named Anubis.

Thus the story was told by the wise ones in Atlantis, for the people found it easier to think of the birth of something they could see and understand; as their mothers had borne them, so did their gods in turn bear godlings. Another interesting point here is that, in ancient Egypt, it was considered that if a child were born malformed or genetically mutated in some way it was the done thing to put it down at birth, just as the animal kingdoms do today. This was done by exposing it in some harsh place where it slowly died before the brain attained to a state of consciousness which could accentuate its awareness of the suffering involved. The idea of a dog or jackal being born to someone frightened the primitives and they thought it natural for any mother giving birth to such a monstrosity to expose it. So, when it was explained to these people that the result of the blending of the rays of Osiris and Nephthys was a manifestation of an archetype representing the animal kingdoms, they invented the story of how Nephthys exposed her son and Isis took him in to rear as, after all, he was of divine origin.

Osiris and Nephthys had created a ray in Anubis which was complementary to the other rays and which helped to compensate for the deficiency of the Set ray. The archetype he represents is the jester, he who laughs in the face of evil, for evil does not like laughter and much wisdom can be hidden behind the jester's stick. Do investigate the origins of a jester's stick for it can tell you much.

Anubis has many functions. He is the escorter of souls, the psychopompous who leads the spirits of the departed to the hall of judgment where Osiris awaits. He is the guardian of Hades, or the lower astral as it is sometimes referred to, and none may pass safely through those regions without his help. To Anubis are known the secrets of science and all hidden and concealed things. He is lord of anaesthetics - in ancient Egypt the anaesthetists were priests of

Anubis - for his ray can relieve pain. He can also plumb the depths of the subconscious mind. He is the researcher, the finder of lost things, the spiritual guide dog to the blind soul.

In this context, the archetype of the clown or fool is important. I use the word 'fool' in the proper sense, not meaning a simple minded person. This archetype brings into human life a concept which creates an anomaly and this, in turn, stimulates thought; for this was the original function of the fool. So, try to dispel from your minds all thoughts of comics and red-nosed comedians. Perhaps the nearest thing in your language would be the old court jester, the one person who could humorously point out to the king the error of his ways without suffering any dire consequences. This can be likened to certain atoms where one of the elements runs haywire but, in so doing, stimulates all the others. It is also an earthing force which can direct the mind into new channels of thought.

Anubis has this light side but he is also very serious. He has the perceptiveness to see what is wrong and to put it over to authority without offence; he earths the throne as it were. This he achieves by allowing higher forces to rid themselves of their inhibitions through him, through laughter. He is the safety valve for authority. He can get over to the king the will of the people when they are unable to express it in terms of the king's court.

Another aspect of Anubis is that he may venture into realms where no others tread. He can 'break the rules', or appear to, but strictly speaking he does not, of course. This aspect is illustrated by the saying, 'Fools rush in where angels fear to tread'. Anubis is the fool in the family of angels and he gets away with his folly for it is the folly of wisdom. If you are ever unsure as to whom to call upon for help, ask Anubis and he will direct you to the ray for which you seek. In olden times, the Anubian ray was the ray of the novitiate who had not attained to the rites of the other gods but who, by calling Anubis, could partake of the essence of higher divinities through his help. He is a great finder of lost things, including lost minds, and like the jester he can bring you back to your senses when you are flying too high. This is why he is depicted with long ears, a long nose and a dog's head.

But although Anubis laughs and wears a funny mask he is the equal of Set, so he may travel through the net woven by Set around this planet which separates the minds of men from the revealing rays of Nephthys; and Set can do nothing about it. Anubis has the power to bridge the two worlds and this he does through the symbology of the subconscious mind. He avoids Set's net by travelling under it, just as your subconscious minds absorb much of the stress of your daily lives to release it quietly during sleep state. Anubis's route is a devious one but it avoids Set. It is the bridge which Osiris and Nephthys created to join man with the gods.

The Scandinavians have a folk song about a bridge under which lurk three evil trolls bent upon waylaying passing travellers. So it is with Set who lies in wait to deceive and distort; but, with Anubis to guide and guard him around or even under the bridge, man may safely reach the higher regions.

It matters not in which guise you think of this archetype, as St. Christopher, patron saint of travellers, as Anubis, or as an archangel. Different languages and different religions, that is all. If you stand alone and proudly say, "I do not need help to cross the road", you will be on your own. But try to realise that you are sometimes a blind man in a country where others can see and you will need a guide dog occasionally when you cannot see what is coming. If you remain egotistical where psychism is concerned and say to yourself, "I can negotiate the psychic worlds and inner planes without all this protection", your ego will lead you straight into the arms of Set and he will imprint into your mind that which he wishes you to receive. You will come round thinking you have been in contact with a great entity as, indeed, you have been, but a fallen one.

Now let us consider Hathor who is a dual-roled archetype. One aspect of her is the beautiful woman, the nourisher who replenishes the soul during sleep and gives nourishment to the body, which is why she was depicted symbolically by the Egyptians as a cow giving milk, or sometimes as a goddess wearing the headdress of a horned disc. In her other aspect she is Sekhmet, the warrior goddess with the head of a lioness who guards the eye of Ra. Like Athene in the Greek myths who was born from the head of Zeus, Hathor was born of the divine eye of Ra. She is associated with Horus because he will need her specific ray, the Mikaalian ray, to help him when he eventually faces Set. So, in her milder aspect, Hathor is the mother who nourishes her young and is associated with the skills and crafts of women and the home, for her ray is an outgoing and positive one which sustains and strengthens. Yet this strength can turn to militancy if the honour of Ra is at stake and, like Athene (Kali in the Hindu myths), when she does enter battle she is terrible to behold. Hathor is strong and reliable and through her ray she extends these virtues to all creation.

The Egyptian civilisation extended over thousands of years and these archetypes were sometimes depicted differently at different periods, which can be very confusing for a student of today. As an example, later Egyptian pictures show Isis wearing the headdress of a horned disc, whereas this is rightfully the symbol of Hathor.

The final seraph is Thoth. Traditionally the magician, Thoth is the Egyptian version of Merlin, but he has many other roles. He is the Lord of Karma and keeper of the Akashic records. He is scribe to the gods, a lord of learning, of medicine, of diplomacy and truth. Where the ray of Set represents the human intellect and reason, the ray of Thoth supplies that intellect with knowledge and information. At a later period, Thoth was depicted as married to Maat, Goddess of Truth, but Maat is purely an abstract theological concept and in fact represents the receptive side of the Thoth ray. Thoth is teacher, repository and messenger, which takes some thinking out. He can be likened to the archangel Raphael in the Christian religion.

Man's idea of these archetypal forces is very limited. They cover a much wider field than he imagines. From the description I have given, you can see how all these rays are interconnected and complement one another, broadly representing a set of cosmic principles which manifest at all levels. Nor are these archetypal spirits I have talked about the only spirits helping in the fight against evil for there are other devic beings from this solar system itself.

Suffice it to say that you are represented by the masculine and feminine aspects of the Christ spirit, which we have called Osiris and Isis, and their band of seraphim who are helping in the battle to restore balance to this planet and harmony within the solar system and galaxy. Call on these archetypal principles in time of need for they are here to restore balance not only to the planet itself but to all individual spirits and creatures who are part of it.

The Atlantean Heritage in Egypt

In the early days of Atlantis they had the highest vision of what they were going to do for the planet but all the light that they were expressing inevitably attracted the shadow. It was the choice of those priests who had authority in that civilisation as to which way they would run it. Sadly, many started to be affected by ego problems, and it was in their inability to effectively balance the male and female energies that things began to go astray. Many of the teachers in the temples were very feminine in their orientation, and this aroused fear in them, fear that they would lose the strength to deal with their powers as they intensified, fear that they would not be respected by the people they served. A man had to be strong, and they felt overwhelmed by their sensitivity, and so, instead of being a simple channel for the divine, they started to control those around them and below them with rules and regulations.

They created false hierarchies, causing the fear to intensify. So, arising out of the shadow there came rebellion, anger and frustration. They started to dispense with the most potent of the energies and gradually all the great philosophies and understanding were abandoned. Their practices gradually became more to show off their powers rather than to extend and enhance them and, most damaging of all, they dispensed with many of the balancing rituals that enabled the priestesses to keep everything grounded. So the yang became out of touch with the yin, and Atlantis became very much like what is happening in your world today.

Oh, they had achieved a tremendous technology, achieved a powerful understanding of many occult matters, but they had allowed it to become very undisciplined and far too open. It had lost its true spiritual dimension. There were problems both on a grounding and a spiritual level, and somehow those who were leading the civilisation had become so directional in their understanding that they had become unaware of the catastrophe that they were drawing to themselves, for it had reached a point in that civilisation where they could not carry on as they were.

I don't want to give you the impression that the Atlantean civilisation could have been saved. It was time for it to end in that form, but if they had not gone so far out of balance, what was to follow on by way of dispersion of the power around the globe would have been far more elevated and lasting, and the severity of the dark ages that much of the globe was to subsequently experience, could have been spared. You see, each period inherits its potency and longevity from the last, and has a certain momentum and upthrust that can keep it going when the inevitable ebbing of the tide comes.

As the destruction of Atlantis became imminent, the High Priest became somewhat aware of what had gone wrong, and as he sent his most trusted priests to safe places in the world he instructed them to strive to keep the teachings and abilities alive, but within a greater balance. And in the early days, after Atlantis sank beneath the waves, there was a resurgence of the power that enabled the enclaves of immigrant Atlantean souls to achieve a great deal. They were to carry forward the teachings sufficiently strongly that these became embedded in all the countries in which they settled and, in the edifices that they built, they secreted pockets of knowledge and wisdom that would be accessible later on for the benefit of you who are incarnate today.

The Great Pyramid
Their great achievement was to construct the Great Pyramid of Giza. Why a pyramid? It was a symbol of the unified power of man, and a pyramid of the right proportions is a protected container capable of holding tremendous energy.

In the building of the Great Pyramid they used all the expertise and occult knowledge that they had brought from Atlantis. I would say that this inspiring edifice had as its most important purpose the merging of the masculine and feminine principles within what is a perfectly constructed powerhouse capable of transforming the cosmic energies into a fusion of peace, tolerance and understanding. This would then ray out beyond into the surrounding country, to bring life into a great harmony of purpose and co-operation in a kind of protected circle of activity. They were able to keep the negative energies from Atlantis away to some degree, for both kinds of power came with them. They were aware that, while the Atlantean priest-hood had been very open, it had become undisciplined, and they were determined not to make that error again.

And so, for much of the next 1,000 years Egypt remained in a stable balance within the whole region and, although there are no historical records, it was a relatively contained enclave running parallel to the less evolved races and communities that co-existed with it. After a while, the Venusian spirits, who had so uplifted the consciousness of *homo sapiens*, gradually retreated back to their planet, and much of the spiritual maturity that they had brought to the planet was lost. This period was to successfully transmute some of what had gone wrong in Atlantis, but much remained that was to gradually lower the spiritual expertise and understanding of the priesthood; until, at the commencement of the pharaonic dynasties, there was not much memory of what had preceded it. It remained an advanced civilisation compared with others on your planet, but it was a pale shadow of what had been there earlier.

The Great Pyramid had been the main focus for the priesthood and it was a place of initiation, where both the priests and the priestesses were to take themselves beyond, and into mastery - and one day this will be reasserted. There is a King's chamber and a Queen's chamber in the great pyramid. Those chambers were originally built with the intention of merging the masculine and feminine energies together. The King's chamber is an initiation room, where the candidate for initiation was put into a trancelike state by the priests and, for three days, had many soul adventures. The soul would leave the body and go down into the chamber beneath the earth as part of the initiation ceremony, making contact with the nether world. These initiates had to overcome a great darkness that rose within themselves and then face some of the darkness associated with the subtle realms.

Many men who have lived in Earth bodies have added their quota to a mismanagement of the planet through not allowing the spirit to come more into operation. So, a candidate for initiation is also working out karma garnered by the planet, for Earth is a great entity with a soul of its own. It needed great discipline in training for this initiation, and not all of the souls returned to their bodies.

The female initiation was carried out in the Queen's chamber where they sent the souls into even more subtle realms, into a chamber which has not yet been discovered, low down. At some time it will be found but the passage to it is now closed off, though there are many who suspect it is there.

Distortions by the Priests

The priesthood certainly took on board the need for discipline and, as time passed, Egypt grew into a mighty empire. All the high priests who were involved in different aspects of the place, developed it in a very complex way; yet by the time of the dynastic period, they had distorted many of the really important issues – and, in recognising the need for discipline, they took it too far. From my point of view, one of the tragedies of the Egyptian civilisation was their rigidity in looking at beliefs such as reincarnation and this is what has caused problems, not only in Egypt but in other countries in the Middle East as well.

You must remember that Egypt was a centre of post-Atlantean energy, both the good and the not-so-good Atlantean energy, and there was the fear element that called for control. Because of this, the priests gradually brought in more and more rules and regulations, which humankind is very fond of doing today and, once again, the female input was gradually diminished.

One of the most harmful beliefs was that life followed life in exactly the same way. It was a restrictive understanding of reincarnation that had the effect of locking many souls into a rigid, repressive scenario. A spirit was expected to reincarnate into a similar body of the same sex with a similar karma and the same physical status in life. A pharaoh returned as a pharaoh, a slave as a slave, and a woman remained a woman of exactly the same social class. It was not possible, they believed, to move away from this. But it does not happen that way and many souls became stuck, creating an atmosphere in that region that held people firmly in their place. Many, when they died could not move away. They remained immersed in the old beliefs and this created a pall of stuckness throughout much of that region. It strengthened the tendency of the Hassidic Jews to incarnate regularly in that form, determined to keep the purity of the line, and the attitudes of the Moslem faith where the old male/female imbalance has become rigidly entrenched.

It doesn't work like that because before a spirit incarnates it looks back at all that it has been, and if it is a wise spirit it will decide that in its the next incarnation it will encounter, perhaps even larger challenges, ones that will enable it to step forward on its spiritual journey. So, it might be a pharaoh in one incarnation, and in the next, a man rowing a ferry boat, or a lady serving a princess.

The one other misconception that has bedevilled that country is containment, which was due to an over-reaction to the lack of discipline inherited from Atlantis. You must remember that the Egyptian religion under the Pharaohs was to become increasingly fixed. It represented a tremendous archetypal Atlantean energy that was saying, 'Never again!'

They became a society that had a structure and discipline, certainly, but it became strict and narrow. It did not allow for change and, in that sense, they went from one extreme to the other, for though they had accumulated power, they were unable to disseminate that power. As they had come forward from Atlantis, they were concerned about not wanting to do what happened before, they wanted to 'put things right' but, in doing so, they actually put things more and more out of alignment. They felt that they had to conquer even more lands to bolster their omnipotent presence. So, what has happened is that there is a tremendous amount of stuck energy in the Middle East, far beyond the land of Egypt itself.

The Great Pyramid was used as a means of storing energy, of preserving the personal authority of the pharaohs and high priests, and of supplying the power that was focused so strongly within the city of Thebes, the base from which the Pharaohs ruled the empire. It was seen as a way in which the religious energy could eventually control the world. But the religion crumbled, thankfully, for people started to move beyond it, as people are starting to move beyond certain religions at this present time. But, of course, the energy they created is still there, and there are those incarnate now in Egypt and in other middle Eastern countries who are carrying a restrictive Egyptian energy from a past life in those ancient times.

The Heretic Pharaoh

I have spoken about the pharaonic dynasties that came and went as the purity of the Atlantean traditions ebbed away and became hidden in the formalised rituals to the gods. It was then that there came to Earth many teachers, such as the Buddha in the East, whose lives and teachings were an attempt to reassert the feminine with the masculine, for this state of equilibrium is an essential aspect of the Horus ray. And there was one in the Egyptian line who fore-shadowed the coming of an even more elevated expression of the fifth plane. I shall let Akhenaten speak for himself:

"It is perhaps with somewhat mingled feelings that we come before you today. For, to look back to the past is a business which has both its happy and its sad aspects. Though when you are able to look back by consulting the Akashic records, you will be quite amazed that so much of what you term failure has not been noted down by the Lords of Karma as you would suppose. Man sees only that which a short sight leads him to see. He cannot enter fully into an understanding of the Godhead. If he did, then he would not need to be in life at all.

"God is boundless - boundless wisdom, boundless love, bound-less life. These things were born in upon me when I was very young in those far off days in Egypt. But I also saw that the priesthood of that time was a corrupt priesthood. When, as was the custom, the Pharaoh, and I refer now to Amenophis III, sat in the Hall of Judgment, there would be the priests who had been bribed to tell untruths. Very often, lives were forfeited because of this fact.

"Egypt had grown strong because of her ability to conquer and subdue the surrounding cities and tribes, and there were many slaves taken. But to lovers of peace, such as we were, these warlike conditions were very frustrating. We wished to remain in tune with the God of Love. And when the time came for the mantle of the Pharaoh to fall upon me, I was determined to rid Egypt of the corruption and vice. But having entered into pharaoh-hood at a very tender age, many were the times when, like the Buddha later, I found myself wrestling with thoughts perhaps too large for the mind to encompass, thoughts that could only be hinted at, glimpsed, thoughts that had a habit of vanishing as soon as they came.

"After much striving to encourage the priests of the 'god' Amun to see things as we were learning to see them, we resolved to move away from Thebes, the capital, and find a place where a new city could be built, where a new kind of expression of the creative arts could come into being.

"There were too many foes, too many ready to pounce upon us when giving expression to what they called a farrago of nonsense. Many who came into the judgment halls were still bribing the priests. But when the sight was clear and the emotion less troubled, we were able to see into the hearts of those who came for judgment, and we would never condemn the wrong man. We would never take the forfeit of any life. But the priests of Amun fought to keep the way of life as they knew it.

"We did not condemn them. They had to grow into understanding, and so we sailed away to found the city of Aten. It was then that the wonderful hymn, with which we were to begin and end each day, started to come through little by little.

Hymn to the Aten
Wondrous you appear on the horizon of the sky,
O living Aten, beginning of life!
You rise triumphant in the Eastern heavens,
Filling every land with your brilliance.
You are beautiful, great, exalted on high.
Your rays encompass all that you have made.
You are the God who makes all laws;
You gain obedience by your love.
You are far away but your rays shine upon the Earth;
When you are with us, your presence is the day,
And when you depart, to rest beneath the far horizon,
The Earth is in darkness like the dead.

"Many of you like to see pictures of the family you look upon as Royal. But how static are those pictures. You do not see paintings of the Queen seated at her breakfast table with the fork raised. But we wanted to create art that was absolutely natural, so that one could look at a picture and feel it became really alive. Of course, time has obliterated many of the most noble works of art that were executed, and the tomb robbers and those who erased the name of Aten from the many works did their bit of vandalism as well.

"You cannot imagine the vast splendour of the city of Aten. Does that city flourish today? It flourishes in that world beyond, but in a very different sense, because the city of Aten was completely destroyed. You see, Amenhophis III had been a great warrior, but Amenhophis IV (or Amenhotep IV) was no warrior at all, save a warrior for God. But why could not that beautiful city have been duplicated? Why was not the dream realised that people would want to come from near and far, would want to enter in and feel the new vibrations, hear the new strains of music, see the new works of art, and sit at the feet of those who taught the way of monotheism? Why?

"There are many who come in their time to pave the way, or to set into motion a stream of thought that has life in it, but a life that cannot arise to its greatness and its glory at that particular time. And such was the City of Aten.

"We tell you now a truth that you can find in no history book whatsoever, that as he who was known as Lord of the Horizon, Akhenaten, was passing into the spirit world, there appeared before him a figure he had seen perhaps thrice before, and had wondered greatly who that figure was. Sometimes the figure would be shadowy with a cross of light behind it. Sometimes the figure would appear full of youthful beauty, full of light, with the glorious Aten shining behind it. Sometimes the figure would seem to be so elevated that the very clouds ceased. But it was only on the couch of death that Akhenaten saw and understood that this was the coming Son of God who, being endowed with the Christ consciousness, would overshadow the man Jesus, transforming him into the glorious Son of the Sun.

"For well did Akhenaten know that behind the Sun that gives life to all, that nourishes and brings into being all that is, and without which the world would be dead, well did he know that another Sun was there, and yet another one behind that one, for the radiation came from the Godhead. And alone in him was invested the power and the might and the glory.

"And so, in spite of the agonies through which Akhenaten had passed during the time when the city of Aten was being overrun and conquered because he would not take up arms and fight; in spite of the great illness that had seized his mortal frame, the son of peace looked and conquered. And it was in that moment of great realisation that the soul of Akhenaten left the Earth.

"You could see it as a failure for the man Jesus to have gone to the Cross when the power was there to command legions of angels to his side, but we would not do so. Something emanates from a defeat that is not really a defeat, something of a lasting quality, something that speaks the message loud and clear to those souls in any age who hear and respond to its call. It may come in the form of a vision of something that lies ahead in time, and there is the impulse to chase that vision, to carry it a little further along the way. Always, man must make the effort, and sustain it, if ever the vision is going to open out and yield its fruits.

"In those far off days in Egypt, if we had made the effort, perhaps a little more, to break through the strongholds of the priesthood, who knows what might have happened. Everything boils down to a resource in the last degree, to the fact that dreams are all very well, but dreams have to be set in motion through effort, through striving. Man is not only a feeling being, whose senses can be heightened and quickened by the kind of life he feels will bring him happiness, but man is also a thinking being. He has to learn to make good thought structures, and then he has to have the will to breathe life into them.

"Be not afraid, for that dim, shadowy figure, the glorious spirit of light that Akhenaten saw on his death bed, was surely the Son of the Sons of the Godhead and will be so to all eternity."

Chapter 6

THE OLYMPIAN CIVILISATION

The Gods of Olympus

I invite you to take a journey with me. Let us travel backward into the past and then perhaps forward into the unseen future. Our first destination will be the realm of Mount Olympus where, for an 'age', the gods reigned supreme. Viewed in a modern light, they may appear to be purely imaginary stories; but all such legends are based on some form of truth or message. As each spirit evolves it ascends to the higher planes, toward the heights of Olympus, and during this journey many assume the roles of heroes or helpers of men. Many of these 'heroes' are amongst you now, helping the planet through its period of trial. For aeons of time, spiritual teachers have found it necessary to speak in parables, fables and stories, and man has enacted these in the theatre of life.

At the height of the Greek civilisation the evolution of the planet was very much in a transitional stage intellectually. It was a time when there were many spirits in incarnation who were beginning to look deeper into the reason for life and to seek some form of guidance which embraced the intellect. The wise ones incarnate at the time realised this and they sought a form of symbolic instruction which would convey a meaning on many levels.

If you look at the Olympian pantheon you will observe that there were twelve predominating deities and many lesser entities, as well as the 'heroes' who represented *homo sapiens*. Throughout the various teachings given on this planet you will find this cosmic number constantly appearing. As I said earlier, there are twelve cosmic bodies in this solar system that represent twelve archetypal principles, with the Sun representing the number thirteen, the Master.

You all know and understand the physical dimension in which you live and most of you realise that there are other dimensions beyond the physical material, for nothing in this universe is limited. Man seeks beyond his own dimension and, because he sometimes tries to measure that seeking with a material yardstick, he comes up against a brick wall. You have been told to "Knock and it shall be opened unto you". Do you dare to knock? And, if the door is opened, do you dare to go through? Can you face the gift you have, which is the capacity to use your mind?

Although there were those people in the days of ancient Greece who understood this, the majority did not, so the teachers formulated stories of gods and goddesses who appeared beyond the reach of man's physical attainment. Gradually it began to occur to the wiser seekers that gods stood for principles, points of light and cosmic actualities rather than exalted human beings.

There is a connection between the Olympian pantheon and astrology, an art which has become obscured over the ages. Man has tended to use it for his own material gain and thereby has ceased to understand its esoteric significance. Let us take the signs of the zodiac; again there are twelve, just as Jesus had twelve apostles and Arthur twelve knights. In Atlantis, the governing body consisted of six administrators and six occultists to govern the land, with one high priest or arcanophus as the thirteenth.

Those of you who understand astrology will know that it is possible for two people to have the same Sun sign and Ascendant, the same background and be born at almost the same time, and yet they will not respond to life in the same way. Why is this? First and foremost, every spirit is individual and on its own journey. Secondly, although their astrological aspects may be similar, these will result in different outcomes because every sign of the zodiac has several frequencies and many octaves and it will be up to the individual evolution of each spirit as to which of these levels it can attain. This is one of the points upon which people disagree where astrology is concerned. It is one of the things that turns the more rational-minded against it, because they cannot visualise the broad sweep of evolutionary distinctions.

You will notice that the characters of the twelve Greek Olympians are identical to the characteristics of the twelve cosmic bodies in this solar system. This is by no means a coincidence, for the Greek masters used cosmic information already known to them about the planets and their devic influences to portray their deities. As for the minor gods, these were either aspects or combinations of aspects encountered on the ascent towards Olympus, in other words, the lesser devic spirits who form part of the retinue of the great ones.

At this moment you are in yet another transitional period. Humanity has dispensed with the gods because he finds them no longer sufficient for his needs as a rational thinker. Yet hidden within those stories are cosmic laws, laws of the universe, by which man needs to conduct his life if he wishes to progress and live in harmony on this planet.

The spirit that has incarnated from the higher spheres must return down the Olympian mountain with its message, its credentials, its teaching capacity and try to convey to man the cosmic principles in a way that he can understand. At different periods during man's recent history great spirits have incarnated for this purpose, giving their own version of the cosmic picture. There are many stories in ancient Greek literature which illustrate the descent of the higher spirits into dense matter so that man can be shown the way. What a wonderful vision these people had!

Take the story of Perseus in his cloak of darkness fighting the gorgon. A wonderful story, but what does it mean? The hero here was able to see beyond the physical and, so seeing, recognise the evil. He could have been turned to stone (a state of mindlessness) or taken under the gorgon's power, but he learned to rise above these dangers with the aid of the gods who lent him the necessary equipment. When evil spreads, many heads must fall, but to know the enemy's strength and position is half the battle; being thus forewarned you can equip yourself with the necessary aids to repel it, otherwise you will become part of it.

The island of the Odyssey is just as much here with you now as it was with Ulysses, especially in the great cities of the world where Circe reigns supreme. The lights are shining and the liquor and drugs are flowing; everything is there. When you are tempted on these levels, pause for a moment and think, "What do I get from it?" Apart from a deteriorating physical body, dreadful headaches, confusion and disillusionment... nothing!

I have tried to give you a tiny glimpse of the Olympian story. The twelve characters represent the twelve archetypes as portrayed in the zodiac, each one having a part to play, a message to give which is important to the whole. Learn to interpret the principles for which these gods stand and to see how they can apply to life today and to your own individual progress on the path of evolution; for at some time in your cycle of experience you will learn to negotiate each of these truths. It may take many incarnations and no two people will experience them in the same manner, but each one gained will enrich your soul and help you forward on your path toward the Ultimate.

Of the twelve gods of Olympus, six are on an outgoing vibration and six on a receptive vibration, thus observing the cosmic law of polarity and balance, a law which operates on all dimensions.

OUTGOING VIBRATIONS	RECEPTIVE VIBRATIONS
Zeus	Aphrodite
Athene	Hera
Artemis	Hestia
Ares	Demeter
Apollo	Dionysus
Hephaestus	Hermes

Footnote: Poseidon, Hades and earlier deities such as Uranus and Chronos were symbols of a solar age rather than a planet. In the age of the rulership of Zeus, Poseidon and Hades (that is, the outgoing Piscean age) the vibrations are as above. The Aquarian age will come under the rulership of Athene who 'sprang fully armed from Zeus's head'. The rulership of the twelve signs of the zodiac ascribed by the Greeks differs somewhat from those used in modern astrology.

Pan

A broad understanding of this topic would surely fall short if I did not include information about the natural forces which guide the every-day running of Earth, those very powers of nature itself without which nothing else could manifest. For these, after all, have been the inspiration for many beliefs, past and present.

As you know, Earth is the Planet of Healing and Music though I would prefer to substitute 'balance' for 'healing' for it describes the action more precisely. In the very early days of this planet, and to greater and lesser degrees ever since, a spirit has worked through nature on the planet, a spirit of great beauty, great wisdom and great simplicity. It has been referred to as the 'great god Pan', and it did not come from another star or solar system for it is native to Earth itself. This is the force of growth, physical, mental and spiritual. Pan represents a form of devic life as manifested through nature.

The planetary Deva, Gaia, guides the planet and this means that such a deva, being of great evolution, a spirit of the higher fifth plane, can by its closeness to the Godhead transmit the love, wisdom and understanding of the Godhead down on to the planet as a whole, through the nature devas. You could say that it uses its thought power to guide the planet on its course, inspiring those forms of evolution which are experiencing thereon. It is like a great beam of light shining upon the planet which all incarnate spirits can look up to; but it is rarely anything other than passive.

Then there is this great elemental force which moves in everyday things upon your planet: the growth of plants, the movement of the seas, the clouds in the air, the wind, and so on. This force draws the attention of men's minds to the signposts which point upward through the beauty of nature; and it has a personality. It is what we call Pan.

Now Pan, as you know, always carries pipes with which to weave his musical spell. This spirit heals through nature because Earth is one of the most beautiful planets in this solar system and beauty heals. It is Pan that utilises the gentle, soothing, balancing force of the tree; Pan that causes grass to rustle and make its gentle, restful sounds and, although Pan encompasses the whole planet, at the same time it will come to any individual upon request and immediately, for it is always ready to sit beside you and talk to you. When I say 'sit beside', I have chosen that expression with care because it never sits in front of you. Its eyes are so beautiful you would not be able to remain incarnate if you looked into them.

I would like you all to get to know this spirit for it is one of the great moving forces upon this planet. Just by sending out the thought it will appear beside you. It is a spirit whose talk ranges from the most mundane matters to the highest philosophies and it is a spirit that every man, woman and child should call upon whenever they feel the need. It is not a spirit that is carefully guarded in occult or mystical places so as to address but a few. It is the spirit for everyone, indeed every animal and every tree, although these, perhaps, have not forgotten it in the way that human beings have. So, when you think of song and dance and sounds of nature you will know that Pan is nearby. In the old religions there was always a horned god and a mother goddess and one day you will learn about the old Earth mother who accompanied Pan.

It is taught to students of the occult that to call upon Pan before you are ready is extremely dangerous. This is true, but only if the caller has not mastered those aspects in himself which are of the Pan kingdoms. If such a person should summon this great being to his presence, the power invoked would rebound upon him, affecting his health and often his reason; not because of the Pan spirit itself, but because of the imbalance in the summoner which becomes quickened or accentuated by the presence of Pan.

The Pan ray is a mirror ray, reflecting back to you what you are. So, if your character is one of cruelty, evil and lack of understanding, then to call the Pan ray will invoke those very aspects of your inner self back upon you to the force of its power.

The Christian Church feared Pan, therefore they used its horned guise to depict the devil, the epitome of evil; but this is pure slander. It was because the Pan spirit was so strong in the minds of men that they needed to debase it in order to frighten people away from it. The Pan ray harms no one who approaches it with the respect it deserves and, by respecting it, I mean not misusing it.

One well-known magical practitioner of the past tried to master Pan but he made the mistake of trying to master the god and not the ray behind it, which is faulty occultism whichever way you look at it; he might as well have tried to catch a nuclear bomb falling from a plane. And yet, a small child could sit in safety with Pan, as can an animal, for they are without guile and receive from this spirit only what they send to it and that is love tinged, perhaps, with a little youthful curiosity.

The Deva Kingdom
The fifth level devic entities have all evolved through the elemental stream of experience and gained their four-fold nature. They include those who oversee the development of the planet, those that help humankind, those that watch over the animal kingdoms, devas of plant and insect life, atomic devas and those that regulate the seasons and elements generally.

You have given them names but, if you wish to understand them as they truly are, this can be limiting, for they are in no way human. The important thing at this time is for groups of you to link up with both the devas and the elementals in their ongoing mission to rebalance the planet. By connecting mentally, healing rays can be sent to areas of impurity and devastation.

Human Evolution
I think it is time to introduce the sixth plane energies who come to help human evolution on this planet. At this crucial time, I speak through many incarnate souls who have chosen to be channels for our initiative to lift planet Earth onto a higher level of understanding. I am part of a composite being that has a slightly wider perspective on things, an older brother, if you like, although on the sixth plane the energy is a union of both male and female. And this is why I have chosen the term 'archetypal energies' to describe us.

It is very difficult for an entity from the sixth plane to incarnate because the energies are so powerful that they could not be contained within a human body. It is important to differentiate between the sixth plane archetype, a collective energy, and the man Helio-Arcanophus, a fifth plane being who incarnated in Atlantis all those years ago and who subsequently ascended to be within that archetypal energy. Consequently, I use archetypal inspiration when working with the medium today. I have not returned into an Earth body since that time, and will not again until the overall human evolution has returned to a comparable level to that which was achieved in those early Atlantean times.

When one speaks about Akhenaten and other such names remember that the inspiration behind the person Akhenaten, which we will refer to as the 'Akhenaten archetype', continues to bring its energies down close to this level that you inhabit, presenting its practical philosophy through many human channels around the planet. It allows itself to be known as Akhenaten only where this is appropriate.

It may interest you to know that the spirit energy that lived as Akhenaten, the man, is indeed incarnate once again on your planet at this time, in the body of what you call a 'Downe's syndrome' person. Every spirit in its journey will choose at least one incarnation of intense deprivation and it will do that because it feels that it needs to understand some of the deepest suffering that humankind can face and, of course, one of the greatest problems humankind has is to be able to respect others.

Many of the souls who are in these bodies with limited mental capacity are young souls on the evolutionary path, but a few are very advanced souls, who have chosen the restrictions of this form as a service to others. To be an advanced soul in a body where it is impossible to express this level requires immense self-sacrifice and, in the case of this present incarnation of the energy that was previously expressed as Akhenaten, this young man is now able to act as an Earth anchor for the Akhenaten archetypal energy to come closer to Earth in order to carry out its mission for humanity.

Every great civilisation has at least one sixth plane presence behind the scenes, supporting it. Behind Socrates was a god of Wisdom, an archetypal energy from the sixth plane, that had come to stabilise and inspire the Greek civilisation. This energy came through Socrates, the man, Plato and Aristotle, and this energy is still there in Greece, but held back. Those people who were particularly involved with the human Socrates would see it as the 'Socrates energy', others the 'Plato energy'. When you go to certain parts of

Greece today you may still be able to be conscious of this energy, but the situation there is still far from ready for it to re-assert itself.

Socrates channelled energy from a higher plane, but the spirit that was in that body moved on and has incarnated since on a number of occasions, drawn to other parts of the planet at times of great need, significantly to South America. He is in Southern Africa at this very moment trying to counter the shadow there that is threatening to take control. His is truly an energy of the light.

The Animal Kingdom

We must not forget the archetypal energy which specifically supports the animal kingdom, for the harmony of the planet includes their evolution and well-being also. I have often been asked about battery farming and my answer always has been that the spirits who come into certain animals know that they are going to be slaughtered for food, and they are prepared for that; but what they are not prepared for is to be tortured to produce that food and that is one of the things that I have tried very hard to bring across. All the kingdoms of life need to work together at this time. The animal kingdom, you see, also needs to understand these issues of the sacrificial life, as does the vegetable kingdom.

We must also emphasise the degree of co-operation there is between we who represent the human archetypal energies and the archetypal energies supporting the various other kingdoms. Indeed, each of us works very closely with one of the Deva energies. For example, Akhenaten has an affinity with Gabriel, the solar messenger. It is on the sixth plane that the devic energies and the energies on the human vibration have their greatest affinity.

Considering the Christ

All spirit comes from the Godhead and has to be tuned down, as it were, before it can influence a physical consciousness. If a high sixth plane energy were to try and use a physical body direct, the physical body would disintegrate because that energy level is much finer, much more sensitive, much more penetrating, much more holistic than it could handle. So, any spirit wishing to channel through a physical body to give a teaching, has to transform itself down close to the vibration of that person.

The H-A energy is a group energy. The Akhenaten energy is a group energy and, on the sixth plane, they come together. Jesus was a man just as any other man. The sixth plane spirit that came to that body channelled a teaching through him to those who were ready to hear; but it was, on its own level, part of a group energy which archetypally includes not only the Christian energy, but the Buddhic energy, the Islamic energy and many others. You see, the Christ energy is a group energy that embraces and inspires the whole of humanity.

Chapter 7

ISSUES CONCERNING RACE

Rhythms of Life

Everything in the universe is a frequency of energy. As the universe evolves there are two aspects of that evolution and those aspects come from the quality of choice. So not only is one looking to the light and dealing with the shadow, one is also looking at resonance and harmony facing discordance and disharmony, and realising that one cannot exist without the other.

So within the concept of harmony there is the idea of rhythm that takes place in a cyclic way and as the frequency becomes finer so the cycles begin to become wider and more spaced out. On the other side of the coin is the process that will try to create cycles of disharmony to offset those of harmony and resonance.

Those of you who are interested in music will understand what I mean and you will see different composers, whether classical or popular, reaching out to one side or the other, or to both. Rhythm can uplift you, taking you onto another plane of existence, or rhythm can imprison you, penetrating those higher levels of resonance within you and destroying them. So let us differentiate between rhythm that creates harmony and resonance and touches the emotions in a deeper and finer way, and rhythm that can touch the emotions in a very destructive way, bringing your shadow to the surface in an uncontrolled manner. Interestingly enough, as music moves into the age of Aquarius you have both extremes.

I want you to hold that in your mind as you begin to observe the evolution of the universe; and then, for a moment, bring it onto a totally personal level - for each one of you is a universe unto yourself. You will know that in your life there are cycles. There are seven-year cycles and, depending on when and how you were conceived and born, you will attract resonances in your lifetime that will make your heart soar onto the highest plane of your being, helping you to understand love in a totally unconditional way. You will also know the other side, facing feelings of failure, feelings of being trapped, stuck, unable to move forward, of putting down or of being put down.

One of the challenges that faces a spirit in a human body is coming to terms with its own cyclic rhythms, why certain things happen at certain times. You may have put out a great deal of positive thought to create a change in your life and you get terribly frustrated and concerned that it doesn't happen. It will happen at the right cycle of energy movement in your evolution. This is really how astrology works; it observes those cycles. Each one of you is a universe within a universe; a microcosm within a macrocosm. In this present cycle of evolution which is the life you are in at this moment – look back along it and you will see how the cycles have occurred; how suddenly doors have opened, how suddenly doors have closed. Accepting those cycles within you takes a lot of understanding. Some people write it off as being predestined but nothing is predestined, nothing is predetermined - everything reflects your choice and the way you move forward within those cycles.

So, when you reach a certain point of resonance in your evolution, at a time when certain things can happen for you, they don't have to happen and they don't necessarily happen, but if the right openness is there at the time, they will happen. And sometimes, when we offer guidance and try to work with you, we gently steer you towards those moments of resonance, towards those cycles which move from one type of energy to another. The whole of evolution is about movement, it is about energy, it is about understanding the energies that comprise you. When you came into this life you brought all that you had been, the resolved and the unresolved, the harmonious and the discordant, the light and the shadow. And now you are trying to deal with those energies, to seek, find and ask yourself, "What should I be doing? Am I in touch with my own mission and the karma that I have chosen for this particular lifetime that I am going to draw towards me?"

In a lifetime on this planet you can draw energy towards you from another planet, from another solar system, another galaxy. Sometimes people feel that they are in touch with extra terrestrials and they may be; but many times it is because they are resonating on a certain frequency level and are drawing towards them past life experiences from where they were on other planets. As at different times in your life you draw towards you different energies, so you will find them building up in you. You meet someone and you develop a relationship with them, a relationship that does not necessarily have to be sexual. It can be a karmic relationship where you suddenly realise that there is something between the two of you that cannot be written in words.

It is important to understand that some of the energy that you draw from that other person will actually impinge on your aura and will touch a note of recognition within you. It will create a development within you. In any deep relationship you each receive something from the other person, you allow it to come to you and become part of you. It begins to develop and grow within you, taking you forward in a different direction, into a different aspect of your incarnation.

Your planet has also moved forward in its evolution because of its relationships with all the life forms that exist upon it. In a sense, all life of your planet is an incarnation of its Deva. As Earth moved forward, it drew different energies towards it that reflected climatic changes and different types of physical evolution, but when Earth became ready to create a strong evolutionary impulse, this was when *homo sapiens* started to develop on the planet. However, this has led *homo sapiens* to think only in terms of *homo sapiens* - and it really needs to expand its concepts now to include all forms of physical evolution on the planet as equal partners.

How have the Different Races on Earth come about?

Most *homo sapiens* spirits, as they have evolved on your planet, have come from other planets - some from this solar system, some from the galaxy, some from the outer bounds of the universe. And these spirits have been drawn to your planet in groups because spirit tends to evolve in groups. Each one of you receiving this teaching is part of a group spirit, a collective spiritual energy.

Cosmically, planet Earth represents a very fascinating experiment, because one area where Earth varies from many other planets in the universe is that it has so many different forms of evolution stemming from so many areas of its experience.

With one notable exception, the various root races on your planet have come from other planets, other stars, other remote parts of the universe. They have come at different times into human bodies to modify the form and accelerate the evolution and, in so doing, have provided an energetic spirit impulse to help the planet move forward. They represent an emigration, not of the physical, but of the spirit – and, in that emigration, they carried with them the qualities of the planet that they left.

Let me explain by taking the oriental races, Chinese, Japanese, Tibetans as well as the Indonesian, and associated races. As I see it, they are not originally Earth spirits. The seed of that evolution, the spirit impulse of Asia, actually came originally from Sirius in another part of your galaxy, but later there was something of a divergence when spirits from Jupiter entered the area causing various separate national identities to be formed.

These races are basically one particular energy force and have a great deal to bring to your planet and, like most of the other alien root races, they have found it difficult to adapt to the planet and to the other energies on it. I would like to emphasise most strongly that there is no quality attached to my comment. It is not that they are good or bad, merely different, and they are bringing with them tremendous capacity for creating ideas in a way that is different from any other race on the planet.

So, when a large group of spirits come together to incarnate on Earth, they seed a particular form of physical evolution. And the type of energies that they bring will draw from the planet certain physical chemicals towards them, which will affect the type of physical body that will grow around the needs of those spirits, and the kind of collective energy that is the race or group identity.

I must now mention two very significant racial streams, the Indian and the Middle Eastern. Over time, however, the influence of the Middle Eastern energy expanded and occupied much of what is now Pakistan and some present Indian areas. This is why you have this clash of energies between India and Pakistan.

Then there is the Nordic culture, the Arian culture, the Mediterranean culture, the Native American culture, and some of the South American cultures. They are all reflecting energies that have come to the planet at different times to become part of the whole. It is like in a large family in which it becomes increasingly necessary to maintain a harmony between all the members.

Then you have the Caucasians who see themselves as the dominant force on the planet. These, too, are from another part of the universe. Some European spirits also came from Jupiter. But it is not quite as simple as that because on your planet there has been so much mix and match, many of these influences have become intertwined. Yet, however intertwined they have become, back somewhere there is a root energy behind their evolution.

Many of the largest problems that face the planet today involve the matter of race and it is the cause of strong emotive reaction. Every being on this planet is a thought created by that Ultimate Thought. All are spiritual brothers and sisters. Yet, as travel and communication have improved upon your planet, and people of different countries have come to mix as a matter of course, racial intolerance has reared its ugly head. Many people have a sense of security in being associated with a particular race, country or continent and, because of the way in which humanity has evolved, there are still, in some people's eyes, certain stigmas attached to being born into a body of a certain colour.

That leads me to reveal the original racial line that began its existence on this planet, and still thrives today. It may surprise you to know that it lies with some of the black races, and it is appropriate that this influence now spreads more around the globe, as also happened when the Atlantean civilisation broke up and spread to many parts of the planet, taking the Venusian influence with them. Today it, too, is everywhere.

It is ironic that those who carry forward the oldest forms of human evolution on your planet are the ones who have been, in so many ways, left on the margins of the global community. On some level, all those who occupy bodies that are, in a sense, alien to this planet, feel threatened by the natural inhabitants, to the extent that they choose to see them as inferior. So, it is not surprising that the spirits in physical bodies which have evolved from planet Earth itself are actually facing the hardest challenge of all. They have been suppressed and vilified by the incoming races, constantly put down, and even enslaved; yet they are the natural inheritors of the Earth traditions.

The influence of both the western and eastern cultures has been very difficult for them to contend with, because they are trying to find their own level of consciousness on a planet when deep down in their root memory it feels as if their right to belong has been usurped and relegated to second class status. These are the original Earth spirits who have formed a line of evolution stemming from the commencement of human existence on the planet. It must be said, that I have a deep regard for them for they have some exceptional qualities to offer which, because of the suppression, have not actually fully developed. They inherit a culture that is very special to them and very important for the planet. Music and rhythm lives in the soul of all the black races, and Earth is primarily a planet of music.

I would forecast that sometime in the future of this planet they will be the race that will take this planet forward because, despite their present difficulties in finding a harmonious balance amongst themselves, they actually have the capacity to provide a stability that no other race can.

Now, you will not be surprised to learn that, as I see it, no one race or culture on your planet is superior to another. They are all different and it is really important that humankind moves towards respecting all other cultures. It urgently needs to do this. This advent of the age of Aquarius is an excellent opportunity to move beyond the need of trying to convert others to your own understanding and resonance; because what is right for you may not be right for them, and what is right for them may not be right for you. It is about respect, it is about true understanding.

I have said that spirits, after incarnations on other planets, have incarnated on Earth to bring the fruits of those experiences to help the evolution of this planet. So, there are spirits from other planets incarnate in physical bodies from other planets at this time. However, you can forget the concept that they must necessarily be wiser than you are. Some may be, but others have come here simply to learn.

There are even those who have incarnated intending to spread destruction.

Of course, there are many wise spirits on your planet today who have developed through human evolution, some of these have incarnated from the teaching planes in order to help the planet forward into the Aquarian age. There are also many advanced discarnate energies that are trying to connect with human beings to bring them this new concept of spiritual enlightenment, one that is angled to the individual rather than to the hierarchical control of the past.

Overcoming Racial Intolerance

Let me assure you that, in response to the present state of evolution of this planet, the forces of light are bringing with them spirits of enlightened evolution that are, alas, struggling to lift the planet above the chaotic state in which it is at present. They are striving to help divert it from a path that is carrying it at an accelerating speed into some kind of world catastrophe. Such is the strength of these forces of light, such is the strength and diversity of these enlightened spirits that they are coming into bodies of all races, colours and creeds; for if man is going to overcome the weaknesses, and the emotions of greed and power that have forced him into the corner in which he now cowers, this renaissance of spiritual understanding must arise in every region of the planet.

I urge most strongly that, for the sake of the evolution of this planet and the balance of the solar system in this particular galaxy, do not leave it to those in influential positions, for there is much that each of you can do in your thoughts and daily lives. With the coming of the new age there are tremendous moves between various spiritual groups to come together, to accept the fact that each of their philosophies presents a different facet, to come to terms with the overall principle of light that shines, or attempts to shine, into each particular philosophy; and to understand that all are part of the whole. Much can be achieved by this 'unilateral' thinking.

Man needs to acknowledge that nobody's ideology is right for everyone and that every spirit has the right to individual expression through the physical body in which it is incarnate. Love and tolerance and working towards mutual respect and understanding should be the prime goals of all people. Let the governments of the world start thinking not about race, but about world resources and the ecological issues facing mankind. These are problems to be shared, problems that all can help to solve, urgent problems that can bring people closer together.

The Semitic Race

Many people consider that the ideal way to find a higher teaching is by means of studying ancient texts, gaining a great knowledge of the works of the ancients, studying their ways, their ideas, their actions and their lives as a whole. Whilst I am not here to refute longstanding conceptions I would like to point out that man, in his search for these mysteries, is going quite the wrong way about it.

The spirits that inhabit men's bodies are capable of expanding. But it is not knowledge that expands them, it is wisdom. In some ways wisdom is a quality that is rather intangible to man. It does not merely consist of having the ability to make the right decision at the right time; it is an awareness of beingness, an acknowledgement of the universe around you.

As you live your life and evolve, so you present your spirit with a chance to express itself. The full extent of that expression is determined by the limits of expansion currently possible within the spirit; and in that expansion lies understanding and awareness that has nothing to do with knowledge. It is not a case of God knowing all, it is a case of God understanding and being aware of all.

Many people do not realise that not only does the spirit affect the body but the body affects the spirit. Incarnating into the body of one racial type is a quite different experience from that of another race, and particularly where the body is of mixed race, even if the karma offered by those different bodies is basically similar. In other words, different physical bodies can offer the spirit different forms of interpretation of the experience it wishes to undergo. However, the more powerful the spirit, the more influence it can have and the more it can convey its will to the body.

There is one race, in particular, about which I would like to speak, the Semitic race, for it has been hounded from pillar to post for generation after generation. It is important to understand that the energy behind the Jewish people is from another sphere of evolution, but whereas many of the planetary groups who have settled here have adapted reasonably well to their new home, the contingent that became the Jewish race have remained more insular. They have never seemed to be able to fit in. And one of the interesting elements of Judaism is that for many thousands of years they had been looking for somewhere to settle and find a home.

They originally came because they wanted to assist the planet, and they felt that what they had to offer could help to bring about a better spiritual understanding. Again, unfortunately, the religion that grew out of it, like many other religions, is thwarted by the extremism in it, although the true Jewish understanding is a very lovely one, a very creative one, and can bring about a great deal of peace and understanding. It is only when it is abused and becomes controlling that the usual problems occur.

The essence of Judaism and what it stands for has become hostage to the extremists, who feel they have to defend themselves against those who would persecute them. But they, themselves, are partly responsible for bringing this persecution about. It is within the beleaguered state of Israel that these extremists feel especially justified in using force against those who would cast them out, and so they seize whatever power and control that they can manage. It is out of fear, always out of fear, that the actions have occurred that have caused some of the tremendous problems and issues with the Jewish experience throughout the ages.

In addition, several thousands of years ago this race of people was used to discharge a cosmic karma. Many of the elemental spirits that had worked with the deva Mikaal received a severe occult shock as a result of the unleashing of occult forces against them during the Mikaal/Lucifer battle. They were bolted from their own sphere of evolution — mainly of the earth elemental form — and caught up in physical incarnation within the bodies of some sections of the Jewish community. They became enmeshed in an evolutionary whirlpool, which caused them to incarnate solely and repeatedly within the same race.

This is why elements of the Jewish character are somewhat of an extreme nature. The exhibit many gnome-like tendencies, especially over possessions, and there is the tendency by many to keep it as a race apart. This does not mean that every Jewish person has inherited an elemental nature, but some have. The religion as a whole has absorbed these 'lost' spirits from a form of evolution alien to the normal human pattern, and is still very much influenced by them.

This displacement of evolution has been the 'cross' these particular spirits have had to bear and many of them have been used as tools for Lucifer down the ages, as at the death of Jesus. When devic spirits - or any spirits - battle occultly, the losing side suffers a retrogression of spiritual evolution that may take the form of a temporary spiritual blindness. Because they fight on the 'right' side does not exempt the losers from this suffering. This was one of the reasons why Jesus did not save himself from his assaulters by the use of occult power and why his true followers have pursued a similar path of occult pacifism ever since, always standing firm but never attacking. The power he could have called, even to defend himself, would have caused great spiritual suffering afterwards.

Many people throughout the ages have wondered why a spirit to be overshadowed by the Christ consciousness chose to incarnate into a Jewish body. "How odd of God to choose the Jews!" wrote a certain Englishman, when it was, in fact, very sensible, for within this race lay the elemental wisdom, accumulated over many centuries, necessary for this particular incarnation. Advanced elemental energy gives a deeper aspect to any understanding and belief. So, the Jewish race was chosen because it was the most suitable race at that time, but this does not necessarily mean that it would be the most suitable race to choose today or tomorrow.

Incarnated elemental spirits are inclined to feel out of place amongst *homo sapiens* spirits and they therefore tend to congregate and find solace in being together. Unfortunately, in the case of close-knit sects within the Jewish race, this is an instance when they should not be together as they only become more and more interbred. Such Jewish people need to break out of this whirlpool, to expand themselves beyond the confines of their immediate understanding and beliefs. They need to cohabit more outside their faith so that their present identity could gradually be intermingled with other races; thus the spirits within them would be able to move on and escape from the trap in which they are caught. But for the elemental spirits that are currently trapped within this whirlpool it will indeed be a very difficult thing to do.

For their future salvation, these spirits are, in fact, looking to the day when their original leader, Mikaal, will overcome the shadow aspects of Lucifer. They will then be released from their karma and able to return to their own sphere of evolution. When this happens the extreme tendencies that can be found in the Jewish race will gradually disappear, and they will take their natural place among the nations of Earth. Indeed, they will be indispensable.

I would like to stress very strongly that none of this is in any way meant to be derogatory to the Semitic people, but rather an attempt to explain why, as a whole, they find it difficult to blend with other races. I have very great love and sympathy for them and would indeed like to see them rise above their present form of evolution and return to their rightful heritage and purpose. If you were working with a Qabalist from the Jewish school of occultism you would notice a vibration that has a distinct flavour of its own.

Because of the refined elemental influence within this race, the Jews have been responsible for much of the great inspiration that has come to this planet. They have contributed greatly to creative expression in cultural fields and in the field of science. Spirits of this nature can often bring with them a brilliance and a dimension that would not normally come with spirits of a purely *homo sapiens* form of evolution. Indeed, it is fair to say that this planet is richer in many ways for the contribution of the Jewish race.

There are a great many things to happen in your world in the future, one of which will be the evolutionary upliftment necessary for the release of the Jewish people, which will be very closely linked to the upliftment that will come to the Egyptian people. This will accompany certain catastrophic events on Earth that will be the forerunner of world peace and harmony.

Chapter 8

MISSION OF THE NAZARENE

The Saviour is conceived

Many of the people who dwelt in the ancient civilisations possessed the power of prophecy, so, when the great teachers such as Buddha, Confucius, Socrates and so on, came to Earth and gave out their teachings, they came not only to assist your world at various stages of its evolution, but also to lay the path that would lead inevitably to a great teacher who would follow. They knew that a man would be visited by a manifestation of an energy source close to the Ultimate, and they realised the difficult circumstances under which this would occur.

So, who was Jesus and what sort of spirit inhabited that body? I would like to approach this subject from a broad viewpoint in order that you can understand the life of Jesus in perspective. Each spirit which has been created by the Godhead has started at the beginning of its evolution with nothing and gradually begun to expand. This expansion is enabled by gaining experience, knowledge and wisdom while undertaking a cycle of evolution which entails many incarnations in a physical body. The spirit reacts and responds to the experiences and, through this, finds understanding.

Eventually it will reach a stage of evolution where it is no longer necessary for it to return to Earth through a physical incarnation; and thereafter the spirit and its mental processes will carry on evolving on planes of existence which are not of the frequency of matter, until a stage of understanding is reached where it is ready to rejoin the Godhead. This process of evolution is continuous, like the infinite universe itself which has no beginning and no end.

I want you now to expand your thoughts and picture this Godhead, a state of beingness that has become all wise. Those spirits within it have reached a stage of evolution in which they have found complete harmony with all other thought, all other beings. Yet this Ultimate thought is not static, for a spirit, once having reached this state of perfection, does not stagnate or remain still. On the contrary the Godhead is continually expanding within itself as, indeed, is the universe, into infinity. As it expands, fresh thought is being created which evolves, eventually rejoining the Godhead and then goes on evolving in complete harmony with this state of beingness.

Now, there is a part of this infinite thought which is responsible for each of the solar systems in the universe. Each of these great spirits is a duality in itself, having a positive and negative aspect. The spirit which is looking after a particular solar system will not interfere when an imbalance occurs, for each planet is evolving and experiencing according to its own free will and, in its wisdom, the Father/Mother God will stand back and watch with love and care. At certain periods in the evolution of some planets, however, additional guidance is needed, in which case this Ultimate thought will choose to bring about guidance to the sphere in question through an appropriate incarnate spirit.

Jesus was a man, who had evolved through earth incarnation and whose spirit came from the fifth plane. One of his earlier incarnations was as Zoroaster - which is why no great movement has arisen out of his teachings in that earlier guise, because these were superseded by those that came through Jesus when it was time for him to be over-shadowed by the Christ energy.

All the planets in your system are 'children' of the Sun which can be considered as the crown chakra of your solar system – with the heart chakra being Earth - and are you not as a cell in the body of this solar system? Jesus Christ often referred to himself as a shepherd looking after his flock and, when one of the flock strays, "Does not the shepherd go forth to seek that which is lost?" The Sun's rulership is one of light and life and love — born of the Supreme Thought, God.

When the time came, Jesus entered into the body of a common man like yourselves and, for one so advanced, it is impossible to find words to describe the sacrifice entailed. Jesus Christ was so powerful that he could have wiped out his aggressors with one flick of his hand, but it was not to be so. It is because he suffered in a physical body, that he understands your problems, fears, jealousies, loves, and so on. It is not God's will that you should shut yourselves away in a hut 'in the middle of the moor.' Jesus did not shut himself away. He entered into the life of the ordinary people of his day and worked tirelessly to achieve his objective, which could not be fully completed at that time.

One of the great drawbacks with Earth people is that they spend so much time looking for detail and so, often miss the important aspect of the picture. Notice how many people are intent upon checking on some small detail in the life of Jesus, or trying to make something of a simple biblical text. Remember, the Bible is true on the whole, but not in its detail. Yet, when a preacher tells his congregation that if they are good, they will all have a little piece of Jesus in them, each one will conjure up something different in his or her mind, but few realise the true significance of such a remark. After all, we are all part of God, and a part of the divine imagination, whether we are good or evil by Church standards.

God is not a person. God is God; supreme thought, wisdom, power and glory, true, but also simple compassion and, above all, unconditional love.

So, in this modern day, there are many interpretations of the teachings of Jesus Christ mainly based on the words in the Bible which do not take into account any of the understanding that I am bringing to you. It was written by hand in an era rather different from your own; the majority of it many years after the death of Jesus. I do not intend to go into details of biblical history. I need only say here that certain parts of it have been omitted and held back and, in general, it is incomplete. I am going to cut away all the trimmings and come down to the man whom you all know as Jesus Christ. Who and what was he?

First, let us turn to the Earth planet where over many, many thousands of years *homo sapiens* has evolved. At various times during this evolution *homo sapiens*, as a whole, has slipped into a state of stagnation where it has been fully set on a form of self-destruction of the soul. In other words, a community has within itself a form of group evolution and, as it undergoes this group evolution, it must move outward, it must grow. Sometimes it evolves in such a way that it turns in on itself and ceases to expand, assuming a state of suspension; and when this danger looms, it becomes necessary for some form of strong external guidance to be given. So, over the history of this planet you will find that, at certain points, various forms of guidance have indeed been given and one of these times was the period, two thousand years ago, when Jesus was born in Palestine.

Now, let us focus on the time which has touched the hearts of so many, the time of his birth. In order to appreciate this, we must bear in mind the fact that this physical body was going to be overshadowed by a spirit of high evolution, that was wise beyond any who had hitherto come to this Earth. This spirit was the positive half of the Christos or solar Christ spirit which looks after this solar system. It descended from the sixth plane, bringing with it all the wisdom, evolution and beauty of that plane, to help this planet in its time of need, but when the Nazarene commenced his mission there was one thing which he shared with other teachers, a normal physical body.

I must again make it clear that the Christ spirit knew that it had to choose a body which would be able to provide a clear channel for the teaching while, at the same time, being responsive to the overall state of Earth at that particular time and its evolutionary needs. It was necessary for an aspect of this spirit to descend, to tune itself down, as it were, to a frequency which was compatible with the vibration of physical life. It did not choose the body of a priest, a king, or leader; it chose an inconspicuous body, the body of a child that was born in the normal circumstances of that time, yet one that represented the frailty of the human condition for, let us face facts, the man Jesus was not strong — in fact, he was very fragile.

Jesus, Jeshua-ben-Josephus, was the natural son of Joseph and Mary, who had specially incarnated for the purpose of bringing this child into the world. First, you must realise that if God, with infinite wisdom, wished to work through the Christ energy, it would not involve a transgression of those very laws that had been created as a part of the Ultimate thought. It would need to be a natural birth in an ordinary place, in an ordinary town. He would certainly not have chosen circumstances as conspicuous and highly suspect as a virgin birth.

Jesus was born when the Sun was in the constellation of 'Virgo,' the Virgin, and it was this that gave rise to one of the early Christian myths. Christianity overlapped with both paganism and occultism in its early days, and many strange beliefs emanated from this mixture. Joseph is always depicted as being an older man, and indeed he was 47 years of age at the time of the conception of Jesus, Mary was considerably younger. Joseph had been married previously, and had children, which explains the Bible quotations concerning Jesus' brothers and sisters. There was only one child born to Joseph and Mary, and that was Jesus.

Both Joseph and Mary were students of the occult, and members of the Essenic order. John the Baptist was also concerned with this community, as were several of the men who later became Jesus' Apostles.

You will remember the story of the Wise Men — the three Magi. I would point out to you that these wise men did come from afar but were not, in actual fact, present at the birth of the child, Jesus. These three Magi had studied the universe, astrology and similar arts. They had seen, in the heavens, astrological signs which they knew pointed to the coming of a Master. From other occult knowledge which they possessed, they were able to pin down where this child was to be born, and it was to this place that they wended their way. Put yourself into their place and consider how much caution was necessary. These men were, what you would term today, occultists, and they were followers of the teachings of Zoroaster. They therefore knew of many things which were to happen, and that their entry into the small town where Jesus lived had to be conducted very carefully, for if it reached the ears of such a person as Herod, he could have put a very great spoke into the wheel of a divine plan. Had the Three Magi not been cautious and discreet it could have stopped the divine plan at the precise moment of his birth.

"But", you might say, "is it possible to put a spoke into the wheel of a divine plan?" I should like to answer this, by saying that the Ultimate Thought created a form of evolution whereby, as a part of its experience, a great spirit had to enter into the type of physical body you know as man. To the spirit of man he gave the gift of free will, and that free will implies that such a spirit can do what it chooses. It can go forward in its evolution or it can go backward — it is entirely up to its free will. That is why evolution is not a straight line. Of course, whichever way a spirit chooses to go, it will eventually reach a point of understanding where it will be able to ascend to the Ultimate.

To give you further understanding on this, I will have to touch very briefly on Karma. There have been a great many teachings in your world on this subject and, generally, they claim that life has a predetermined plan. In other words, your life is a series of events which you are fulfilling. Those of you who strongly support such a belief may find what I am going to say difficult to accept; but my work is to give you an understanding of the universe. It is up to you as individuals as to whether you accept or reject it.

Karma is not a fixed plan. The karma of a life represents what that spirit in that incarnate body intends to do. Karma does not take into account free will. In fact, a spirit can enter into a physical body and go right through its life without fulfilling its karmic intention in any way. In humankind's continued rejection of God by invoking free will, it has sought the power of materialism and selfishness. To open oneself out to the wisdom of the universe is always a hard path — it always has been and always will be.

The physical body has its own temptations, those of intolerance, pride, cruelty — everyone has them in varying degrees. It is up to your free will as to whether you allow yourself to follow them, or to try to uplift yourself. Just as it is up to each and every one of you now, so it was with that physical body which housed the spirit of Jesus. It was limited and if these conditions had been changed, it would have been going against the very cosmic laws which it was bound to obey. The Christ consciousness, with all its great wisdom, does not do such things. Free will has given man the chance to find himself, and it is therefore up to each one of you to do so.

Indeed, as I mentioned earlier, when Jesus was born, the receptive or feminine half of the Christ spirit, known as the Sophia to the early Christians, should have overshadowed a female affinity to Jesus intending to be born in India at the same period; but, due to the shadow forces, acting under Luciferian influence, this plan was thwarted and Jesus was denied a living polarity. Here, indeed, was a spoke in the wheel of the Divine plan.

However, the feminine side of the Christ spirit was able to work through her after she successfully linked in with Jesus from the spirit side, at the time of his baptism by John, after which he was able to proceed with his occult work and undertake the purpose of his incarnation.

The Life Unfolds

At this point, I would like to stress how that great spirit was limited by the physical body of the man Jesus. In his early childhood, Jesus had many unusual experiences, as the spirit within him started to express itself. He used to see what you would term 'visions' and, because of these things, he became a laughing-stock. "You are mad", they told him. Think how easily this happens today! Man has not changed very much, you know. That spirit strove to control its body, to help it through its youth, a frail body, whose health was not always as it should be. All the time the spirit was trying to effect a complete harmony with its shell, for harmony is essential for the well-being of any physical body. Harmony is one of the most important things needed in your lives today. Everywhere there is noise. Even in your fields you have mechanical tractors. Your evolution depends on the balance between your spirit and its physical shell, and such noise can jar that balance.

When the boy, Jesus, reached a certain age, a state of awareness came to him that he had to reach out to the world. Gradually the spirit had begun to communicate through the body. This communication started by merely realising that he had some form of duty to perform in the evolution of the planet. He felt a responsibility, a sense of urgency, and knew that there was some special task to be completed. So, at an early age, he left home.

Joseph and Mary, being wise and evolved spirits, knew that Jesus needed to travel in order to gain the necessary spiritual understanding, and he needed to learn how to meet the harsh contingencies of life on the physical plane. In allowing Jesus to go, they incurred the criticism of their friends and many people condemned them. "Fancy letting a weak child like that travel," they said. You can imagine it happening today. But Jesus went with the blessing of his mother and father, because they knew that it had to be.

They played an important role in bringing to his conscious mind the part he had to play. They knew why it was necessary for other people such as teachers and advisers to be involved, and Jesus was ready for this.

The Journeys

All those of you who are honest seekers will well know that the path is a hard one, beset with pain and doubt. It was not a case of Jesus leaving his parents and going to a school of learning where everything was unfolded to him simply and he could accept it all without question. With every step that this boy took he had to know the reality of what he was doing. He had to be able to understand, and when I use that word I use it with the full weight of its meaning in the widest possible sense. Knowledge is insignificant without understanding and Jesus, the boy, had to learn to understand. So, whilst that spirit, at any one moment, could have forced its wisdom upon the physical body, it had chosen instead the path whereby it only gently induced within the boy this longing, this urge for responsibility toward mankind.

You will readily appreciate that in those days it took many, many years to do this. It was rather like a form of treasure hunt because he had to find each key in turn. He visited many monastic orders and houses of learning and, particularly, he spent quite some time with an order known as the Essenes, which did indeed awaken much within him, because the spirit within that body had to become manifest so that it could express its great wisdom through the physical shell. But the Essenic order and its doctrine had limitations, and the teaching which this man had to give was to be anything but limited.

So, he travelled to other fields of learning including Greece, Egypt and the land you know as India. During these so-called 'missing years' this boy, as he grew to manhood, travelled a tremendous distance on journeys that were necessary in order that he could believe in himself. He had to realise the many paths to the Ultimate and, as he journeyed, his own spirit was gradually brought closer to the body. In certain of the places he visited, power centres were energised, one of these being in the south-west of England. He did not journey there purely to energise a power centre but rather to find a key to one of the doors which he had to open. The people Jesus met when he came to England might have appeared primitive from the point of view of your modern civilization, but their priests had an occult tradition dating back many thousands of years which was taught by word of mouth. They had part of the story and from them he gradually learned to activate his own telepathic senses and to harness and use psychic power.

Each order with which Jesus came into contact tried to create a link that would protect him when he returned to Palestine to commence his teaching. Unfortunately, to a certain extent, this linking failed, which is partly why his life had to end in the way it did. Whilst he did not wish to call on his own powers, he could have accepted help sent to him from these various centres which he had set up. And the most important of these was in the West Country of England, particularly the area around the village of Glastonbury.

When he arrived, he found that the sanctity of that chosen place had been greatly violated by members of the black brotherhood seeking to find the entrance to the power they sensed was there. All of these special places on your Earth are afflicted by conflicting attitudes. While there may be a certain quality of aliveness from energetic streams that are flowing through, there is likely to be a sinister aspect present as well. Now, put these two qualities together and you have a picture of Glaston as it was at that time, for indeed the records of the past are not such that would appeal to a true seeker, for the ravishment and pillaging, and the unholy things that happened there, had brought into being a very great miasma of darkness.

On the more psychic and spiritual levels, those who visit even today can feel this. It enters into them, seems to engage the soul, for as they look around at the beauty of the countryside, they feel this ugliness, the depravity that has existed, and they are aware that this place on Earth that should be truly beautiful, certainly needs healing.

Whenever you go into any place of worship on your Earth, of high spiritual power, you will nearly always find mixed vibrations. Your spirit inspirers will need to be asked to be with you, so that you may be led to link up with those there who are striving to raise the vibrational tone. You take a higher note in with you, more resonant than you can normally manage but, once there, you are certain to come up against those who are supporting the ones who are planning to bring about negative events, even catastrophes on your Earth. Those who delight in going against the plan of God are there, but they cannot remain if there are a sufficient number of you. They must go because a stronger power has come in and is easing them out. And so it was, when the Master Jesus came to Glastonbury, he was able for a time to completely uplift the energy, in order to set into place a refined purpose and a new blueprint for the future that awaits mankind in this coming age.

Today, certain orders and individuals are still searching for some of the entrances to these repositories, because they sense that with the right key they can tap power that was concealed there, but which they would never use as intended. They are unaware that the key does not allow desire, and so, their quest remains a futile one, but they can still do much damage to the surrounding atmosphere. This is a very important factor to remember. What happened nearly two thousand years ago has a great bearing on the state in which your planet is today and on what is to happen in the future, and it is connected to these places of spiritual antiquity within which the secrets lie.

I have not placed emphasis upon Jesus' Egyptian studies and there is a reason for this. Although the teachings of early Egypt were the closest in existence to those of Atlantis at its height, in later times the occultism of that country became polluted and the strains of the true priesthood were lost and swallowed up in the manoeuvrings of men greedy for power. When studying Egyptian occultism the student should be wary, for there are many traps. The earliest system was the purest and this was associated with the old Atlantean solar cults.

The body of Jesus did not have a brilliant technical or mathematical brain. He was no genius. He was not even a particularly good speaker, for he suffered from a speech impediment which had been caused by an injury he had received during childhood when a missile thrown at him damaged his jaw. Even in those early days they mocked him.

However, that great spirit still continued to push through and manifest itself and, by attending these many halls of learning, Jesus was able to find that peace, harmony and balance which aided his spirit in the control of its body. He then returned to the Middle East, because he knew that the time for his teaching had arrived.

One of the many significant episodes in your Bible is where Jesus is said to have gone into the wilderness. As you must realise this is a metaphor, for Jesus did not walk a few hundred yards to a piece of land or a mountain with a few trees and a river. It was, what you would term today, an occult initiation, for in his own land, in his own body, he had to face fully those spirits you would know as evil, who were determined that his teaching should not succeed.

Some of the greatest tests faced by the man Jesus were not at the time of his teaching in Palestine, but on his journeys away. These lower forces, in their attempts to stop the spirit of God from manifesting, tried everything in their power. On one occasion when he had come through the northern parts of a land you now know as Italy, Jesus was set upon by bandits. By the sheer magnificence of his wisdom he was able to stop those men attacking him without the need for belligerence or force! Such was his power that he was able to make these men see him for what he was. It is interesting to note that two of these men came back with him and were present throughout his ministry.

The Teaching Begins

When he had reached the stage where he had a complete awareness of why he was here and of the task which he had to undertake, he knew that he was ready to return whence he had set out, not simply to give a teaching but to take part in what was going to be a tremendous occult battle. This was not just a case of good versus evil. It involved the uplifting of the evolution of the whole planet against tremendous odds, against forces which wanted to subjugate Earth and use it for their own purposes to add to their already borrowed power. This is one of the reasons why his ministry was so short.

Most of you have read of the many incidents which occurred in Palestine and around the Sea of Galilee. Many of these happenings were of an occult nature, in order to encourage those close to him to open their minds and allow each of their souls to really grasp wisdom and gain spiritual perfection for itself. Such was the idea of his teachings, but of course the men who reported them found it only natural to pick out, and indeed exaggerate some of the things that happened. His teaching did not go at all smoothly. Most people rejected him and he was treated as a crank, just as he would be today. But slowly and surely, after facing the most terrible odds, he commenced to make his presence felt.

I have been asked on several occasions whether at any time Jesus was involved in any emotional relationship with another human being. My answer to this is a definite "No!" Let me put it to you this way: within him he knew that he had very little time in which to give forth his teaching and build something which was to last for a very long time. He knew that this influence he was bringing to the planet was not only going to continue after his incarnation but had to grow a hundredfold; so the emotional expression in his life was restricted to a tremendous compassion for humanity. He was a person of strong emotions and had great love and feeling for many people but, by the time he returned to Palestine to carry out his ministry, the communication between the spirit and the physical body had become very closely aligned and, therefore, his strength of purpose was predominant in his personality; thus he never really had time to indulge in the usual human emotions. Also, as I have said, his female affinity was not incarnate so there was no partner available for him on his level.

During his ministry Jesus went about healing the sick, teaching tolerance and understanding and explaining the laws of the cosmos in parable form so that they could be understood by all. He did not perform any feats that were humanly impossible for he came to show man that all such 'miracles' were within the bounds of cosmic law and possible for human beings to achieve. "Go ye and do likewise," he said to his students.

There were other things against him besides the people who would not listen to his words — there were those twelve apostles who gave him many headaches. I know that most people have an idea that he met each of them in turn and so impressed them with his wisdom that they immediately trotted along behind him. Those apostles were twelve human beings, and they, too, faced the limitations of their bodies. There were many times when they found it very difficult to follow Jesus. They wanted more proof, just as many of you do today. When a teaching of God is given to the people, it is left to the wisdom and understanding within the teaching to make its mark. Such is the way of God, for he has given man free will with which he may accept or reject wisdom.

The spirits incarnate in the bodies of the eleven apostles, other than Judas, had all been in Earth bodies before. Five of them being especially inspired by planetary devas, while the other six had links more directly with archetypal energies from the planets Venus, Uranus, Saturn, Jupiter, Pluto and Pan.

Matthias, who replaced Judas, was greatly influenced by Mikaal. Many Earth schools of theology consider that the apostle Paul was the rightful twelfth, and that Peter and his friends made a mistake in choosing Matthias, but this was not so. They were inspired in their choice in this particular instance. The spirit of Paul, or Saul, was under Neptunian influence. This spirit has a special task to achieve after the eventual release of your Moon, and he will be connected with its rulership after the return of Lucifer to its rightful position in the devic kingdom.

Whenever a high manifestation of the sixth plane comes to your planet, he/she is always attended by the devas of the solar system. These 'archangels' had devoted a great deal of their spirit evolution in preparation for these tremendous tasks. They knew that they would have to stand by Jesus and assist the apostles to attend to him with selfless sacrifice. Yet the temptation upon these men was too great so that, in a moment of weakness, each denied him and one was turned cruelly against him!

Lucifer could not incarnate and so chose to fight Christ from a distance, where he felt he had a greater advantage. The Moon is the sphere which influences the mind, and it is through the minds of men that its fallen deva has perpetrated his machinations against the Godhead.

Judas was not deva inspired, but was a spirit who had recently been incarnate upon the planet Mars and was well aware of the disruptive influence coming from that planet. He came to try and make up for the deficiency, but he could not really enter fully into the community of the apostles and always felt something of an outsider.

Many people feel a bitter resentment against Judas, but I feel very sorry for him. As the one who failed, he needed help and guidance, a little extra tolerance and kind thought. While you are in a human body you will make mistakes as you have not achieved a state of perfection. Judas was, in many ways, a beautiful soul and he did love Jesus. His spirit has greatly suffered since in repentance, yet if Judas only knew and realised that he is forgiven it would make a tremendous amount of difference.

Jesus continued against all these odds. He had several very difficult times with Peter. Peter was a very lovable soul, but he was one of those people you find so often today who worry a lot. He used to worry over small things that were not important; and of course Peter worried about himself, for he was never quite sure as to whether he was doing the right thing. It was a difficult decision for him to make, but as time showed, he did stay with Jesus, and eventually became a very powerful figure in the events that were to follow. Then there was John who was rather different. He was stronger in character, but a little headstrong. John had a good physical brain and wisdom, but he loved Jesus so much that he was inclined to accept him blindly in some ways, and not really look into the consequences of his teaching. Then there was Matthew who had a great sense of humour, and a keen sense of perspective, which often helped to keep the others down to earth. Andrew took things too seriously, and yet achieved much wisdom. He was a faithful member once he was convinced.

It is the man Jesus we are focussing on, and I have emphasised the weaknesses which beset the band of people who followed him, these human beings with human failings, because Jesus, too, had the physical limitations of his body with which to contend. For instance, the love of God would not inspire a man to go in amongst money lenders with a whip and turn over their tables, but the mind of a man would consider it a logical protest. God teaches humility, under-standing, and no belligerence, but the very human Jesus, in this case, allowed the emotions within him to respond in a human way.

At one period, Jesus suffered from the disease which you know as tuberculosis, but by his profound self-healing he was able to step beyond this condition. It came upon him at a time of stress, for he was always being turned out of towns and villages, and so had to travel on much against his better judgment. This caused his health to suffer.

The Last Days

I have tried to give you a broader picture of Jesus Christ than is given in the scriptures, to uplift your appreciation and show you how that spirit felt when it was betrayed by one to whom it had given nothing but love, tolerance and understanding. Yet, on another level, it was not a betrayal really, for Jesus knew in advance that Judas was under the thrall of the deva Lucifer. He did not condemn him because he knew that it was a human weakness inherent in many people, if not in one way then in another. Is there anybody who can honestly say that he has never been tempted to do or say something against his better judgement?

I would like you to pause for one moment and picture the scene when that poor tortured body had to carry the Cross. At one time he dropped it, for his physical body was in such great pain. After all he had been tortured for many hours. He was helped to lift the Cross so that he could march on with it. There were kicks and jeers from the crowd, for to them it was a great sport.

When Jesus came to the end of his physical existence, he did so knowing that he had not completed his mission! Of the many occult tests or initiations which Jesus Christ underwent, the greatest was his suffering and death on the Cross. With the powers he possessed he could have released himself at a moment's will, but his test was to suffer as an ordinary man, and refrain from using his occult knowledge and power to gain any advantage over others. Had he called on these forces, many people would have suffered severe retrogressions in their evolution, for an occult attack damages not only the physical, but also the etheric body. He also knew that in order to stop the crucifixion he would need to inflict such a heavy blow upon the evil forces around this planet that it would have seriously affected its whole evolution. It would have caused a tremendous catastrophe on many levels. So, regardless of what was best for himself at the time, he had to surrender to the situation in order to save the world from the terrible results of such an interplay of occult forces. This he did and you all know the events that followed.

And what of the Resurrection? The physical body of Jesus never came into action again after it had died upon the Cross — such a thing would be against cosmic (natural) law. Friends took the body away and buried it in a cellar. It was never found. Jesus did, however, materialise to his apostles and disciples, and the form of materialisation he used was the highest possible, as no physical medium was used. Although it appeared with such reality to those who saw him after the crucifixion, it was nevertheless an etheric impression, and *not* the physical body arisen. The most significant thing about the crucifixion was that it came at a time when Christ's teaching had only just begun; that is why he has to come again.

Let me put it this way — there is a part of that Infinite Thought which looks after the planets in each solar system of our infinite universe. It is a very broad subject, but I am limited to words and can for the moment do no better. The Infinite Thought which is looking after your own solar system will not interfere, for Earth is evolving and experiencing according to its own free will, accepting or rejecting, and your Master will stand back and watch it with love and care.

At certain periods in the evolution of some planets additional guidance is needed, in which case this Ultimate Thought will choose to work and speak through an incarnated one on the sphere in question and giving the guidance which is necessary. Here, I am going to make a statement on which I do not intend to elaborate and in which I shall ask you to bear with me, for I feel it will give you a clearer picture of the mission of Jesus. When the Christ spirit came to the body you know as Jesus Christ it was not the first time it had come to Earth to give a teaching, it was the second. I say this to you because of certain events which will be taking place soon when the meaning of such a statement will become more apparent.

Jesus will return eventually, in his etheric form, to continue the work that he started on the physical plane 2,000 years ago, that is, when the Luciferian energy is ready to be released from its current state of alienation. Until then, those who work with him, will continue to support and influence the ones who relate to the Christ message through the Church that celebrates and interprets his life and teachings, and those outside it who recognise their link to him and wish to further his plan.

I hope that I have helped you to understand Jesus Christ as a person by encouraging you to feel for yourselves the conditions surrounding him, the limitations that such an advanced spirit suffered in incarnation and the occult battles that had to be fought; not fought in an aggressive way, but defended spiritually. For, when a higher teaching is given, it cannot be spread through belligerence. It has to be offered with tolerance, understanding and humility, and it has to be in accordance with the overall evolution of the world at the time. It is not God's wish that there should be doctrines and dogmas, but merely that the teaching should be carried forth with firmness of purpose and an open mind. Then, everything is there for you to accept or reject. It is entirely up to your free will, for the Divine Creator will never force you.

I am sure that you will know and understand a little more about the spirit that was incarnate in the body of Jesus by transporting yourself into spiritual meditation, taking your thoughts away for a while from your material surroundings and opening out to what it means to be truly human.

I can assure you that as he comes again into close contact with Earth to carry forward his mission, he will not speak exclusively through any individual, certainly not the head of a government, nor a church dignitary or even a guru, as you might expect. His words of inspiration will be communicated in an ordinary way through a very large number of ordinary people. Many of these are already in position and something extra is beginning to pass through them as an inspiration to many others who are ready to accept a teaching with higher resonances of truth that will, collectively, provide a comprehensive direction for the planet.

Chapter 9

THE RISE OF RELIGION

Prophets and Teachers of the Past

During Earth's history, great prophets and teachers from the higher frequencies of the fifth plane have incarnated to give guidance in accordance with the evolution of the human race, at the time and place in which they appeared: Buddha, Mohammed, Zoroaster, Confucius, Jesus of Nazareth and others. They came to assist the world at various stages of its development and each of them was intimately guided by one of the great planetary devas. These 'archangels', as they are called, are responsible for the guidance of the planets and many of them, from this and other solar systems, have come to Earth to try to heal the divisions caused by the fall of the devic aspect known as Lucifer.

Some prefer to know Lucifer as Mephistopheles, Beelzebub or Satan, but these names are only appropriate to the planes below the sixth, where these energies have been personified and where imbalances are magnified and isolated. I think you will find, however, that these names are used in orthodox occultism to depict certain of the 'dark masters' of the so called 'satanic hordes' in particular ages or periods of time; while they are not exactly fantasy constructs for particular energies, they are, as I see it, largely misunderstood. While you choose to relate to it as the Devil, or any of the other names used to denote its influence, you will be giving credence and therefore power to this influence.

The planetary devas are advanced fifth plane spirits that Christianity has named Mikaal, Gabriel, Uriel, Raphael and so on, though they are known by many other names in the different pantheons; thus you may encounter a name such as Mikaal associated with any of a number of planetary devas in the various schools of occult thought down the ages, not always accurately. It is up to each one of you as to which names and explanations you choose to accept or reject. Basically, it is the principles behind the names that are all important, so by all means substitute your own terms of reference if you wish. They all work in the service of the spirit that is under the direct guidance of the supreme presence in this solar system, known to you as the Christ, whose power is symbolised at a physical level by the Sun.

During his life, the Buddha was influenced by the archangelic deva who guides the evolved planet Orpheus. The deva spirit which worked closely with Confucius held a similar position in relation to the sphere, Neptune. The influence behind Zoroaster connects with the planet Mercury, and behind Mohammed was a deva linked to Mars. You are probably aware that the Deva of Earth, in what would be recognised as its masculine aspect, is Mikaal, known in the Bible as St. Michael; and its feminine counterpart, Gaia.

There have been many other great spirits who have taught man wisdom, and have come from the advanced levels of the fifth plane of spirit existence. You may call them adepts or initiates, as you so choose. They all serve the Solar Ruler, who is the representative of the Ultimate or Godhead responsible for your own solar system. So, in addition to those masters who have initiated the great religions of the world, there have been many other outstanding spirits who have also incarnated from the fifth plane to bring light and understanding to mankind, the great composers, philosophers, architects, scientists, artists and so on.

Your ancestors were not as naive as you might think when they considered the Sun as a manifestation of the divine thought. All the planets in this solar system are 'children' of the Sun and you are a life form that has evolved from one of those planets; Jesus often referred to himself as a shepherd looking after his flock. The Sun's rulership is one of light and life and love, born of the Ultimate Supreme Thought.

The Early Church

Returning in our minds to Glastonbury, we discover that there is much legend, much tradition, but also much romantic nonsense that is talked about that place. However, St Paul did actually visit Britain, although the visit was very fleeting. He came at the time when the fifteen disciples were massacred for not bowing down to the forces of opposition, fifteen of the fifty who were sent out by the Master Jesus to lay the foundation in Britain. (Twenty were sent to other places on Earth). He came to comfort the remaining ones, because they had had a very grievous setback and St Paul, through his letters and his visits, was always keeping his eye on his flock and the shepherds who looked after these flocks.

He did not want them to return. They had a vital task to do there because, through their ministry, the gospel did come to England, and the Christ figure became a figure of great glory. Many people had visions of Jesus Christ at that time, and many souls were led into giving their time and their energies to bring about a truly Christian religion at Glastonbury, for that is where Christianity started and, for a time, thrived.

There was much thanksgiving and praise, for you see, many of these people were the descendants of the Atlantean settlers of the region, and they could sense this past still there within them and the purpose that was being enacted through them. They would meet in the little Church of St Michael at the top of the Tor, and there they would enter into a great silence. St Paul blessed a bishop and sent him to look after this little flock at Glastonbury. Huts were made of reed and wattle, and some of them are in a state of preservation today.

Then there was the healing ministry at what was to become known as the Chalice Well. It was a great baptismal font, much larger than it is today, and baptisms were frequent in the early days because the disciples trained many to carry out this work. Crippled people emerged from the water healed. The tradition of healing is very strong there, even today, and all who go and participate with an open heart and who enter into that mystical element of the spirit, will find that the healing waters do not flow just for the body, but for the mind and the soul as well. A soul that has become very downcast and depressed, or frustrated at the way life is proceeding, can open up and draw on the transformative power of the water of spirit that was associated with the healing ministry of Jesus.

But always there were some who came in to disrupt. Simon the Sorcerer, mentioned in your Bible, came and set fire to the little Church because he was refused the laying on of the disciples' hands to give him the power whereby he might heal. So, you see, the first Church was destroyed, but that only confirmed that this is a blessed place, and the persecutions and the sacrifices that were made then, served to lay the foundations of Christianity.

Christianity: an Examination

Is Christianity a philosophy of life, or a teaching based on the ideas given by a man called Jesus Christ who existed two thousand years ago? Does Christianity need the past existence and divinity of that person Jesus to make it work?

Many people claim to be Christians but the doctrine they follow differs considerably from what was taught by Jesus. These people are neither tolerant nor humble, nor full of understanding for their fellow men. On the other hand, many non-Christians do in fact employ the principles which Jesus taught, in their everyday lives, although they may be hardly aware that such a person existed.

Christianity has not developed into what was intended at all, due mainly to an infusion of the Pauline teachings which inhibited the true nature of the teachings of Jesus. What then was originally intended? There was a devotional side, which nurtured a harmonious family atmosphere within the general public; and an inner or mystical side for those who were destined to study the universe so that they could act as elders of the family.

There should have been a strong matriarchal side to balance the ultra positive characteristics of man who tends to become too dominating and aggressive, causing an imbalance. The whole approach should have been gentle and in no way belligerent or warlike, for religion cannot be thrust upon people by the sword. Christianity should have grown from the old Sun religion of Atlantis — which was echoed by the Pharoah Akhenaten in Egypt — and merged with the kinder nature religions to embrace the unified human family and its relationship to all living things.

When a very powerful, highly evolved spirit comes into incarnation it can be likened to a tank of water entering a tiny vase; only a fraction of the contents of the tank can be taken into the jar, while the remainder is left outside. The amount of Jesus' spirit which could manifest through the limitations of his physical body was very small, so consequently, the majority of the ego, including the feminine half of the polarity, was outside, overshadowing the body and guiding him. When you plunge your hand into water, the disturbance causes ripples which gradually subside unless further movement is created. This is very much what happens when the vibration is increased in the physical body; with an occultist such as Jesus, it was inevitable that his body suffered each time he was able to draw a little more of the wisdom from his great spirit.

The Bible and the Ten Commandments
The Old Testament was written many thousands of years ago by many different people. Some of it is in poetical form and many of the accounts are in example form so as to make it simple for the uneducated people of those days to understand. The theme of the Old Testament is, of course, the history of the Jewish race and, while some of its prophecies must be regarded with respect, no one part can be taken as accurate as the original contents have suffered severely in being handed down from generation to generation. Even so, there is much in it for people to learn if they have discerning and practical minds and do not allow themselves to be influenced and carried away by many of the fanciful fables and the hyperbolic phraseology employed.

The Ten Commandments are but a rather incomplete set of rules that can be interpreted in many ways. Though not wrong, they are not expansive enough to address the complex moral issues of the present time. You only have to look at the way in which "Thou shalt not kill" has been misinterpreted over the ages by people professing a devotion to God, to understand that. When they were originally compiled, they were intended to help people according to their lives in those days. But the world has evolved and they are in need of

118

some broadening and widening, for now that man has advanced enough to understand that the Ultimate state of being is infinite, he has also grown wise enough to understand that the teachings of the cosmos are also infinite. These teachings that I give offer a way of life, a philosophy of cosmic religion which is being put forth into the world to help people to see themselves as they are, to see others as they are and to see the universe as it is.

Although commandments such as "Love thy neighbour" give a basic guide to moral behaviour, they do not go far enough, for the laws by which man should live are the laws of God's universe, cosmic law, and these unfold as humanity progresses.

The New Testament
Now let us consider the New Testament. Most of it was written many years after the death of Jesus Christ, earlier gospels and writings having been discarded by the Church. Many of its contributors, whilst fervent followers of Jesus, were not great literary men and the minds of those who were gifted in that direction tended to be clouded by the lapse of time. I am not wishing to devalue this book but merely to put it into perspective; for let us be sensible and admit that it is, in many places, exaggerated and incorrect.

However, the authors did manage to create a story of the life of Jesus which, although inaccurate in much of the detail, was an effective record of his works. Unfortunately, as the years rolled by, many of these teachings were corrupted and large, important portions omitted by power-seeking men who wanted the teachings to be as they would have them instead of as Jesus wished.

Now, I have not spared my remarks here, for I feel that it is most essential that people should see the Bible for what it is. Providing it is read sensibly, it can definitely be of great inspirational benefit to any true seeker. What people must remember, though, is that one cannot take any one particular sentence from its context and use it to prove anything, for the Bible is a document which is right in theme but not in detail. Surely, what is most important is the message Jesus gave. This message, this teaching, was in accordance with the Piscean age in which he came and the stage of evolution of the world at that particular time.

As well as having male followers Jesus also had female disciples, although this information only appears in those books and writings which were once part of the Bible but which have been discarded for totally unethical reasons. The attitude which discouraged women from priestly office was certainly not part of the teaching given by Jesus himself. It came from Paul whose prejudices are quite clear to the unbiased viewer.

Christos and the Sophia

The Christos and the Sophia, the male and female aspects of the Solar Logos, were an accepted part of early Christian teaching. Your theologians refer to the period in early Christian history as the tunnel period when little is known of the movements within the growing corpus which was to become the established Church. The gospels emerged many years later, by which time a definite line had been adopted. The two influences predominating in those times were the Judaic or Pauline and the Hermetic or Gnostic. The Gnostics had a gospel which they called the Pistis Sophia, or faith/wisdom, but as this, like many other early Christian documents, was seen to be incompatible with Pauline teachings it was ignored by the main body of the Church as time went on.

The conflict between these two factions continued for many years until slowly, one at a time, the Gnostic teachers were declared heretical and the pattern was set for what was to become the Church of later years. The reason why this first hundred years is called the tunnel period is obvious. The train is seen entering the tunnel; let us say that when it goes in its funnel is green; but upon emerging at a later moment in time its funnel is red and that is exactly what happened to Christianity in those early days.

The original gospels were far more comprehensive than the collection of scripts which comprises your Bible today. Gradually pieces were omitted or rejected; a king disposed of this piece, a pope of that piece, an egotistical cleric of a third and so on. Collectively, those rejected fragments are known as the pseudoepigrapha and there are translations of them in your museums today should you be interested in checking them out.

It is of great significance that while this metaphorical train was in this particular tunnel that it contrived to lose the essence of the Sophia. I could tell you the details of what happened but it would only add to the confusion of mistrust and disbelief; suffice it to say that the subtle distorting influence set in at a very early period and the deviation, although small to start with, became magnified by the passing of time until it ended up with the dogmas of present day orthodoxy.

Scholars over the centuries noticed these discrepancies in Christian teaching. Some, like Giordano Bruno, spoke forth about them and were burned for their pains. Others, like John Dee, commented on them under the guise of academic exercises and were humoured as cranks but nevertheless allowed to live.

So where did the mother disappear and the dove fly in? In some branches of the Christian religion she didn't disappear completely; she was relegated to mortal status and became 'Mary, the virgin Mother of Jesus'. Subtly the archetype contrived to exist, even if only on the finest of threads. Mary comes from the name Marah meaning 'bitter sea' and as Stella Maris she was star of the ocean; but, in an earlier period, she was Isis in her role of Divine Mother. So one religion superimposed itself upon the other and took along with it much of the symbology of the original.

It is interesting to note that, symbolically, the sign of Virgo is sacred to Isis or Demeter and the glyph shows a young maiden carrying either a sheaf of corn or a cornucopia, a horn of plenty. There is something for you to work out if you are interested in ancient symbology.

I have explained that there was a belief in the existence of the Christ polarity from the earliest days of Christianity which, in turn, came from even more ancient teachings and was embraced by Jesus himself. Let us now consider a little more closely these two polarities as archetypal forces. Here are a few associations which will help you to understand how each aspect of the polarity works and blends:

THE CHRIST POLARITY

CHRISTOS The Logos or Knowledge The Great Power	SOPHIA The Wisdom The Great Love
Associations:	Associations:
The Father	The Mother
Healing	Channelling
Light	Love
Music	Nature
Teaching	Intuition
Occultism	Mysticism
Strength	Inspiration
Leadership	Regeneration
Will	Understanding
Knowledge	Imagination
Scholarship	Wisdom
Discipline	Compassion

The idea of a Divine Son of God is not confined to Christianity, it appears in many schools and systems. Sun gods and heroes who came to save mankind and who suffered death and torture for their pains were well known to the ancients. All arose triumphantly again in spirit; all possessed healing powers and all were purportedly born by some magical means, following the death of a father, as with Horus, or out of time, as with Apollo; and so forth. In the interpretation which I have chosen, Isis discovers and Osiris crystallizes. The ankh represents the seed of love and wisdom, the Isis; and the Sun represents the Osiris, the light and warmth by which that seed grows and manifests.

Let me make it clear, however, that whether you use the old Egyptian names or whether you choose to refer to these principles in

Christian, Hebrew, Chinese, or Hindu terminology does not matter at all. God has many names and, no matter how honest you feel your belief or religion to be, it is ultimately your personal approach to the Godhead that will determine whether you touch the archetypal force of light or of darkness. You, and you alone, are responsible for yourself and your evolution.

Rome

After the crucifixion of Jesus, the concept of life after death lived on, as did the idea that if the spirit concerned had dedicated itself to helping humanity, it would come back at some point to help the Christian impulse spread around the planet. To this end, the Jesus/Christ energy realised that it could not continue to manifest where it was, so it looked for a country that was suitable, where it could base itself and thrive. Greece was not appropriate because already there were strong spiritual concepts going back many, many centuries that would prevent a new philosophy taking root; the same was true for Egypt and the surrounding area. So, Italy presented a very interesting possibility, because it did not have as many entrenched spiritual concepts as these other countries.

Thus the descendents from the disciples and many who wanted to further the teaching of Jesus settled in Italy. Rome was chosen because it was a powerful energy point. There was another energy centre in the north of the country, but the major one is in Rome. So, they were able to use this energy in an occult sense to gain a foothold. In addition, the Roman Empire had established tentacles reaching out into many other countries, and these could be used again to expand the word of Jesus far afield. These were the main reasons to choose Rome and it has since become a very concentrated energy source with strong links worldwide which can be used more wisely in the future.

The Growth of Christianity

I would like now to consider briefly the history of Christianity as a teaching, the growth of that teaching which Jesus instituted. A detailed examination uncovers a story stained with blood and darkened with vice, yet a story whose sordidness is brightened by the glory of the stalwarts who have kept its true meaning alive.

Christianity first became a state religion at the time of Constantine the Great. Its early days were riddled with so-called schisms and heresies and anyone who disagreed with the established body was pronounced a heretic or schismatic. One example of this is the teaching of metempsychosis (reincarnation) which was declared heretical by the Second Council of Constantinople in A.D. 553. This Council marked, in fact, the end of a bitter struggle between two contingents in the Church, one side being backed by the Emperor Justinian and the other represented by a very famous person of the time, Father Origen. The Council was called by the Emperor Justinian and only a few bishops made their appearance.

The reigning Pontiff, Pope Vigilus, was remarkable for his absence, even though the teachings of the Church stated that the Pope's presence was essential because of his infallibility when speaking 'ex cathedra'. Nevertheless, he refused to attend. Yet, despite his absence, and through pressure exerted by the Emperor, the Council declared the teaching regarding reincarnation heretical. And so, just as easily as that, one of the great and major truths of the cosmos was dismissed through a personal whim and the absence of the reigning Pontiff.

In the first half of the 3rd Century A.D. Christianity started many schools of thought within its own realm. For example, there was the doctrine of Neo-Platonism which emanated from the teachings of Plotinus of Alexandria who was himself a pupil of another great occultist, Apollonius of Tyana. Neo-Platonism was a step to combine Greek philosophy with Christian beliefs, which was admirable, as a close study of the earlier philosophies shows quite clearly that they are basically all very similar and only differ in detail of application. The teachings of Jesus are, after all, of a universal nature and any attempt to establish a link between them and the teachings of earlier masters was surely a step in the right direction. The Neo-Platonists inevitably became sectionalised, with individuals pulling to extremes and spoiling the plan.

However, Neo-Platonism was the foundation of Christian mysticism and the work, once begun, was later taken forward by Dionysius, known as the Aeropagite, to whom is owed the nomenclature ascribed to the nine angelic choirs: Seraphim, Cherubim, Thrones etc. In other words, he was saying that there are other forms of evolution which have specific duties to perform and a role to play in the universe and its work. He lived at the end of the fifth Century and brought Christianity into line with the Hermetic 'doctrines of successive emanations', which was why he was known as the Aeropagite.

Later developments in Christian beliefs were marked by the divergence of the patriarchal See of Constantinople from the pontifical See of Rome. The point of separation occurred in A.D. 1054 when Pope Leo Xl excommunicated the Patriarch of the Greek, Greco-Roman and Russian churches and certain oriental groups which remained faithful to the patriarchal cause.

Time progressed and Christianity spread, splitting into many different paths according to the personal beliefs of certain strong-minded characters amongst its ranks. As different countries and states adopted different branches of Christian beliefs, these were used as an excuse for persecution and many men gave up their physical bodies in great pain and torture to a state which used religious backing for its own exterminatory purposes. I put it to you, should any man have to die for a belief?

As I said earlier, the Christ energy and the Jesus teaching went to Italy because of the influence of the disciples who were interested in presenting it in a more controlled way. They chose Rome, because Rome had some very interesting energies that they could sense, going back many thousands of years to Lemurian times. Italy was not part of the Atlantean civilisation and energy, but it was part of the Lemurian civilisation and energy. The Lemurian philosophy was not totally different to the Atlantean, except that in certain respects it was more disciplined and one of the things that let down the Atlantean civilisation was its lack of discipline. In other words, those who were working for the light in Atlantis were not putting enough energy into finding a balance between the light and the shadow, so eventually the shadow took over.

The original Atlantean energy came out of the fact that a large number of spiritually-minded people were concerned because they thought that the Lemurian civilisation had failed due to its excessive control. That is a complete circle, is it not? So, when those followers of Jesus Christ went to Rome, it was because they were attracted to the disciplined energy that was there. And they wanted to establish a philosophy and a regime so precisely directed that it would encourage more people to become followers of Christ.

Now, there are other branches of the early Christian Church that, as you know, went to Egypt and many other places; but it was the centre in Rome that grew very strong because it utilised the Lemurian type of control, which meant that if anyone disagreed, they were sidelined. It was a great challenge to the Greek civilisation, but that is another subject. So, the Christian Church settled in Rome and drew on the energy that was there to build up the rituals and systems of support that would attract adherents. The general practice of disallowing birth control became a doctrine, thereby encouraging large families, and the rapid growth of Catholicism.

Now, let us glance at the principles of Christianity to see how they have worn with the passage of time. Let us look at the ministry which is no longer as it was at the time of the apostles. Do the vicars and priests heal the sick? Do they cast out invasive spirits? Do they go into trance like the apostle Peter? There are many instances of the disciples speaking in 'divers tongues' and taking on guiding intelligences to help them with their work. In his first Epistle, John, speaking in his capacity as an occultist, warned the Church not to allow their psychic workers to become involved with spirit entities without first challenging their intentions. "Test ye the spirits, that they be of the light."

If any of you had lived in Palestine during this time and were troubled by bad dreams or strange voices you could have gone to Peter or John or to one of the other disciples of Jesus. You would have been comforted or had your karma explained to you. Obsessing entities would have been cast out, in the way that the Master had exorcised evil spirits so many times. "Go ye forth and do likewise," he said. Where today can you obtain these Christian services? Even if a man training for the priesthood does learn about exorcism, how much of what he learns does he understand - and has he the occult power to apply his knowledge in ways that are needed now?

I would like to make it clear that the term 'occult' simply means 'hidden'. An occultist is one who studies and mentally uses the forces of the universe, these being neither good nor evil in themselves, simply forces that need to be kept in balance.

Is Christianity Supreme?

The majority of people in the western world have been accustomed to a Christian way of approaching God. I should like to put this implied superiority into some form of perspective. Why do its followers seem to think there is something special about it, and are they are right in their thinking? To an outsider this could well be regarded as arrogant and pompous? As usual, the whole matter is not quite as simple as it would seem.

Let us examine the Christian religion as it is today. First we have the established Church, divided between Roman Catholicism, the Protestant beliefs and the Free Churches. The Catholic Church has very cleverly adapted pre-Christian rituals for its services, notably the Mass, and it uses these various methods of spiritual expression to convey to its followers its own interpretation of the life and purpose of the person on whom its teachings are founded. Strict dogmas are used to convey to its members a picture of the Trinity and to give them a philosophy of living.

The idea of a sacred trinity was pre-Christian and originated in occult teachings of a profound nature. Later it was re-echoed in the pagan fertility cults. Some early communities were matriarchal while their later conquerors slowly imposed a patriarchal system and infused their beliefs into those already existing. This resulted in the Father/Mother God theory. The 'Son' aspect, or 'proven fertility of the ruling union', was then added and examples of this may be observed in most of the earlier writings and myths of the world. But the concept of a trinity dates back to before early man for it is basically a cosmic principle which states that when two forces unite a third is created. This may be evidenced in science, biology and all aspects of life within the universe.

When Christianity spread across the world it embraced many of the beliefs already prevalent in those times, pausing only to reconcile them with its own dogmas. The idea of the Father, Mother and Son was adopted early in the Christian era but, due to views regarding an immaculate conception held by the main orthodox Christian body of the time, the 'Holy Spirit' or 'Holy Ghost' gradually replaced the 'Mother' aspect which was relegated to mortal status and became Mary, the 'virgin' Mother of Jesus. The Churches employ the term 'holy spirit' to denote the third person, the balancing one, but what was originally said was "and I will send you a paraclete". A paraclete is a mediator, advocate or go-between, so what was really being said was that a mediator would be sent to speak to the Christ on behalf of mankind, once his spirit had passed into the higher realms from whence it had come.

Trinities occurred in other religions and are by no means the prerogative of Christianity. Egypt had its Isis/Osiris/Horus, Ptah/Sekhmet/Imhotep, Amun/Mut/Khons to name but a few, while in the Far East there is Rama/Vishnu/Shiva and so forth. The sign of the triangle has occult significance in itself, representing the number three, and is often employed as a protective symbol.

Another symbol which dates back to ancient times is, of course, the equidistant cross. Since Mu-an times the four arms of the equidistant cross have been used to denote the four elements of earth, air, fire and water. The power of the symbol lies in bringing these elements into balance and, indeed, the whole planet into balance. Contained within a circle, the equidistant cross is the symbol of Mikaal and of planet Earth. The cross was to be seen at the summit of the great temple in the capital city of Atlantis and its significance was known at that time; prophecies concerning it were passed down for many thousands of years, the later ones appearing in the Old Testament of the Bible.

Other pagan festivals which were adopted by the early Christian Church were Christmas and Easter, both of which can be traced to the occult rites of ancient Egypt carried out by the priests. Let us take Christmas; in many of the old religions solar festivals were celebrated shortly before December 25th to denote the return of the Sun after the shortest day. As students of the occult are aware, Jesus Christ was not born on 25th December, but on 19th September, when the Sun was in the constellation of Virgo, the virgin; this is an ancient teaching which subsequently gave rise to many of the dogmas accepted by Christian schools of thought today. The sign 'ascending' at the time of Jesus' birth was Aquarius, the water bearer, which is also significant. However, the fact that his birth is commemorated on a different day is of no importance. It is what actually occurred that we are concerned with.

Easter is the time when followers of the Christian religions celebrate or, shall we say, remember, an event which happened two thousand years ago. We know that a man called Jesus was crucified, although some people have chosen to doubt even that. But let us assume that it happened. What we must ask ourselves is the true reason why.

The future of religion
It is indeed difficult to see why religions all over the world are incapable of preventing man from hurtling forward at an ever accelerating rate in pursuit of his own doom, because, although all religions have within them the same fundamental message, they are all ineffectual when faced with this momentum. So where have they gone astray? Does it mean to say that a philosophy of goodness, a teaching which tells you to do the sensible thing, is not strong enough? Is it merely because each one of you has been granted free will, the free will to accept or reject the Godhead Itself? Is the challenge too great for the human species or are the forces of evil so strong that they override all other considerations, man being too blind to grasp the obvious? These are questions that have been asked from time immemorial and which are especially pertinent in this day and age. Let us look a little deeper to see if we can find an answer.

Your planet is part of something much greater, as you will appreciate, and as each one of you is only a small part of this planet it is interesting to consider the natural force that brings people into groups and the contrary force that can so easily lead individuals and factions to move against the running of the tide, against the flow of cosmic law. Is it the evolution of the individual or is it the overall evolution of the people on this planet that must take precedence?

When the crucifixion took place there were many ramifications. It is very easy to blame the circumstances of the time. It is also easy to say that it was part of a much larger plan, that it had to happen.

Assuming that it had to happen, how many things in this world do have to happen? Do all things have to happen? The answer is, "No, they do not." Let me digress a little.

Each one of you has a karma, a plan of your life which sets out certain milestones for you to reach. Your spirit has, of its own free will, chosen its particular karma in this incarnation. But although a spirit sets out to complete its karma it does not always manage to do so in a particular incarnation for, as your spirit has free will while working through a physical body, it is not always able to impress itself clearly on the physical mind. To a certain extent it is limited by environment, circumstances and so forth. Also, each one of you has a spirit guide or guardian who is trying to help you to discharge your karma; it may be that you allow it to help you or you may resist and close yourself down. Whatever the reason, the final responsibility lies in your own hands as to whether or not you achieve those karmic milestones and learn the lessons your spirit originally set for itself.

The picture I am trying to convey to you is of the evolution of the planet as a whole being shaped by the way in which man is using his free will. We come across belligerence, fear and greed and all those things which have brought the planet to the state in which it is today. These are evils that have been brought about by man choosing to work against the impulses of cosmic law, rejecting God and going his own way.

It is the spread of these evils that we, who work for the light, are trying to prevent; this is the darkness we are trying to lighten. I do not wish to criticise any particular belief, but it does not need me to tell you that if organised religion had succeeded - and I speak not only of the Christian religion but of every other major religion - then there would be no need for spirits like myself to be giving you a teaching now.

Remember that the Godhead is a unified force and a unifying force; in other words, it offers unconditional love and any form of assistance that will bring forth the qualities of patience, tolerance, understanding, forgiveness and respect in you. The Godhead will never interfere with man's spirit, and this is the basis upon which we must work. We are coming up against forces of evil which are so strong around this planet that they will not stop at the niceties, nor will they observe the rules; they are quite happily prepared to interfere with your free will. It is up to you to step beyond such influences. You have the choice.

When Jesus Christ died on the cross nearly two thousand years ago he did so in order to save the world, yet not quite in the way in which it is generally understood. He knew the forces of evil had been marshalled to prevent him from carrying out his teaching, but because his spirit was under the unified Christ influence, he offered no resistance. He knew that if he summoned the legions of light in order to save himself, he would shatter the planet and set back the evolution of every individual upon it. He wanted to give *homo sapiens* an opportunity to redeem itself of its own free will.

Broadly speaking, religions fall into two categories that reflect the two principles of the universe: the outgoing and the receptive, the active and the passive. Christianity is an active religion, but it has tended to become an assertive religion, a crusading religion, a polarised religion. When anything was seen as sinful, something had to be done about it, in contrast to the Eastern, more receptive approach where they are content to sit back and allow.

Buddhism is the perfect example of a passive religion, being mystical in the receptive sense. The mystic, as distinct from the occultist, can afford, metaphorically speaking, to sit in his hut on the mountain and do nothing but meditate, because his is a receptive role. But the occultist has to move and progress with time, as do the teachers and healers because they share an active intention.

Nevertheless, there comes a moment when the two roles reach the point of imbalance in their respective directions and this is when each needs to learn from the other. So, the time has come when the peoples of the East and West would be wise to learn of each other's religions, for they have much to give each other, in their beliefs and in their approach to God.

The spirit of Jesus was influenced by the masculine and the feminine aspects of the Christ spirit; in fact, this was a moment in the evolution of this planet when a spirit manifested through a physical body more strongly and completely than it had ever done before. This was what was significant about it. The Christ presence is certainly of the finest sixth plane energy, and every religion draws inspiration from it in its own individual way.

The Christian religion has no cause for complacency, particularly as the interpretation of the teachings as originally given has been distorted down the ages, often by men seeking power and, in some respects, it bears very little resemblance to what was originally taught. It is not the religion that you follow that matters, it is how fully you live the teachings, how completely you love your neighbour as yourself.

Chapter 10

THE SOUL OF AVALON

The English Heritage
There are some countries that have a great stabilising influence on the world while there are others that have the opposite effect. I am not including the rest of the British Isles in this presentation — Ireland, Wales, Scotland and the smaller islands — and there is a very good reason for this.

In area, England occupies a very small portion of this planet, yet its impact in world affairs belies its size. England started its evolution in a very mundane way until a period in prehistory, many thousands of years ago, when a certain race of people landed on its shores. They came from the continent of Atlantis. These settlers brought a new teaching and a new way of life that did not last very long owing to the constant influx of lesser developed immigrants.

During the ensuing centuries there were many invasions, wars and squabbles and a glance at recent mediaeval history leaves little to be proud of. However, from these numerous ups and downs and ins and outs, a personality has emerged, a character that can only be described as English. Scotland has a different form of esoteric significance from England. Indeed, so has Wales, and especially so has that other island to the west, Ireland.

When the Celts came to Scotland and Ireland, they brought with them a very specific kind of energy that has caused these countries to develop along lines that have been sometimes very much in conflict with those of England. Even today, the Celts, particularly in Ireland, have a much more pure, solid tribal energy.

One of the reasons that England has always emerged as a very strong energy in the spiritual field is because of the mixed nature of the people who have inhabited it. You have some very powerful, yet different, tribal energies that came together in England long ago, the Normans, the Saxons and so on. England has become very multi-cultural and this offers tremendous opportunities. I think it is very important that people have come here from Eastern Europe and from the old British Commonwealth. They are all playing a part in building a strong multifaceted energy that is going to become the new England. However, it is very important that, in the process, no one energy becomes predominant.

Looking at it purely from a practical viewpoint, the English people have many faults. They are rather slow in some ways and they are also inclined to find it difficult to accept anything other than that which is their own. There is a defensiveness that is common with the inhabitants of small island states, and they can be quite definitely pigheaded. Perhaps I appear to be a little unjust here, but it is deliberate, as it is partly through these characteristics that the English have found a certain balance that has served them in very good stead. The Scottish influence has been beneficial for the English people, so indeed has the Welsh, for they are both far more extreme than the English and, consequently, they have brought a double influence into England which has again helped to create a form of stability.

I should like to touch briefly here on the subject of astrological influences and their effect on countries. Each country comes under the rulership of an astrological sign, which stems from the time when it came into being as a nation. These rulerships are not easy to determine and many astrologers are divided in their opinion as to the signs associated with the different countries. With England, I would definitely consider the predominant influence to be a Taurean rather than an Arien one. There are other influences, for it would be wrong to say that only the Sun sign exerts an effect, whether it be on a country or an individual. But the stubborn characteristic of Taurus is very evident in the English character, as is also the external reserve that reflects the subrulership of Uranus. At the same time it conceals a true Venusian warmth at heart. (Venus and Uranus are the two ruling planets of Taurus.)

From an esoteric point of view the Atlantean group that landed in England was no ordinary one, for they had chosen this island as a centre for a great deal of power. It was known even at that time, many thousands of years ago, that this country would be the root from which Mikaal would reappear to renew his endeavour to guide this planet onto an even keel.

King Arthur and his Knights

In order that this Atlantean beginning could be moved forward in its preparation for the events that will come about in this country quite soon, we turn now to the place that was Camelot and the legends that surround it. I wish to pass the recounting of this to my colleague Akhenaten:

"If you were to ascend the Tor to the top, keeping that peace and quiet and stillness within your hearts and minds and souls, as you gaze out over Glaston, you would see that, in the past, that region was laid out in the form of a zodiac. The twelve figures in the zodiac can be traced, being a configuration using the many waterways and canals around the area which is about 10-12 miles across.

"Here it is that we link with the first of the three 'Arthurs' who had their influence on the myths and the legends that have been passed down and that you know today. He was actually King Uther in those ancient days following the destruction of Atlantis, and he was the first of what would much later become the Knights Templar. He had twelve companion 'knights', each related through their Earth mission to a particular sign of the zodiac, and they knew that by their adherence to that, much streamed through from the higher beings. So, they sowed the seeds of the spirit, which subsequently developed and contained a power source, encircled by the circumference of the Glastonbury zodiac.

"The labourers got to work and carved out signs. And they were very conscious that, as they worked, they were tuning into a strong creative element that would bring aliveness into the souls of men long after they had accomplished their mission. The ravages of time obliterated some of this, but the early abbots and others tuned into the records and restored the markings and, today, if you could view it from an aeroplane, you would see the whole pattern which links man with the cosmos, for it is from the cosmos that occult powers proceed.

"Now, these knights of King Uther knew that they had an important mission to perform. They had to invoke powers that were much greater then themselves, and that is what they did. At one time, in the very early days, when the purity of the Christian tradition was strong, men could see and feel that there was a certain pre-Christian element coming in and helping. It was coming through from the days of King Uther. Some Christian celebrations have pagan names — Easter was from the Goddess Oester — because the Christians realised that they had to link with the good vibrations of the pre-Christian era, allowing these fine qualities to invade, in order that a good foundation for the future could be built.

"Also linking with this King Uther, is the place known as Camelot which is near the periphery of the Glastonbury zodiac. When they were in residence there, they would allow everyone to come in, rather like the early courts of Ancient Egypt. They were the guardians of the people, who would come in with their grievances, seeking justice. Indeed, with their occult powers, the knights would be able to discern the truth and put right these disagreements. All the important issues were decided within these councils, for they were regarded as the peace keepers, the trustees, who cared about the whole realm over which they ruled. But alas, other men came after, stepping into the shoes that were left, who had not the same degree of integrity and, by accepting bribes, they were able to mete out punishments and laurels whether merited or not. And corruption entered in.

"These were the ones who were conscious that if they were to have workers from the spirit world with them, then they had to sacrifice to the gods of the Netherworlds. You see, the shadow influences of the Atlantean degradation were still there in the atmosphere. They even performed the black mass, and you will find that there are many unholy places where such an enactment occurred. If any one of you should visit this place that was Camelot, first walk right around it, and then gather and concentrate quietly, asking that the power of God can come in and release those souls still held in bondage. They are still there because the shadow influences that they invoked from the spirit world are continuing to use these souls to reap further havoc, and they are afraid to displease their masters.

"So, we could say that Uther was a very fine and noble King in the early days, who looked after the poor and the sick and did many fine works, but who unfortunately became somewhat other before the end of his rein because of those around him who rather led him astray.

"Then there was also a military general called Arthur. A very accomplished commander in the field who lived around 300 A.D. He was a very rigid, dogmatic, stick to the letter of the law kind of man, very stern and very unforgiving to those who went against his wishes. He did not have the spiritual stature that was needed, and yet he would have the priests come and bless his sword, and bless all his soldiers before they went into battle. He had somewhat of the ruthless zeal of St Paul before he became a Christian.

"And the Sword Excalibur? Now, the general had his sword put in a case in the church when he departed his life, and he said that whoever should open the case, and who felt that it was his by right, should have that sword. And that is how the third Arthur came to possess it.

"This legendary Arthur was born more than 500 years after Jesus left this Earth. He was a great and mighty leader, but only within the very localised area that we have mentioned. His reason for incarnating was to further the establishment of the twelve pillars of truth in the realms of energy very close to the physical. It was a very concentrated mission. It was not the time for it to spread far afield, and Arthur was well aware of what this mission entailed.

"You see, when the spiritually advanced members of humanity today are ready to be participants in this very important outworking, they will be lifted up by the band of refined consciousness now encircling the Earth into contact with what could be seen as a temple in the spirit realms, and will be able to direct the power contained within to really transform this planet. So, it was important that Arthur and his fellow occultists, working in the guise of knights, carried out their allotted tasks in a very precise manner.

"These men and their ladies for, of course, there had to be both, were some of the most evolved on the planet; they incarnated through the families in the area who were direct descendents of the Atlanteans, and so could access something of that power which had been held dormant in the DNA. This was a small and advanced community of souls who were overshadowed by the twelve archetypal consciousnesses that endowed their charges with the qualities that legend attributed to the knights, although they were not as flamboyantly expressed.

"Arthur was particularly gifted psychically and when he laid his hands on people, they received very profound healing. The knights sat at a large table, and it is true it was round and had all the signs of the zodiac carved into it. Each sat according to his allotted place, never at any of the other signs.

"And that wise old sage, Merlin, who represented a powerful archetype from the sixth plane, had much to impart to this Arthur of Camelot. He instructed him and helped him to understand his psychic and spiritual gifts, so that he could do a mighty work for humanity. This he did, for he laid the foundations for a more important expression of the work that was to follow. But again it was not completed, because one of the twelve did not respond to the expectations and so, a relative outsider, the Lancelot figure, was drafted in to help. So you see, legend has become intermixed and interwoven, but much of the truth remains.

"At Camelot there would be much frolic and fun, with jousting and great revelry, and the echoes of this rejoicing can still be felt at the Cadbury Castle site. Those with special sight will be aware of the spiritual purpose enacted by these knights that was to carry the work, started by the Atlantean immigrants in Uther's time, forward into a much more mature form appropriate to the times that are still to come. But alas, one can also feel how the members of the black brotherhood have accessed and used some of the peripheral power that was held there. They were unaware that the really important energies were not accessible to them but they used what they could for their dire practices. They would put human sacrifices on the altar, often people they knew were associated with the Camelot knights and who used their power for the light. As you know, the dark brotherhood, of those times, needed a victim when they enacted their black mass.

"Today, most of this kind of shadow activity is happening on the astral level, and some of those who were caught up in evil at that earlier time, the victims, who allowed hatred and resentment to remain with them, are still held to a past from which they feel they cannot move. They feel chained and sometimes when those Earth people who do rescue work are there, they can hear their cries for help. It is not until they are ready to be released, that we on this side can help them to walk into the pathway of light with us. Though, when one has been held in anything for a long time, it is not easy to realise that the freedom is there.

"When any archetypal energy comes to this planet to work through a human vehicle, it has to acknowledge and accept that in trying to lift the planet onto a higher level of spiritual energy, it will know in advance that the planet may not be totally ready for what it has to offer, but that it still needs to do the work in order to lay the foundation for other energies to come in later. In other words, it was an aspect of the Christ energy that enabled Arthur to fulfil his mission, which was to set into place conduits for energy in precise patterns; but because of the shadow element that would inevitably come in as a response to humanity's unreadiness, these could not be used at that time. In any group of twelve there is one who is unwittingly linked to the shadow, one who will 'let the side down'. It was there with Judas, and with Lancelot. The shadow band wants to destroy what any group is doing for the light and so they build a lot of energy around a member of that group whom they feel is most vulnerable.

"Now, a word of warning, powerful though the energies are, they, like everything else, have a shadow side and so there is every reason to be cautious. There are many members of the shadow band, the perpetrators of the past, who have not seen the error of their ways, and there is definitely a very strong occult brotherhood on the black pathway that is still in operation behind the scenes working through the chink opened up by Lancelot. It is common for these places of spiritual significance to become diverted from their true path into a whirlpool of sensation. We do assure you that this is no place for the thrill seekers and the drug takers. It is much too dangerous."

Power Centres

Many of the power centres on Earth are beginning to reawaken after a long period of dormancy. These centres are closely linked with one of the fundamental tasks of those people who are studying the occult. The word 'occult' suggests hidden mysteries and the many different approaches man has made to them through systems such as the Qabbalah, Hermeticism and, of course, Alchemy. I would go so far as to say that an understanding of occult principles is essential for advanced evolutionary progress. A person who is deeply spiritual without entering the world of occultism is really eating the bread without the butter. He is trying to experience on a finer level of understanding without really registering the subtleties; whereas a study of the occult is designed so that you not only access the higher frequencies but you can understand what you find. This is the difference and it is very important for me to stress this.

Many spiritual groups carefully avoid a ritualistic approach, not because it is necessarily wrong but because they are endeavouring to be more flexible; for any set system, however conscientious, is always limited by the very rituals it employs. It is time to take a new look at occultism, unfettered by time-honoured tradition. There is nothing new in the teachings coming forward for the Aquarian age because there is nothing new in the universe. The fundamental principles do not change. So, although you may try to dispense with tradition, you cannot eliminate that which is history and has formed the milestones; for the milestones are not tradition, they are the points which have been reached by those who have preceded you, that you can learn from and carry forward into more subtle expression.

You may wonder what a statement like this has to do with power centres. You see, basically each one of you is a power centre giving out your own little force field, each of an individual pattern and density according to your individual stage of evolution. You all understand in your own particular way, which is why each person interprets a picture individually. Thus it is with a teaching and thus it is with power centres. They exist on different levels and they can be understood on different levels.

As the planet has evolved, certain civilisations have grown up, each with its own type of culture and power. From an occult point of view these powers accumulate with each successive generation. Let us take an imaginary example. If you were to build yourself a little hut in the middle of your garden, or set aside a small room in your house purely for psychic use, you would find that in time an atmosphere would build up, for the power generated in that room would accumulate and make its mark. When you do psychic or occult work you create a web of power with its own magnetic field that exists over many octaves at its own point in time and space.

I have often explained to you how every thought goes forth into the universe to exist there for eternity, gradually decreasing in intensity. Similarly, when you speak and create a sound in the way that I use the voice of this sensitive, the sound continues to travel on and on in an ever-widening arc, growing fainter to human ears but nevertheless existing. When you send a thought, distance is no object, but only from the point of view of someone who is using thought in a trained manner.

Picture a series of shock waves all proceeding outwards, gradually spreading and dispersing as they go. This is what happens when the average person sends out a thought. But, supposing you are an occultist, is there a difference between your thought and a non-occultist's thought? Yes, there is; not in the basic creation of the thought but in the precise way in which it is used. The thought sent out by the trained mind proceeds in a single concentrated beam to the point at which it is aimed, without diffusion. The thought sent out by the healer also does this, but to a lesser degree. Therefore, those who are completely untrained in the art of thought projection will find that their work is more effective on a localised basis, because it will not have had a chance to become dispersed. There are, of course, exceptions to all rules and one such exception owes its existence to inheritance from previous incarnations. However, you do need to take full responsibility for your thoughts, at whatever level.

You may have noticed in our example that I have emphasised the smallness of the hut or room. There is a reason for this, for when you are in a confined space you will find that it is easier to build an atmosphere because the magnetic field of each person easily reaches the corners of the room and rebounds back, thus enabling those taking part to concentrate their thought with greater ease. So, if you continually build your thought power in this small hut or room, a magnetic field is gradually built up inside that confined space until it begins to have a life of its own. Although I use the term 'magnetic field' I do not wish you to take me too literally and ally it with the normal scientific concept of magnetism. It is one of these illustrative examples which serve to present a reasonable mental picture of this build-up of psychic power.

Suppose that, at this juncture, you invite a friend to your small hut, perhaps to do some psychic work or healing there; then you introduce a third person, and another. All the time, this force field of power inside the hut is building up. More people are drawn to it and soon there is a thriving community involved. In your hut you have started a power centre. Whenever you want to do some healing or psychic work and achieve the best results, the hut is the place to use because of the atmosphere which has been created. Those of you who do psychic work regularly will know that, for this reason, it is always helpful to use the same room.

This is the way in which certain power centres on your planet have evolved: through the build-up of power by constant use over many years, perhaps many centuries, in one definite place. Stonehenge is a perfect example of such a power centre.

Let us now look at another type of power centre, one which has originated in a different manner. In the cultures of certain civilisations which existed thousands of years ago there were some highly potent occult forces in use. The most powerful of these occult dynasties existed on the continent of Atlantis. When Atlantis sank there were many who were forewarned of the disaster. They also knew that the power which they had accumulated over the centuries would retain its potency if it were correctly planted and sealed in a suitable location. So, this tremendous power was concentrated into certain centres around the world, some of which were planted by the priests of the path of light and others by those whose intentions were of the shadow. Glastonbury was one of the most important of these light centres, and still is, due to the work of consolidation done quietly by King Uther, the disciples of Jesus, and King Arthur.

However, do remember that where the power is expressed is not necessarily where it is generated, and the Atlantean elders knew what they were doing when they sealed off the power from grasping intentions. They always chose quiet places of support that resonated out of reach of the unscrupulous and the casual seeker. You will find none of these places in your books and records. The true facts have been relegated to the realm of legend.

As a matter of interest the only other part of the British Isles where there is still a strong Atlantean influence is northern Scotland, but there again other influences have been set up to counteract it to a certain extent. In the South West of England there is one interesting place of uncorrupted power, near a town called Tintagel in North Cornwall, where the energies of Arthur were buried and subsequently found.

Chapter 11

THE NEW EARTH

What does the future hold?

The next phase in the evolution of this planet, up to the year 2012 and a little beyond, will be the period of greatest opportunity. In a few short years we will finally enter the age of Aquarius, and the world is experiencing an influx of new energies into the Earth's etheric body and into the soul of humanity. It is the degree to which these are embraced by those of you in physical form that will determine the unfoldment of the future. Progression is a spiral, and the progression I have passed on to you of past civilisations will be revisited but on a higher rung of experience made possible by this new Aquarian energy.

As I see it, this new and uplifted period of Earth experience will come out of the old, but not as if by some magical waving of the wand in one designated year of Earth time. There will be a change in 2012 on many levels, but for there to be a full manifestation, this has to come through the whole evolutionary cycle of humankind, and that will take, quite frankly, as long as it takes. Certainly, special dispensations of power do come in from higher levels, from time to time, that are intended to give Earth a boost; but these do not happen in a very complete way until humanity and the other streams of evolution on the planet are ready to ensoul them.

If you go back in time to Lemuria, to Atlantis, to Egypt, indeed to all the important periods of human history, you will find that there is still a considerable weight of unresolved issues and energies held in those countries, and these will have to be worked on before peace on Earth can come.

Of course, there is a quickening in the energies going on now, and there is an opportunity to tune into these higher frequencies and so transform this planet without too much ado, but humankind may not choose to take up this opportunity. If you go backwards in time and forward in time you find you have a balance. There is talk of the new Atlantis, that will be a time of great spiritual achievement, carrying forward the old Atlantean energies into even higher expression, and this will be done, in part, by spiritualising the many advancements of scientific discovery that are with you today.

This will only be achieved through finding a balance. The final throes of Atlantis and Egypt saw the complete degradation of what had come through from the early days of Atlantis. So, before there can be the new Atlantis in its full glory, there needs to be a resolution of that degradation. I have spoken of the pall in the Middle East, a heavy fog that is there, which needs to be lifted. There are many spirits, on Earth and in the spheres beyond, still caught up in that condition, who were participants in this fog coming into being.

Following on from there, you find your great Roman energy today languishing in a spiritual backwater, due to the debasement of the power that was entrusted to it. The new Rome is to rise up to balance the old Rome at its most refined, and become a place of great influence again; but before a new Rome can come fully into being, there must be a resolution of what caused that lowered state. All of those places on Earth that received the Atlantean energy, need to come into a state of full expression again, because in the ethers of those countries, in those special places, a profound purpose remains dormant and needs liberating.

So, nothing is going to happen miraculously, no moment, no year when 'the lion and the lamb' will lie down together; nothing like that, at least, not in your lifetimes. There is so much of this resolution to be done first, before you can see the essential patterns of the past reflected in the refined patterns of the future. Of course, it is in the present that everything is worked on by you Earth people, and all around your planet today, particularly in those countries with strong Atlantean heritage, there are many people trying to bring up the secrets hidden in the Earth.

Part of seeking out the truth and accessing these power points are about connecting with the seeds of secrets, held in what have been called 'orbs', golden orbs which contain much powerful information for humanity in the future. It is at these points on the planet that inspiration is being accessed by many seeking the truth, spiritually guided to them, either physically by visiting, or by connecting through the subtle levels and layers. These points are strongly linked around the planet by lines of power. In order to anchor this network of light and information, so that it can be more readily accessed by spiritual seekers and made manifest, a few intrepid souls are starting to anchor themselves within those places of high importance, by first energetically balancing physically in the body and the mind to a very precise degree, thereby bringing a maturity through into their own lives. It always starts with the self.

So, 2012 can be seen as a high water mark, and as a turning of the tide. The great civilisations that emerged out of the destruction of Atlantis, did so one after the other, and this will happen again, but in reverse. There will soon be a new England emerging to take prominence in world affairs, followed by a new Rome, and a new Jerusalem. Then there will be a new Greece and a new Egypt, but these are still quite a way off in the scheme of things.

Nevertheless, there are cycles within cycles, and no matter which one of them is taking centre stage, all will have to go through further rounds of resolution in a spiral of release behind the scenes, a preparation for the time when the Christ energies can finally re-emerge into full expression through the coming into being of the new Atlantis.

The New England
Some people are concerned at the moment because they know that a tremendous amount of light is being brought to bear upon planet Earth and this is arousing the shadow very strongly. All over your planet there are groups seeking to work with the light; perhaps the teachings differ slightly in detail, but that does not matter. The point is that there is the same basic intention behind each group, the desire to cleanse this planet; the desire to start people thinking and to open their minds to the infinity of the universe, to the unconditional love,

understanding and tolerance that is eternally issuing from the Ultimate.

Events are mounting in tension and, from the esoteric point of view, the danger spot is not a certain western power, nor even a certain eastern power. A great many people worry about these two giants at the moment, because one exudes a policy of expansion born out of fear and the other a trigger-happy policy also based on fear. Strangely enough, these two do not concern me as the focal points, for they are too obvious.

From the point of view of those higher spirits which desire that people should be given true freedom and a true love and understanding of God, there is a country about which they are concerned, a point of focus that is going to be the vortex of this rising tension. Extremes will become increasingly obvious . . . more light, more dark, more light, more dark; and the place where all this will happen will be your own country — England.

Oh yes, England has a special spiritual significance, and certainly many spiritual battles have been played out within these islands to prepare for this. And the interesting thing about England at this time and, to some degree, the British Isles as a whole, is that the quality that has enabled it to provide a stability between some of the extremes on the planet, and must do again, has come at a price. It is something that could actually turn in on itself at any time, and, to avoid this, it needs to allow itself to expand. It is imperative, in my humble opinion, for the British Isles to expand its concepts.

What do I mean by that? Well, there is a great insecurity mixed with arrogance that encourages many people who are born in these islands to see themselves as being so special that they need to be apart from the rest of the world. When the concept of a United Europe was first discussed, this was a fulfilment of something I had talked about years before. I think that England definitely needs to remain a part of Europe in the sense that it can provide a balance between some of the different temperaments that make up Europe as a whole. England has grown beyond the need to be independent, and what it can offer spiritually needs to be part of a whole, instead of separate and aloof. Indeed, if it is separated now it will become lost.

There is a tremendous linking between the great spiritual sites of Stonehenge, Glastonbury, and so on, and powerful centres of energy in France. England is part of Europe and needs to be part of Europe. And it needs to be sure of itself to let go of what it calls its heritage and its tradition because, if it doesn't, that tradition will strangle it.

I deliberately do not intend to predict in any way here, because I want you to understand that whether or not Mikaal is eventually able to influence the physical realms strongly enough to uplift those who could be the ones to unlock the power, and to convert those who still wish to misuse it, this is not a predestined issue and it does not depend only upon England. It is an issue that depends upon all those incarnate throughout the entire planet.

Many people worry because they feel that the Luciferian legacy of materialism and sectarianism is increasing in England. It is certainly on the increase all over the world, but I think it would be true to say that its increase in England calls for more concern than it does in many other countries. When speaking of the Luciferian adherents, I am not referring to small groups of people who indulge in perverted rituals and practices for these are small fry in the Satanic regime. Groups of this sort are often composed of a few young people in search of excitement or physical stimulation who do not really understand what they are doing. Unfortunately, however, in this ignorance lies harm, because the power generated at this physical level is often utilised by spirits from a much higher level of evil and by unscrupulous occultists who do understand what they are doing!

In some ways it is encouraging, from my point of view, that the vortex of all this increasing trouble will be centred on England because, overall, the people in this particular country are better equipped to take it than those in many other countries. I shall not give you any further details of the part you will play in this battle, but I do wish to emphasise the points I have just made, in the hope that it will instil into all of you the urgency and necessity of the work you are doing. We are trying to open people's minds, hearts and souls, not necessarily to accept our teachings or our way of life, but to receive the all-embracing wisdom of the Ultimate and become aware of their responsibility towards the whole.

There are so many different movements, societies and religions that exist even in this small country of England; but, after all, it would be rather boring if everyone thought in exactly the same way, would it not? Bearing in mind that each of you is in your own stage of evolution, treading your own path of spiritual progress, then you will see that there must be all types of approach to cater for people on all evolutionary levels. The essential thing is that they each have the same basis of love and understanding and, most important of all, genuine tolerance and acceptance of each other.

I am very concerned about those groups in England who are using what they present as a higher teaching as a mask to disguise their true intentions. It is up to your own powers of discernment to decide which these are, but if you bear in mind the principles of God that should not be too difficult. One of the dangers to look for is egotism in the society, church or religion that 'knows all', the one that gradually infiltrates a little intolerance and a good deal of fear into what on the surface appears to be good and spiritual; the one that claims to be the only one that can save the world. Now, I must qualify that a little here, because many groups make this claim of specialness quite innocently. They are not necessarily inspired by the Luciferian consciousness in any way; it is just a misunderstanding. So, it is up to you to examine all aspects, and listen to your deep intuitive feelings, before you arrive at your conclusions.

The Chakras of Great Britain
There is a chakric system within every form of physical evolution, for this is the link between the spirit and the mind/brain physical part of that being. So the planet, like you as a human being, has various chakric levels and each one of these represents an energy. Every country has created its own energy centres, each brought about by a group of spirits coming together and creating a powerful focus of spiritual intention.

Taking the land mass which includes England, as the example, the base chakra is expressed most significantly in Edinburgh, but for the nurturing Gaia aspect you have to go to the far north of Scotland, at Forres, tended to by a large and very important spiritual community, Findhorn. They are linked energetically, with the Edinburgh energy slightly more elevated and the Findhorn energy slightly more earthed. In Findhorn, they have done a wonderful job to help stabilise the whole of Great Britain.

The sacral chakra can be found at the other end of the country, at St Austell in Cornwall. It is from this centre that the Eden Project gets its inspiration.

I would like to mention that the chakric system of a country is not in a line, as they are in the human frame. Chakras certainly have to be in balance within all forms of evolution, but not necessarily in a line.

To make contact with the two highest aspects of the solar plexus chakra, you would look towards Manchester and the Lake District. Then I see the expressive heart chakra energy as being located in Birmingham. Many of the energies in that area have been trapped, they have been subdued, and so I consider that it is really important for it to open out. On one level, Birmingham holds part of the secret essence of the country and, going back into the past, it is one of the reasons why it has been very difficult for people in this country to find that heart area within themselves except in times of crisis.

There has already been one major opening out of the compassion-ate element in recent times and I am referring to the tragic events which lead to the death of your Princess Diana. Look at what that did to the heart energies, not only in this country but throughout the whole planet. In that sense, she chose what needed to happen with great compassion and, at the moment of her death, great under-standing of where she needed to be. In her own heart and mind she knew she had to give up her physical life and, in the period leading up to her death, she found what she had come into life for. When a spirit in a body reaches that stage it will draw towards itself the very circumstances that will enable it to fulfil its destiny.

The death of Princess Diana enabled millions of people to see how, together, they could grieve, they could weep, and they could begin to understand why she did some of the things that she did. I am not sure that Diana, herself, knew why she did them but, nevertheless, she did. When she found that her own personal love was rejected, she suddenly realised her own anger at the failure of her marriage and she redirected that energy into wanting to help mankind through compassion and understanding. People admired the way she sometimes flirted with death in her associations with people who had infectious and contagious diseases; but Diana knew that she was flirting with death. Deep inside she knew that she was heading for something that was inevitable. That was the whole power of the situation. Her death was a part of the move towards people power, people understanding that the world can be moved with flowers, much more effectively than by demonstrations and protests against guns and truncheons and instruments of torture.

What is interesting about her death is that whereas when a death is traumatic the spirit often becomes earth-bound, traumatised by the actual manner of the death; in the case of Diana this was not so, because that spirit had made a decision, and was ready to move on. The strength of that decision was going to resound and touch the hearts of millions of people, and it has brought to the fore some of the very difficult situations that surround the whole planet, where there is this conflict between spiritual motivation, personal motivation and that of power through money.

Over the years, mainly because of media pressure, your Royal Family has cocooned themselves somewhat; and if you look at your Queen today, you will find someone who is much more withdrawn than when she was first crowned. So, the events around Diana were actually about opening up the heart centre of the monarchy who are, in a sense, the custodians of the heart centre of the country. It is very sad to reflect on the way in which it happened, but you must understand that spirit has a very different view to life in a physical body than you do. On one level, I compliment her on the bravery of the decision that was made deep inside, and it is very important that the whole country continues to reflect on it, in its understanding and its attitude.

Although the age of Aquarius is to be one of the mind, the imbalance created by England moving away from the emotions — which was, in itself, an attempt to not fall into the passionate excesses of other countries during the Piscean era — has led the people to overdo this and so, understate and frustrate the heart. There is a great need to bring the heart to the fore at this time, to understand that spiritual wholeness and spiritual enlightenment is just about being yourself; of perceiving, understanding and sensing your own inner beauty, your own inner wonderment, your own inner being.

In this period leading up to the Aquarian Age, the heart centre energy is going to permeate all strata of society and arouse great excitement as you become your true selves. Culture in this country is going to become more heart centred, business will become more heart centred, politics is going to become more heart centred, right across the British Isles. It is all about heart, heart and heart!

If a country has not achieved balance it cannot exist in harmony with its neighbours, and so, the newly aroused heart and the very effectively functioning mind of this country need to find a way of working together. I feel Birmingham is to be a very crucial part of this transformation in the coming years. But then, all parts are important. They are all crucial because one affects the other.

Then we move down into the south east, to London, with its business activity and all it has created around that. It is very left brain and very cerebral and yet, in another sense, it is the seat of certain kinds of emotions. It can be all things to all people and nothing as well, just depending how you look at it. It is an area of centralisation and communication, for I certainly view London as the throat chakra.

Moving over to Glastonbury in the West Country, we encounter the brow chakra, very psychic, very open, very mixed, very ungrounded. It is not surprising that the wisdom eye is located at Glastonbury, that area crossed by such important ley lines, including the Michael line, passing on through many small communities, all linking in.

Today, Glastonbury is a focal point of what you call 'new age' activity, though to a great extent that is a diversion. As always, when people contact the energies of light this will awaken the shadow aspects because the two go together. Glastonbury will certainly have a pivotal role to play in the future but, just because people want an awakening to be there now, it does not mean that they are ready to be crucibles for it.

Indeed, most people are wasting their time visiting there and other such centres of repute, because these important places need to be protected from abuse. The grasping of the uninitiated to draw on and use the power for themselves, only causes the power to retreat, and that is what has happened at Glastonbury. Oh, there will be a few very pure and sensitive souls who, when they visit that holy place, though they are not conscious at all of the great enactments of the past that are there, will still bring away with them something that lives and grows stronger with the passing years, a link to the greater power. Most find that there is a compelling force that reaches out and says, "We want you here again". It is some of these people who will begin the time of awakening of this most important centre a little later on, so that the Arthurian enactment can, at last, reach its apotheosis.

Spirit is actually diverting attention from many of the inwardly active places towards those well known spots where people are attempting to promote spiritual matters, such as Sedona, in America, which are, to a great extent, playgrounds for the unready. Even many of the ancient sites, such as Ayers Rock in central Australia, have experienced a diminishing, because the people going there have been far too dependent on the old ways of seeking for the self. So many of these sites have been sealed off against further encroachment. Glastonbury is awash with desire, inundated with people wanting to be part of a spiritual uprising, to be in the thick of it, and so it has, of necessity, been spiritually cut off from them.

Don't forget, the Master Jesus went to some of these secret sites, and put into place the hidden keys for the future. He sealed them, as did the Atlanteans in a very strong way, so that nobody without proper training could get access to them prematurely. People say, "That's where King Arthur was", "That's where Jesus went", but they are looking in quite the wrong places. Spiritual centres are there for service primarily, not for the self. Esoteric things were always for the few, and while these realms of higher knowledge are opening up to many more today, when desire comes into it, this will always attract the shadow of that knowledge.

Then I see that the crown chakra of the country lies in the Malvern Hills. It is something that has developed there because these Hills are very old. It is the oldest part of the country, it holds the deepest wisdom, it holds the greatest light and it holds the greatest shadow.

Malvern, if properly understood, will reveal why it has been necessary to preserve that ancient energy at a very deep level. There is a close link with Gaia in the guardianship of the country and of the planet. It is not the only place on Earth that offers this guardianship, but it is one of them, and it is an important one.

It is certainly not a place to feed the ego. It is one of reality. If you study Malvern you will find how much has been drawn towards it by way of elevated creative thought: it has drawn music of the highest inspiration, and many of the arts, it has even drawn the ability to create scientifically on electronic levels. This is because of the very subtle and balanced energy that is buried down below, right under the Hills. It is a very profound place, very deep, very empowering - but very challenging. It will reveal your light, it will expose your shadow so approach it with care; approach it gently, and see how it affects you.

Malvern is a place for people who wish to express their spirituality in a humble and loving way. The energy will rebound on anyone who goes there for selfish reasons, to play with the energies or to take them for personal reasons, as it has to so many who have visited Glastonbury over recent years.

These special pockets of high energy, Malvern and Glastonbury and the others, need to be linked up on a very subtle level. This hasn't happened yet because of the tendency of the protecting ones to seal the sites off from intrusions and so, instead of integrating the energies throughout the country, those in human form who look after them tend to operate in their own individual way. The time has come when there should be much more energy put into linking them up actively, bringing them into a state of mutual respect, and here we come to one of the bases of my teaching which is about balance and harmony in one's spiritual understanding.

There are certainly some beautiful and exceptional energies at Glastonbury, but they are out of balance with each other and with the sacred sites - the Chalice Well, the Tor, the Abbey. If the Glastonbury energies could be linked up with the Malvern energies, this would help the Malvern energies by making them more evident, and the Malvern energies would help the Glastonbury energies by bringing them into a more balanced and harmonious level of being. The two power centres could help each other, and so on, linking up through the whole chakric system, to the very isolated region in Scotland which is so cut off spiritually as well as geographically from its partners.

Behind every thought there is another thought. When the master Jesus taught, it was given on many levels at the same time. Those of you whose senses are tuned to cover the widest range of frequencies will receive it in the greatest depth. Some may prefer to hear it on an etheric level only, although most will hear it on a physical level only. Though the development of your physical senses limits you to hearing on one particular wavelength, this does not mean that others do not exist, for indeed they do. I would like to apply this as a simile to the type of power which exists at a power centre on many levels.

It is those who are aware on a subtle level and are properly trained, who do the most important work; people able to be quiet and very still in what they are doing. And, if you are one of these, we hope that you will visit soon, either in your physical body or in your meditations. The others of you, who are not yet ready to play your part, I do entreat you to leave these centres in peace till you are ready to participate in a constructive way. Until then, it is enough to send out loving thoughts each day to help bring balance and joy onto the planet.

Power centres are places where it could be said that the power of many, many generations of universal seeking has accumulated. Each power centre has a unique vibration and pattern, and they all form part of a greater picture. Simply to analyse the 'feel' of a single site alone is not enough, as each location must be taken in relation to the complex as a whole. You would need to spend a great deal of time there if you are to unlock any of its secrets and discover the network of influence that extends far beyond its borders. These patterns, I speak of, are in reality thought lines which link through to other power centres, some call them 'ley lines'. Once you realise how they connect up in a certain grouping, you can then endeavour to find the key to the group so that you may link up with other like-motivated people on a mission to constructively harness the power from the complex to reach out and liberate some part of your country from its resistance to change and inclusiveness.

The thought-patterns within power centres exist on all levels and are intercommunicative; thus the lines of power are multi-directional in the sense that the links which they form must be on various levels of existence. So, if an occultist is really going to make the optimum use of a power centre, he must learn to understand its many facets or frequencies according to his own capacity.

Each power centre is a universe in itself, a pulsating, living thing which, if treated and nurtured correctly, can help to bring love, understanding and healing to the world; but should it be used improperly it becomes a diabolical weapon. This is why it is important that these centres fall into the right hands. You must remember that all forms of universal power are neither good nor evil in themselves; it is the use to which they are put which determines their 'shade'. Evil is an intention; you either want to help somebody or you want to hinder them; you choose to be selfish or selfless.

The type of key to these power centres is very involved and, for the uninitiated who try to tap them, the results could be violent, because they would be playing with powers which are beyond their understanding and their ability to cope with. It is vital that the power in these centres is used in the right way. If healers who are working for the powers of light worldwide were able to amass the force from these power centres, and link up, then it would be a tremendous aid to bringing the world back into a state of balance. However, should these centres fall into the wrong hands, the thought is too terrifying to dwell upon; for, remember, the powers of darkness do not observe the moral codes of the workers for the light.

So, when you consider these power centres, remember your own personal responsibility, remember that your thoughts and actions can affect all others, whether in Earth bodies or in spirit, who are involved there; in fact, they can affect the future destiny of the planet. These are forces greater than many of you could imagine.

It is said in India that if you want to find a good guru, go to one with only one other disciple – do not go where the masses are. That is not to say that it is in any way wrong to go into these mass movements, for that is what is needed at that time, but the Aquarian age is about individuals working within small groups, so that is the approach to take.

Many countries around the world are going to experience an increase of energy, accompanied by its shadow, in this period leading up till 2012 and for some years beyond. If you want to be a participant in what is coming next, and feel you are ready, do not just look where the present activity is. And remember that you will need to become sensitively aware of the nature of the task, working on many levels.

The destiny of England requires it to be an example to the rest of the world, but it remains an interesting contradiction. On one level it holds the key to a tremendous spiritual force. On another level it wants to isolate itself. Spiritually, as a country and as an energy, it needs to integrate, it needs to live by example. This is a time when secrets and lies are being exposed, and all your structures of power are under constant review. Those in authority slip and slide trying to keep the show on the road, but without really trusting the people they serve nor understanding the new energies that are fitfully flowing into the country. But there is no avoiding the Aquarian energy, and anyone in authority who tries to do so will not remain.

The New Rome
Some two thousand years ago a man gave up his life in a most cruel and defiling way in order that humankind should have another opportunity to try to build the world in peace and harmony. Did it take this opportunity? No; it went on in its greedy, intolerant, unthinking way, and the world accelerated into its present state. Was the crucifixion in vain? No, it was not, because it provided a symbol of selflessness, love and compassion to which humankind can still rise.

Much has been said about whether there is going to be only one more Pope. If the Catholic religion is not prepared to really open its doors, to open its whole concept to a much more sensitive, gentler understanding then it will be doomed to extinction. Of course, a lot of energy and effort has been made to try to bring into the establishment of popes a more inclusive understanding that would open the religion out to a much wider range of people. For obvious reasons, I do not wish to enter into the politics of why the reign of John Paul I was so short, but the fact was that he was providing a challenge to the way that they had built up their organisation. If future Popes are not of the John Paul I calibre and prepared to open up the Roman Catholic doctrines to bring them in line with the free and flexible energies of the Aquarian Age, then I am sorry to say that their survival is doubtful.

So many spirits of people who were caught up in the abuses of the Church over the centuries are back with a great deal of guilt and a great deal of anger. You must also understand that the Christian religion has a lot of past karma to deal with. For example, the suppression of the Cathars was very unfortunate for the Catholic Church and built up a tremendous amount of negative karma that the Catholic religion now has to release by asking for forgiveness. Although certain aspects within Catholicism have asked for that forgiveness, it has to be much stronger, much wider and from the helm.

It is important for all regimes to engender forgiveness. So, to some extent, the various streams of religious power that have arisen out of Rome need to be sent a lot of healing, a lot of unconditional love, because there is a tremendous stuckness which needs to be moved on. There are intermeshed energies there which have been misused for a long time, going right back to Lemuria. But if that blocked energy could be released then that country could be a leading force on the planet to help a new understanding come into being.

With the advent of the Aquarian age, the type of approach to spirituality employed by the Catholic hierarchy is going to be challenged, and in some places it will disintegrate more quickly than in others. What we are anxious to see is that, as more and more people become confident on an individual basis, this does not create a war with established religion. We are not wishing to see that happen, and that is why the energies that I represent and Akhenaten and many others are trying to bring about a gentle understanding of the rights of the individual and their responsibility to find their own spiritual path – not one that is dominated, controlled and limited by any form of established policy.

I should also like to say that it could be advantageous to read some of the equally inspired ancient historical documents which have been preserved in other religions, for it will help you not only to broaden your minds but to extend your horizons.

A teaching should not bludgeon you with a set of dogmas which you are forced to accept, but instead it should encourage you to think honestly and without prejudice. I and my colleagues have always tried to give you a basic understanding upon which to build your life: a set of values, ideas and an open-mindedness. You are a collection of individuals applying these ideas, each in your own unique way, and I respect each one of you for it. It is only in this way, by people respecting one another, that there is any hope for the future.

To what extent has Christianity maintained its designated role? I would suggest that the Christian hierarchy, and here I am referring to the religion as distinct from the teaching, has made the mistake of not moving with the times. By this I do not mean that you should conduct Mass to the latest pop record. This is not moving with the times, it is merely desecrating an atmosphere. It is all a question of approach and of how you present those teachings. Restructuring the Old Testament is not the solution. Rewriting the New Testament in modern prose is not the solution. What have you achieved by doing this? You have altered the meaning yet again and destroyed the beauty of the ancient verse. It is much more a question of attitude, of taking a lead, of showing that you are a prominent force.

The Christian teaching is an important one and it can it be brought to life again. I could not do it; you could not do it. It will need a body of men working under pure inspiration over many years to bring the right sort of life back into the Church. Unfortunately, as things are progressing, religion is going to lose more ground in the future. It is going to lose ground where it matters most, that is, amongst that solid block of uncommitted people who present the real challenge.

Mikaal and Lucifer

There is one crucial thing that the religions need to understand, all of them, for now we have reached the point where I must explain something that will totally alter your understanding of my teaching. You see, the occult battle between the two opposing devic forces has already been resolved in the highest reaches of the fifth plane, not by the defeat of Lucifer, but with Lucifer drawing into a close affinity with Mikaal. You need to remember that every guardian, every angel - and this is what has not been appreciated in orthodox religion

- is both light and shadow, otherwise it could not work. This is why the guardian Deva spirit of planet Earth is both Mikaal and Lucifer. Now, that has given you something to think about, hasn't it? Oh yes, Mikaal and Lucifer are the light and shadow aspects of one and the same spirit.

That Lucifer was to become the alienated aspect of that important archetypal devic energy was probably inevitable, given the degree of disruption wrought on the universe from afar. It needed an evolved devic spirit to ensoul it, in order that it could be resolved and harmony reinstated. You see, the light in harmony with the shadow is not destructive. It brings the two polarities into a resonance with each other. Now that this important relationship has regained its balance, it needs to filter down to the lower levels of energy. This is the first step towards establishing a degree of global unification that has not existed before, but which will eventually engage the hearts and minds of humanity. It is part of the influence as you progress towards the age of Aquarius in 2012 and beyond.

Imbalance created on one level can only be resolved on that level. That is a part of free will. The higher will not impose on the lower, and so when the disruptive influence swept in from far beyond this solar system, it caused the Lucifer shadow to be drawn away from a natural balance with the Mikaal light aspect.

Those were dark days in the heavens. It seemed as though there were two incompatible and separate forces on the planet battling for supremacy, yet both of them were aspects of the ruling Deva of planet Earth. But the Lucifer element, though being part of the same spirit, was unable to maintain an integration with its counterpart and so, on the physical plane, it was forced to become allied to the Moon – where it resorted to sending its baleful influence from a distance, which others took up and used to try to control the people of Earth.

I am sure you realise that this explanation is a simplified view of what actually happened when Mikaal became unable to effectively support and balance Lucifer, but it is close enough to the truth for you to understand. The degree to which the shadow Lucifer was able to influence the malignant energies at the time of Atlantis, was to determine the strength of the evil that was subsequently built up around this Deva as it fell from grace; particularly when that influence drew in other supportive entities from the shadow side of the fifth plane.

It stands to reason that Lucifer did not remain alone, and the seductive nature of its message would capture many spirits in its thrall, with converts subsequently joining in on all lower levels to form what has been termed the 'Luciferian hoards', collectively caught up in a force of controlling evil intent that became self-perpetuating. Many of those who joined in those early days, have not yet followed Lucifer back to a state of balance with Mikaal. But the call is going out to them and, hopefully, they will respond in time to lift the last surge of the unbalanced Piscean age into a truly redemptive initiative.

When God created spirit and gave it the free will choice to love or not to love, it established the influence of Mikaal and Lucifer within each person. And over the last few years we have seen the containment of Lucifer by Mikaal - the containment of the shadow by the light – however, when it is registered on lower levels this containment is creating a great deal of rebellion by those who cannot accept. A vengeful, angry, negative energy has been aroused in many who feel this to be a denial of their individuality and worth.

This is creating a great deal of international tension because the fight to get back in control, by the remaining undisciplined Luciferian influence, is generating fear, control, denigration and the denial of personal choice. The shadow comes from fear, the light will arouse fear in humans where the shadow is still dominant, but the light itself contains no fear. They must realise that when Mikaal lifts his sword above his head it is to use that sword as a symbol of healing, love and forgiveness, not as a weapon to strike back.

The physical plane is still a particularly fertile ground for the missionary zeal of the shadow band. In the ethers surrounding your Earth, the veil of forgetfulness is almost complete. Only a spirit operating on a very subtle level is going to be fully conscious of both aspects, the light and the shadow, and will choose the level of balance that it feels coincides with its own true motivation.

However, many spirits have found themselves focused into the darkness, unable to reach up sufficiently to their own body of light. So, they have become caught up in one of the illusory worlds created by the disciples of Lucifer. And this explains why so many horrors are still happening on Earth today, why there is such a fascination with the shadow in Earth people and why, when law and order breaks down, so many are unable to resist their base nature. And, in succumbing to the primitive instinctual forces, whether in the tribal wars in Africa, or in the more sophisticated West, men without the spiritual maturity that they profess to have, carry out acts of false leadership that are far reaching and reprehensible. The more power a person has, the more the responsibility and diligence they must exercise towards the rest of humanity.

It is because the fifth plane Mikaal/Lucifer entity has now achieved a high degree of harmony, that it is only a matter of time before this filters down through the spheres into the collective soul of mankind. Whether there is enough time left to avoid some of the more destabilising natural disasters poised to occur is yet to be determined. Alas, many of those who accompanied Lucifer into the darkness are still there in the shadow realms of the fifth plane, and each plane beneath it, continuing to perpetrate evil, loyal members of what you could call the self perpetuating 'shadow army'.

And in counteracting this, it has been the mistaken belief that evil has to be destroyed that has led to so many retrograde attitudes and mistaken acts.

If Lucifer is the shadow aspect of the Mikaalian energy, what then represents the shadow aspect of the Christ energy? This cannot be easily isolated in the way that you can with the shadow side of Mikaal. Suffice to say that all the accumulated unresolved karma, of a negative nature, incurred by humankind over time, is held by this Christ shadow. Look at the crucifixion of Jesus, and all the atrocities that have subsequently occurred in his name, and in the names of many other great spiritual leaders, such as at the time of the crusades, the Spanish Inquisition, the crushing of the Cathars, and in the terror attacks and subsequent bombing of Iraq. Put them all together and you will get a small inkling of this shadow aspect of the Christ energy as it is polarised in your human world today.

The New Greece
The Greeks revealed a great wisdom in their philosophy and understanding. They communicated with some advanced archetypal

energies, whom they called the Gods; but somewhat like the Atlanteans - for they were of Atlantean heritage - they eventually sabotaged themselves. Their levels of protection were not strong enough to maintain what they had started, so the energies became dispersed.

There are still parts of Greece where there are some deep, beautiful energies, but somehow the country has never come together again, and today, it is quite fragmented. It is necessary for healing thoughts to be sent to Greece by those who were there in that time of greatness, because locked within its borders, and on many of the islands that are Greek, there are some very important energies for the future. Like many countries, they have been going through a very tricky period and it has been difficult to consolidate progress and find a new direction.

In some ways the Greek energy contained more of the Atlantean energy than the Egyptian, because the Egyptian approach became very complicated. This is why, in my teaching, I have tried to keep things simple, because the tribal approach on this planet has unfortunately involved intense polarisation. In other words, it has supported ways of expressing spirituality through structures that alienate and control. As a result, in both Egypt and Greece you had this reflection of what happened in Atlantis that has prevented a further arising of the energy in both those countries, and as I have indicated, it will be quite a time before this will happen.

In Greece you have these pockets of very fine energy, and if you could work towards linking up some of the power centres that are active there, then it will result in a better integration spiritually. It will take the emphasis away from a tribal approach and more into a unifying purpose that will release a tremendous amount of power into that country.

One way that the strength of the Greek civilisation of old reaches into out into a global initiative of today is through the Olympic Games. What a very wonderful initiative it was envisioned to be and, indeed, despite political intervention, still is. And the fact that they were given to China to hold in 2008 was of tremendous importance, because China has been isolated for so long and this provided it with an opportunity to open its doors and understanding to the rest of the world. The country in which they are held is always significant.

So, I am delighted that the Olympic games are still continuing. I would like to feel that those of you who have spiritual understanding and wisdom will do your utmost to send loving thoughts for their success when they are held in England in 2012. It will be a significant factor in assisting this country to fully integrate itself spiritually and to take up its rightful place as a leading influence in world affairs.

Chapter 12

THE ATLANTEAN HERITAGE

The New Egypt

Many of the pharaohs who ruled Egypt were very concerned about the acquisition of power and sought to hold onto what they had by force. Indeed, this holding on became endemic in the Egyptian civilisation, and though the civilisation crumbled eventually, in the Great Pyramid that power remains there still and continues to be generated.

The misuse of the Atlantean ideas that came forward into the Egyptian civilisation created this terrible stuckness, a framework of stagnation, where spirits are still existing very close to Earth on the astral planes. They are bewildered, they cannot see their way forward. I am sure that you know what it feels like when you cannot see your way forward but, in most of your lives, you have hope. Alas, those Egyptian spirits are manacled to their own beliefs; they can see no hope, they desperately need whatever we can do to release them from their predicament.

I have, for some years, been trying to encourage many groups to work on releasing some of the stuckness of spirits who were incarnate in Egypt, especially those who held positions of authority - priests, pharaohs and so forth – including those who are back today in new bodies unaware of their responsibility. If you are part of a group that works in this way, let me offer you this advice: don't try to tackle the problem en masse. Just try to help individual spirits who come into your consciousness. For with every single spirit we help to release, to move on, others will see the light and be encouraged to follow, helping to relieve the Middle East situation and, indirectly, the whole planet. It is important work, it is urgent work, but it is difficult to do while the energy in the pyramids is held in. You see, the pyramids are the focal point of the stuckness and restriction.

A pyramid is a very containing structure but in the wrong hands it becomes an inhibiting structure. It takes the energy and, if it is not allowed to flow out, it preserves it, it holds it, so that, as time goes on, the energy actually increases. The pyramids inherited the Atlantean energy, and that energy has accumulated, it has matured for thousands of years, and when most people go into those pyramids, they are actually adding to the intensity of that power.

There is still much to be revealed in Egypt, for as you start to work on these Egyptian spirits who were originally responsible for the enforced containment and are still there on the inner planes, you can help them to release and move on. And that will release some of the secrets underneath the pyramids.

As it is today, it is not a structure that is compatible with the age of Aquarius, for control is a distorted Piscean trait and this, in itself, has created great tensions. The pyramid is very protective and, in that protection, it is not allowing the energies which move within it to spread beyond it.

Those of you who have been to Egypt will know something of the purpose of the temples and the pyramids. Certainly, if you are sensitive, you can go into the Great Pyramid and visit the King's Chamber and come out feeling quite uplifted; but it is lower down that the stuck energies essentially lie. I would like to see more of those people who are good at releasing energy to start releasing the pent up forces in those pyramids that actually need to come out.

The pyramid power, the energy that accumulates within that shape, relates to a period that is past and because those in authority at that time controlled the power that they had amassed, it created a stuckness, a rigidity, a fear of moving forward in the whole of the Middle East.

It is important that the hidden chambers are rediscovered soon, and that the energy is released from them in a focused, loving, open way, in order that it will not be commandeered by some dictator or regime and used to gain power over people, over the environment, over the nature kingdoms. It is important that these energies are released at the right time, and it will require very specialised ability and understanding to achieve this.

The safest way to release the energy from the pyramid is to see it coming down into the earth, and then moving out from around the base. In that way, it can be done in an unpressured and entirely non-confrontational manner.

There is no such thing as an accident, or chance. As humanity evolves, so the collective energy of the planet is all the time affecting it. We are facing this vital need to balance the energies of our light and our shadow, both on an individual basis and on a collective basis. This can only be done by actually facing the shadow, understanding why it is there and acknowledging the energies within you that have accumulated over many incarnations. It is time to tackle the fear that has permeated into the events that are taking place in the Middle East at this present time.

What is interesting about these chambers, is that they are, in combination, the source power of the rest of the pyramid, and the energy was locked in the chambers situated at the bottom of the pyramid, sealed in by those who knew how, for future generations to discover and use appropriately to help move the whole planet forward. When this happens, it will release a powerful energy, but the energy will come out in a rush. It will need a great deal of careful handling, and it could easily ferment an international situation that is even less open than the present one.

You could imagine, those of you who are healers, what it would feel like if you had accumulated all the healing energy that you have ever channelled in your life, into one part of your body, into one part of your spirit? Yet that is what has happened in the pyramids. It has to be tackled slowly and gently, and with compassion, for within that energy there is a terrific healing power.

You are aware of how the healing movement is expanding in this country, and in many countries of the world. That expansion is being helped by the new energies forming around the planet, some of which are coming in from higher planes, some of which are coming from within the many spirits who have incarnated purposefully to play a part in this transition into the age of Aquarius. So, do what you can to try to release that pyramid energy, but remember that it needs to be effected without causing distress or anger in the country in which the pyramids are based. It needs to be done in a way that is not confrontational, in a way that is not 'them against us'.

If the stored energy of those hidden chambers had been released before this time, the results could have been horrific, because the world was not ready to take that energy fully. The energy in the pyramids can be used to harm or heal, and there is a great need for light and shadow to be expressed in balance within its boundaries before it can be allowed out into the world.

It is the responsibility of those who understand this, who feel drawn to do this work, to invoke 'pyramid healing energy', and use it to gently and gradually download some of the accessible energies of the pyramid, releasing them downwards and then outwards using the balancing symbol of the equidistant cross within the circle, to be administered by others in a responsible way. It is not good to store energy in one spot; it becomes very concentrated. Good energy is not concentrated energy, it is balanced energy. It is the energy of unconditional love, moving beyond judgement and manipulation, moving into an area of absolute forgiveness. These are the qualities that are needed in the Middle East at this time.

It needs some very strong healers, working as a group, to do this type of healing. It needs precise attunement. It is about placing themselves in a divine protection and then going into the pyramid in love, either in person or through mental projection, in a very disciplined, very structured way. They are dealing with energies that could make nuclear energy pale into insignificance. So, it is not a 'rush in and get it out' job. It is something that needs to be thought about, and carried out in a systematic and planned way.

You could start, always in groups, never alone, and don't try to run before you can walk. These things are not achieved overnight. For me, the single most debilitating energy on your planet is fear, the fear of moving forward, the fear of moving into the unknown, for it is in the unknown that truth lies, it is in that unknown that you negotiate your way forward, it is in the unknown that miracles occur. But do not attempt this if you are fearful, for your fear will make you vulnerable.

I have tried to show you how stuckness can be created in a whole country, in a whole region, and the way that this can come forward into future civilisations. In the case of the Egyptian civilisation, I hope I have given you a clear picture of how that rigidity has been built up. Believe me, many of those spirits are there now; and I am talking not of tens of thousands, I am talking of millions. They are there all around that Middle Eastern area, searching, seeking, confused, stuck. I think it is great that people, in their spiritual and psychic seeking today, are beginning to recognise that they can help those on other planes, as well as people on this one. This work of spirit release is very important, it is urgently needed.

The Legacy of 9/11
The world at this moment is reaching a climax over a series of events where there has been a need for clear thinking, openness, and forgiveness on all sides. This pyramid power has affected the whole of the Middle East area and it has exaggerated the difference between the light and the shadow of Islam. I would see Islam as a very passive, gentle, non-judgemental understanding. When you have energy like that, the other side of it is going to be the opposite, and this is exactly what is happening now.

One issue that they are needing to understand is the relationship between man and woman, two complementary beings that need each other in order to take the planet forward on the physical level. One is not superior to the other and, in order to harmonise, they each need to find the two polarities of the masculine and the feminine within themselves.

It is interesting that with all that has happened in the Middle East, there has been little focus on Egypt, and yet Egypt holds the key to its resolution. It is holding the destiny of so many souls, so many spirits, who are so rigidly caught up in their beliefs and their fears that they are frightened to move on. They hover around the whole of the Middle East hoping that something is going to happen to take them into what they think they deserve, and this is where the problem lies. Rather, they must allow themselves to be taken to where they need to be.

When you get this accumulated, stuck energy, which is underwritten by the fear of reaching out into the unknown, this draws negative energy towards them. That is what the shadow wants, that is what the Luciferian energy delights in because it is about control. We are moving into the age of Aquarius where the challenges will be about finding that individual directional impulse, instead of collective control. The days of the charismatic president or prime minister will go. How many people really believe in them anyway? Wisdom needs to be the hallmark of any leader.

People will begin to understand how each of you, individually, can affect the entire planet. Every thought that arises in your mind goes out into the universe for eternity; so if you want to heal, if you want to play your part in relieving the tension of international conflict, it has to be done through love and forgiveness. I look at what happened on the 11th of September 2001 as one of the greatest opportunities that humankind has been presented with for several thousand years. It presented a challenge to the world to recognise that everyone is part of it, that everyone has a right within it, the challenge of seeing that one can move forward in love instead of the anger and seeking retribution that the negative energies want. If you want to empower the shadow, fight it. If you want to disempower it, give it love, because it doesn't know how to handle that.

I look on every spark of evolution as being a microcosm and a macrocosm of something else. Just as your Earth planet is part of a solar system, part of a galaxy, part of a universe; each one of you is a universe. Each one of you is made up of many spirits, not just the spirit that came into you at the time of conception. All the different parts of your body are carrying different forms of spirit evolution, all the cells within you are living beings, experiencing in their own particular way.

The age of Aquarius is of the mind, of the individual, of humanity, and of freedom. It is a very different age, a more open age. Yet the latter day Atlantean influence remains caught up in many religions, especially those that are more extreme in their demands, in their attempts to control; they have this Atlantean desire to put right, to purge the impurities in the system, as they see it. This, of course, only creates more polarisation.

So, dear friends, this is a time in your evolution when holding on to the past, to old traditions, to old beliefs, is not the answer. This is an age of finding individual freedom. It is an age of letting go, of understanding that what was created in your particular religion or belief or system in the past does not necessarily apply now, because the whole evolution of the planet is moving on.

The future of your planet is not fixed. It is your choice as to what happens, whether or not you have the willingness to say, "I am prepared to change, I want to see the planet go forward in peace, I want to understand what unconditional love means. I want to learn how to forgive myself in order to forgive others." Sometimes, when I look at very sincere people who want to keep everything just as it is, I think to myself, why don't they let the energy go? Why don't they let other people use it? Of course, some will abuse it, but others will use it.

Looking at your present civilisation, you have something that you call the internet. I believe that this is a great opportunity for the truth to surface. But as the light surfaces, so will the shadow. You will get pornography, you will get subversive beliefs being posted on it, you will get anger being expressed through it - but you will also get love, you will get knowledge and a seeking for truth that will surface some of those unnecessary secrets and fears. The more these things come to the surface, the more it will enable you to deal with the many secrets inside you.

Remember what I said about Uranus, the planet which rules the sign of Aquarius, and its influence that can create disruption, that can turn things upside down. If your planet is to remain on a stable course, it needs to let go of all those past tight, lack-of-vision ideas and beliefs, to understand that every human being is vulnerable and fallible, and that it is OK to be vulnerable and fallible. It is also OK to do or say something that you feel strongly about, that your fellow beings may think is wrong; because this is where you are, this is what you are. It is a time to think with vision.

You need to move beyond incarcerating people in prisons; instead you need to help them to understand why they committed what they did. Often it is a crime against authority, especially with political prisoners, rather than a crime against humanity. And so it is about tolerance, and understanding that everyone has a different perspective. You are each unique, you each have free will, you all have choice whether or not to take yourselves forward. This is going to be a great new age.

Everywhere I look on this planet I see so many beautiful people, so many beautiful spirits, and inside some of you I can feel this need to find and express a direction which can give you fulfilment. I want to say to you, "Yes, you can have it. It is not a hidden treasure that mustn't be opened or touched, it is not a Pandora's box. It is about your own willingness to deal with those inner fears." So, say to yourself, "Yes, I can release my fears, my stuckness, and when I breathe in deeply and release them on the outbreath, I am not only helping my fellow beings, I am helping some of those trapped Egyptian spirits, and those held within any religion or belief that is very rigid."

When those spirits leave the physical body, they have to deal with that rigidity; or else when they do reincarnate they will bring anger, bitterness and resentment with them. Even worse, if a spirit doesn't reincarnate, it will be there on the spirit planes arousing the shadow and creating heaviness, which will not allow *homo sapiens* to move forward, or any of the other kingdoms which make up your planet.

The 11th of September and its aftermath epitomised two sides at loggerheads, each believing it was right, each providing a polarised reaction to the other; when what was required was to exhibit the qualities that can bring a new era of love and understanding onto your planet. I do not view the destruction of the twin towers as an accident, I regard it as an action that involved peoples of many races, of many spiritual beliefs, who were trying to enable the world to see how small it is, how it needs to move beyond isolation.

It is fear that has driven the leaders of both sides to react in violent ways. If you become physically ill, you are taken to hospital and they love you and care for you. Surely the same should apply to anyone who commits a crime against humanity; they also need help and healing. I accept that you have to have structures and laws and if people are doing things that create pain and disharmony in society then they need to be restrained, but they do not need to be condemned. They need love just as much as the person who has been taken to hospital, in fact, more so, because it is on a deeper level.

Maybe, you could find the time to spend a few minutes once a week with one or more friends, sending thoughts of love, balance and harmony to that power-house that is the Great Pyramid. And you could extend it to those hidden chambers to relieve the pressure. Then you could allow that energy to spread right out, so that it reaches the hearts of humankind. Feel it in your hearts, let it go out to the hearts of people in places like Israel, where there is so much pent up anger and hatred. I am not here to criticise or condemn either side, but I do recognise that there is an urgent need for both sides to listen to each other, to hear what they have to say, and if they believe in a God, to allow that God energy to fill their hearts. If a small group of you did this every week you would find that it would also help to change you.

When they stored the power in those pyramids in their idealistic way, they saw it was for everyone but they felt that it needed to be controlled. And so, the distorted energies of Atlantis that have come forward, have somehow accumulated considerably in the age of Pisces. Symbolically, I see the age of Pisces as a triangle, for this represents to me the height of autocracy, where the power was enshrined in the few. I could have chosen a pyramid.

But we are now moving into an ambience of self-empowerment, where we find that divine energy within, as opposed to finding it without. So, symbolically, I see the coming age as a circle made up of many small circles – epitomizing the power of many individuals working in consensus.

As you continue to channel that healing pyramid energy as a group, you will find that it will challenge you, for it will make you realise that there are two sides of yourself, the light and the shadow, and somewhere, in the balance between the two, you will find your own beauty, your own love and, as you offer that out, it will affect all the countries in the Middle East, including Afghanistan. Because of your effort, the rigidity there will begin to soften, and people will begin to hear each other instead of condemning them. And include America, for they also need to listen rather than condemn. Of course, terrorism has to be dealt with, but it needs to be understood. So, it is a pretty big task I am asking you to do, isn't it?

I have often been asked about the capstone that was originally at the apex of the pyramid. It was a means of bringing down even more power from the elevated planes; but that is hardly what is needed now. And what about the inscrutable Sphinx? As I see it, the Sphinx was put there to guard the pyramids. There are a number of discoveries that will be made concerning underground chambers and passages leading from one site to another, and all of these were linked up both physically and energetically. I haven't mentioned the Sphinx before because, if the programme of healing is carried out on the pyramids, the Sphinx will lose its power, its reason for existence. I do not personally believe that the Sphinx is the key to the pyramid energy. The type of energy contained within it was put there to guard, so that if anyone tried to interfere it would confront them and deal with them.

That is why I emphasise that any healing initiative must be done in an atmosphere of compassion and love, and not by trying to put something right. The whole pyramid/sphinx energy is the epitome of putting things right, and that is what we have to move beyond. The planet needs the freedom for every spirit to experience in its own way, not in someone else's way. Liberated, the pyramid energy can be used to empower the world.

When a planet moves through this transitory stage from one great age to the next, an energy field is created in which transformations can happen, but which become more difficult once the next age is established. At the moment, the energies around your planet are neither Piscean nor Aquarian, and yet they are both. So, it is an opportunity for energy to lift, it is an opportunity for you to lift; it is an opportunity for fulfilment, for you to help yourself, to help your planet and to help every energy therein and thereon.

So, this is the time to release yourself, to let go of the past and say, "This is where I am now". Sometimes you might need help and it is not wrong to ask for help. Remember, "To give is an indulgence, to receive is a gift". So, if you think deep down that you need help, allow yourself to be open to that help. A miracle can occur when the love and the fear in a person come into perfect harmony – it is as simple as that. Let miracles happen for you, and all that you hold dear.

As that pyramid power is released, and it will take quite a time because it is going round in a vortex - as the release gets properly under way it will create tension in the whole of the area for a time, and that is what is needed. Beyond that, Egypt will eventually once again be the focus of power and energy in the Middle East, and that will reach out beyond, to England, to Europe, to the far East, to China, Russia. It will become a great civilisation once again and that will provide a spring board for moving into the new Atlantean age.

The Transition

For Atlantis to continue its evolutionary journey it may be necessary for some parts of it to rise from the sea. This has been predicted by many, and the impression has been that it will happen very soon - but this is a misinterpretation of the time element. Nevertheless, the reaction by the various kingdoms to many of the things likely to happen to this planet within most of your lifetimes will determine the likelihood of this kind of dramatic event.

I would like you to remember that your solar system is in a precise magnetic balance, thus if the balance of one planet should be upset, the effect will reach out to all the others. I mentioned earlier that twice previously in the history of man's existence upon Earth, there have been major cosmic disturbances caused through the influx of powerful new energies that were intended to lift the planet up. But, because of the unreadiness of the planet to receive them, this instead caused an upset in the magnetic balance within your solar system, first when a large portion of the Continent of Mu, or Lemuria, sank beneath the Pacific Ocean and, secondly, when most of the much smaller area of Atlantis sank beneath the Atlantic.

If Earth were to change its position in the solar system in relation to the Sun and other planets, no matter how slightly, the influences cast upon it would change, and this would tend to alter the character of man somewhat.

There was a period quite recently when many seers, some of them very spiritually immature, had 'revelations', telling them of the end time, and some even named that it would happen on a specific day.

Various groups then went up to the top of a mountain to prepare for the expected cataclysm to occur which would cleanse Earth of, as they saw it, less worthy citizens and would, naturally enough, lift them up mightily into the protective arms of the angels of light. Nothing happened, of course, and they came down again from the mountain. Their revelation had let them down, for they had picked up thoughts and visions influenced by the shadow ones. And all these thoughts of impending global destruction have collected in banks of thought that grow in intensity each time they are tuned into by yet another psychic or mystic, who is certain to embroider and exaggerate the deceptive message even further.

There are always those, unable to distinguish between high revelation and the shadow forms, whose burning desire is to be singled out as a special channel for divine wisdom, and this will inevitably cause them to bring through these distortions. Many false teachings are still circulating on your Earth today, along with those that are true and profound in their heart resonance. It is vital to challenge any that should come your way.

There are many prophets of doom and destruction around, and I do not want to be seen as one of them. I certainly would not wish to give the impression that any future event is inevitable in its exact form and timing. Even though there are forces moving evolution towards particular spiritual objectives in your planetary affairs, the activities and responses of all the kingdoms of life connected to the planet will determine the way that the planet will be affected.

In your Christian Bible, St. John described a series of tumultuous happenings in much detail, and his writing concerning the 'sixth seal' is one of natural disasters and upheavals. Many people today, some of them are in positions of considerable influence, believe that these prophecies of catastrophe, doom and destruction that have been forecast over the centuries, relate to the present time.

You are already wondering what could possibly cause such a happening. I will tell you. There is within your solar system a planet which you know as Uranus. Now Uranus is a very old planet, in fact it is due to break up fairly soon, for each planet that is of physical matter must meet such an end when its period of evolution has run out. Astronomers will tell you that Uranus is an extremely erratic mover. Astrologers will tell you that it stands for upheavals, sudden happenings, radioactivity.

When the magnetic balance of a planet is irrevocably upset, it slips from its normal orbit and is drawn in towards the Sun. A planet running thus will hurtle through space, burning as it goes, and any unfortunate sphere which happens to cross its path will be affected slightly or severely according to the proximity of the pass. Uranus will pass very near to Earth. Not near enough to "bump" it, but sufficiently near to spin it on its axis and cause great disturbance. Very soon your planetary observers will spot Uranus off its course. Already some scientific observers have noticed that the movements of Uranus have a very definite bearing on earthquakes and physical catastrophes occurring in your world.

Looking at it in what you might call the 'worst case scenario' I will trace what the Book of Revelations is referring to. Events will work up gradually. There will be industrial unrest throughout the nations and instability in all governments. The average man in the street will become more unsettled because the knowledge of these happenings is there in the subconscious minds of all people.

There will be earthquakes where they are not normally experienced; volcanoes will become active which have been extinct for centuries. Abnormal weather conditions are already prevailing, and will get worse as time progresses. The seasons will appear to have no more significance, for there will be warm days in winter and cold days during the normally warm periods. As the time nears there will be increasing darkness, for the rays of the Sun will be blocked out. A substance commonly known as 'black rain' will fall from the skies and there will be considerable chaos.

It will be during a final great war that the massive tilt of the Earth's axis will take place, for this culmination will be a cosmic one, a decisive one. When these events have risen to a crescendo, the island group of Atlantis which did not complete its evolution will return to the surface to do so. Of course, there will be many people who will pass from their physical bodies during these happenings.

That is not a certain prognosis, it is merely one of the possibilities. "When would these events happen?", you might be asking yourself, "in 500 years, a thousand, or at the end of the Aquarian age which is ruled by Uranus"? You don't really expect me to give an exact date, do you? I will, nevertheless, tell you what you need to know.

I have indicated that there is this vast unravelling of past karma running through the great civilisations that must happen first, before Atlantis could once again rise from the depths of the ocean. Until then, there will be no major realignment of the poles that would compel the physical Earth to follow suite. Always time in man's thinking is telescoped and it has been difficult for him to perceive an accurate time for these possible happenings, for it is the evolution of the planet Uranus, not Earth, that is the critical factor.

The Tilt Today

That is an axis tilt for the future, but I must now return to the present period. Some thirty or so years ago, many of those in spirit were transmitting messages to Earth through mediums and psychically sensitive people, warning of the possibility of Earth's surface erupting and changing its form. Then it was a very real prospect, and these messages were to try to awaken humanity to its slothful attitude towards proper planetary stewardship. It would have been a cathartic response to the pressure being built up on the etheric level caused by evolutionary necessities of that time. Then, a sudden release of that pressure would have resulted in a great deal of upheaval in the physical makeup of planet Earth.

These axis tilts reflect the overall energetic/spiritual situation on the planet. They are particularly pronounced at a time of the transition from one solar age to another. As energies come down, filtering level into level, with different emphases and polarities, this causes great stress for all created forms as they strive to make the necessary adjustments. Although this was conceived to be a gradual thing that would not lead to a great cathartic release as the new power moved down towards the physical, certain blockages were becoming so severe that, if they continued, a catastrophic reaction may have been the only way out.

However, much pressure was subsequently taken off though the liberation of so many people around the globe: during the fall of the Berlin wall and the disintegration of the Soviet Empire, but mainly through the liberating effect of release from some of the limitations of materialistic living, by means of meditation and spiritual practice. The pressure was also relieved through the many severe illnesses that have occurred in *homo sapiens,* and indeed amongst the animal and tree kingdoms as well. These have reflected this inner tension, this inability to allow spiritual evolution to take place in a natural rhythm, a rhythm that resonates with the rhythm of the planet as a whole.

So, the original prognosis was changed as Earth's future outlines took on a clearer shape. The work done by *homo sapiens* and other forms of evolution on this planet had actually created an energy that had moved the planet beyond the need of a catastrophic reaction at that time.

When I talk of a tilt of Earth's axis, I am talking about something that is reflecting the needs of the human race, the needs of the animal kingdoms, the needs of the mineral kingdoms, the vegetable kingdoms on many levels. On the physical plane it is registered as the difference between true and magnetic North, but on the etheric level the present tilt is much more pronounced. This has created an uneasy tension between the etheric and physical bodies of Earth that resonates through all forms of life.

It has probably not escaped your notice that governments, commerce and individual complacency are still strongly resisting change, and this increased pressure has returned the planet to a state of alert. You are certainly seeing many dramatic upheavals as the karmic energies realign.

Your current extremes of climate are reflecting the energy tilting that is going on beyond the physical but, of course, these weather patterns are also being aggravated by humankind's persistent abuse of the planet. However, I would like you to understand that it is through these climactic outbursts, the hurricanes, the tsunami and the earthquakes that the pressure is relieved, not increased. For that reason, more can be expected.

The most pressing challenge now is in man's blinkered approach to the way he is handling nature and natural things. It would be inappropriate for me to suggest that a catastrophic reaction to global warming is likely or not likely to take place, but as we go forward over the next fifty years it will remain a possibility. It is not predestined or predetermined and I am saying that it can be avoided if all forms of spiritual evolution on your planet can hear, accept, feel and sense the higher levels of spiritual energies coming onto the planet. It is about flowing *with* the directional impulses of cosmic law rather than against them. It is about releasing your deepest fears and about having the courage to be true to yourselves.

So, despite the continuing unrest and the conflicts erupting around your globe, I face the future with optimism because of the many inspired individuals who are providing a call to action, and the many spiritual and ecological groups all over the planet that are beginning to gain ground. The world is becoming smaller. Gentleness is beginning to manifest.

Towards the Aquarian Age

Yet, as we approach the Aquarian Age, the levels of fear that tend to amplify negative energy have intensified and became much more confrontational. In many places, regimes are brutally holding onto power and, in others, the fear of terrorism has been deliberately heightened. All forms of fundamentalism are based on extremes of fear, and the weapons that mankind has at its disposal reflect that fear. When a 'weapon of mass destruction' is created, it cannot be taken away, it cannot be undiscovered. It is there for all eternity and it needs to be handled wisely.

If you choose to lead your life constructively without fear, it does not mean that you need to become anarchistic; you do not abandon rhythm and order in your life. The exploration of one's own being-ness needs to be done within a framework of wholeness and rhythm. If you abandon that, you will have chaos.

When one looks at the acceleration of the evolutionary path of humankind over this period, it is not surprising that this has brought about tampering with the ecology of the environment. The use of chemicals to aid growth, to control certain forms of life, are often promoted without any true understanding of the dangers of interfering with the cycles of evolution; that if you change the chain reaction, whether it be in the human body, within an animal body, or within horticulture, you are actually creating something which is going to reverberate through every other form of existence.

Clearly humankind does not understand this. It does not understand it in its symptomatic treatment of illness through modern drugs and medicine. You'll never find drugs that will totally cure illness. If they block, then they stop something developing. It will still have to come out somewhere else because of the chain of reaction and response. To date, orthodoxy's efforts with drugs and chemicals are crude, they are naive, because they are only concentrating on the symptoms rather than the causes.

I want to paint a picture of how every little action causes a reaction that goes on and on, affecting every other level of being and every part of the universe. Around 2012, this incremental process that is unbalancing the etheric body of Earth will be complete, but not the working out of the karmic response to this, for it will force to the surface more unresolved energies from the past. You can see these taking hold of communities today, causing them to attack even those who were once their closest friends.

As the Aquarian energy increases, it is allowing the light to shine; but also, it is bringing up the shadow in a very dramatic way. The Godhead itself is light and shadow that has perfect balance and wholeness, but we on levels below this have not yet been able to reach a comparable state of unconditional love. How then can we?

Detachment has been practised by spiritual seekers in many Eastern countries, but this has usually resulted in a passivity that is not useful. However, during the liberation of India from colonial rule, Gandhi demonstrated a form of involved detachment that neutralised the Piscean ways of control, but this approach needs to be re-interpreted in ways more appropriate to the Aquarian nature.

The Atlantean Heritage Today

The shadow elements that are coming up today are from the recent past as well as the distant past. When the Atlantean civilisation ended, they had created a precedent on the planet that they felt needed to be put right. In sizeable groups, they reincarnated several times and, again today, there is a great deal of Atlantean influence on the planet. It is an archetypal energy and it has a very definite feel about it. For some of you it can be an almost solid energy like a crystal. It is brilliant, it is bright, it is laser-like.

The interesting thing about Atlantis, and this is advice I would give to any of you who feel that you were incarnate in that civilisation: if you can, let go of it, release it. Don't feel that you have to put it right, because this can be a trap. It can be the very thing that is stopping you from moving forward because, in effect, you are still locked into that civilisation. This is the moment to release yourself, to move forward, to be in the present day, to take yourself into a new consciousness.

Because of their philosophy, Atlantean spirits have no difficulty in reincarnating because they are beset by this 'need to put right'. But what does 'put right' mean? What does redemption mean? It is about releasing, letting go of the past and being fully in the present. You are all looking for freedom but freedom is a state of mind. Freedom is being aware of the spiritual impulse inside you which is trying to synchronise your whole being. Allow that inspiration to come forward from deep within, and allow it to motivate your conscious mind.

Freedom is, above all, about simplicity. For within simplicity lies a very pure, unadulterated beauty, a beauty unaffected by others' lack of self-esteem, unaffected by manipulation or fear, a beauty that is just there.

Genetic Manipulation

As we watch over humanity, and particularly those who are in the forefront of scientific and political responsibility, we are concerned that so many of the mistakes of the Atlanteans are once again in danger of being repeated, and the experiments in human genetic engineering are among the most serious. They reached a point in their scientific understanding where they felt that by manipulating the genes in the body they could produce a superior form of physical being. It was like creating a robot, and the spirits who were attracted to these bodies were usually those who were very unbalanced in the first place, or unevolved.

Today, there is so much disregard for the natural rhythms and patterns of evolution. The area of cloning is a particularly disturbing development. Science will not discover all the secrets of creation until it chooses to recognise the spirit. Cloning is not about the flow and impulse of life taking its own course; it is about manipulating forces.

It is an example of where left brain thinking can lead to tremendous ramifications for the plant and the animal kingdoms, because this travesty is happening now. It is creating a ripple of imbalance that is affecting the whole natural order.

I am also very concerned about any form of genetic manipulation such as GM crops. They will never succeed, and it is a very healthy sign of the Aquarian age that this has started to become exposed, for those crops are not as good as they are claimed to be. These are the types of things that were the downfall of the Atlantean civilisation.

It is vital for the scientific community to become aware of the sanctity of human life. It is not something to be disrespected, to be played around with for gain, for achievement. To say, "I have created life" will certainly create a backlash. It is not for humankind to take that sort of step. Quite simply, I feel that this kind of experimentation is reaping a whirlwind. There will be much need for resolution karmically in all those instances where science does not allow spirit to use its free will.

The elemental kingdoms, the animal kingdoms and the plant kingdoms are working very hard to try to restore balance, but it is at a critical point. Unfortunately, on the etheric levels there is still not a resolution spiritually and, certainly, little understanding. It will take a concerted effort to bring back balance and harmony.

There are many groups of people on your planet striving to reveal the truth and their influence is increasing. This is why so many of the machinations of power in your political and business worlds, connected to these matters, have come to the surface. So often the two are in collusion, to the ultimate detriment of the planet. It is never easy for people of goodwill to achieve anything without arousing negativity. Merely sending a thought of opposition will only add to what is happening. Allow yourselves, if you can, to send thoughts of unconditional balance, and if you have an opportunity to express your spiritual views to people in the scientific community, then by all means do so.

Scientists are obviously making great strides in many ways, but the moment they get involved in health, they seem to go horribly astray. The human body needs to grow in a way that is natural for it; and whilst, obviously, you have doctors and hospitals to help alleviate suffering, people need to understand why they are ill, why they are suffering and why, in many cases, their spirits have chosen what is happening to them. So, I understand and appreciate the need to help people, but not at the expense of cutting them off from their natural evolution.

Energy should be directed towards helping people to eat properly in the first place, to eat food that has been naturally grown, and not artificially stimulated with chemicals. One thing that is not often understood is that when you grow vegetables using synthetic fertilisers, when you grow chickens using artificial chemicals to make them grow more quickly, apart from the fact that the birds are being tortured, you are also torturing the vegetables; because a vegetable, if it is going to evolve, needs to have natural stimulation around it, not artificial stimulation that is far from holistic. So, one of the problems with human health today occurs not just because people are eating chemically stimulated foodstuffs, it is the effect of that on the spirit within the cabbage. When you eat a cabbage that has been grown artificially you are also taking in the anger of the manipulated spirit that was in that cabbage, and the fear. It is not only a chemical thing, it is also an energy thing.

There was a time when humankind could respond to the essence of a plant or animal with their own essence and there would be a blending of essences. Unfortunately, we now have a separateness, a separation of essence, a failure to understand the essence of the plant kingdom, the mineral kingdom and the animal kingdom. This also applies to the different races upon Earth. There is a subtle fragrance, a subtle emanation of essence that comes off all living creatures which can create a resonance of understanding and acceptance.

As you grow in sensitivity, enough to sense another's essence in the same way that you would the fragrance of a flower, then there is a quantum leap in consciousness, a quantum leap in the capacity to love in an unconditional way. The subtle energy influences that are around this planet at this time are leading many to discover a new level of resonance, particularly through their psychic, receptive gifts, which will enable them to become full participants in the wonders of the natural world.

Chapter 13

RETURN OF THE CHRIST

The Forces of Light Prepare

I now wish to go a little deeper into the cosmic participation on the part of those in the heavens and a few on Earth who are direct channels for an aspect of the Christ energy. Through them, a pulse of divine upliftment reaches out to the many manifestations of God's creative love who have volunteered to participate at this critical time in Earth's evolution, and it does so at exactly the level and strength that is needed.

Humankind believes that the plane occupied by the Christ consciousness visits its species alone. Cannot the animal kingdom also receive an appropriate visitation from a higher source? Of course it can. And it is important to know that, in many ways, some of the other kingdoms of life on the planet are further along their evolutionary path than most human beings. How else could the devas oversee the planet, if the elemental kingdom had not progressed as far as it has. The human ego has become far too arrogant and that is one of the issues to be addressed at this time.

It is very relevant because of the developments which are taking place in the evolution of the planet and those which will follow. These special dispensations from the Godhead come along very infrequently and they usually accompany a crisis on the planet that also provides a great opportunity. However, at the time of Jesus, the dispensation was not received. It came in above the heads of humanity, a preview, if you like, of what would happen 2,000 years later.

Earth is the Planet of Music and Healing. Music, amongst its more obvious qualities of giving pleasure and stirring the emotional and spiritual depths of human beings, also enjoys the role of being a form of interplay between the spiritual world and the material world. It is one of the few links between those two worlds which humanity can readily understand; it is a vibration, a sound which can inspire, uplift, soothe, heal — and, in its distorted forms, depress, deprave, degrade. Music as you would understand it is unique to this planet in the solar system; and it is because of these qualities of music and healing that in the days of Atlantis a spirit from the sixth plane successfully impressed its presence upon this planet to prepare it for what was to come, and also to give out an influence of healing to the entire solar system. And this influence needed to be reinforced and grounded through a human vehicle.

A planet of Healing will naturally attract the sick, the sick of spirit. This would obviously present a comparatively young planet with many problems, as it would not only be coping with the normal flow of spirits, but also with spirits of considerable evolution that had gone off the rails and had come to be cured and rebalanced. It was for this reason that this Ultimate impulse came in to help the planet in its very difficult role. In the early days of Atlantis a cleansing of the planet was carried out, which extended to the universe. Yet, there was still more sickness to come, more than Earth was easily able to deal with, and it was this that sent humankind and the planet into an apparently retrograde spiral.

By the time the Christ spirit returned again to Earth to channel through an evolved human vehicle, the Nazarene, things were very different. The influence of Lucifer predominated and all attempts to stem his infiltration were failing. The great civilisation of Egypt which had arisen after the fall of Atlantis was now in ruins. The civilisations in the East which had started so well were declining. What could have been the great civilisation of Rome was now degenerating into a barbaric, sadistic regime.

However, there was one spot on your planet which lent itself to this incarnation and that was Palestine. The Jews, because of the type of evolution from whence they came, had within their consciousness a belief that an avatar, some day, somehow, would come to save them. One could say that, because of their behaviour towards their neighbours, they had placed themselves in a position where they required saving! However, that is somewhat irrelevant, the main point being that they did have this belief and were virtually unique in this respect.

Palestine stood at one of the crossroads of the world's trade routes, a very important factor in the world, as it was then, for information travelled with traders. It was also under the occupation of the Roman civilisation which, although it was not functioning as it should have done, provided a vast network of communications through which the traders travelled. So, you see, this particular country and these particular people were very suitable. Also, it was close enough to Egypt to provide a link with the ancients for, although Egypt was in ruins, there were still a few wise spirits there who could impart their wisdom, knowledge and understanding.

So this Christ spirit came to overshadow a human incarnation in Palestine. Jesus came as a teacher, it is true, but do not forget the healings, for he was, above all other things, a healer who came to sacrifice himself to a greater purpose. The various groups of people at that time were fragmenting, forming themselves into enclaves and separate units; only by a supreme sacrifice, made after first showing that he intended no ill will toward anyone and through the expression of his boundless love for all human beings, could they be brought together once more.

This great love was demonstrated to the full by Jesus in his forgiveness and compassion towards those who crucified him. Try to imagine the mind of a person not all that different from yourselves, a person who possessed great sensitivity, but to whom the realisation came of the terrible suffering that would be inflicted upon his body, of what he must undergo. These were great challenges to the mind and to the spirit and, when the spirit allowed its body to be brutally executed, this decision released from the planet to the entire solar system, a fulfilment of that force of teaching, healing, music even, which had first been given to Earth those many thousands of years before.

Everything in your universe is an ebb and a flow. Planet Earth benefited considerably from the cosmos at the beginning of the Atlantean era, and this beneficent energy was absorbed deeply into the soul of the planet, into its very essence. When the axis shift came, the shadow was drawn into Earth's atmosphere and, with it, a new influx of energies that needed healing. So strong was the force of this, it was to take hold of humanity to such an extent that the Luciferian forces were able to take charge and bring this sickness into manifestation through a new swarm of incarnations. But that wasn't the end of it, for at the time of Jesus' death, Earth was able to release a vast amount of healing through him back to a troubled solar system, still reeling under the effects of the malaise that had come from the planet Sirius.

Such an act of unconditional love cannot go unrewarded for, in the greater scheme of things, there must be balance, and so, 2,000 years later, this generosity is returning to heal this planet in its time of need. So, you see, this present stage in the history of Earth, that seems so beholden to the Luciferian influence, when seen with the eyes of wisdom is something quite different.

When the going becomes difficult, when the crops fail and the tempests rage, and the righteous are persecuted, it is not unusual to feel abandoned by God. But those who believed and felt bound to support the teachings of the Master Jesus, were forced to put aside such feelings in their struggle to keep the mission going, and many of them followed in the way of the cross. Nevertheless, the teachings were gradually asserted against the odds; but so great was the shadow force, that they were obliged to create religions, fortresses almost, against the encroaching darkness.

So, inevitably, after the spirit of Jesus had returned to its own sphere of evolution, the forces of darkness which had contrived to bring about the end of his incarnation moved in upon the teaching he had given. This they were able to do through those people who, by their own freewill, chose to reject the simple truth in favour of a path which was more satisfying to their personal egos.

These forces of darkness, being of considerable evolution even though they were on what you would call the 'left hand path', realised that if they reconstructed the teaching rather than suppressed it, it would, from their point of view, be much more damaging to the evolution of this planet. They set about this task and, as time passed, they were able to remove the key pins of the teaching. Reincarnation was first to fall under their influence. Then they started to elevate man above the animal kingdoms, the plant kingdoms and the elemental kingdoms, by encouraging him to think of himself as a superior creation. Intellectual ability is not the main criterion of advancement. I would look upon the plant and flower kingdom as being more evolved than the human kingdom, overall. Man should be the guardian and keeper of this planet, not its master.

Many centuries went by and the logical outcome of this distorted teaching was that their horizons became more and more limited. The true meaning of the higher teachings faded away in all but the minds of a few. The evil forces engendered the idea that one particular line of thought only was correct, and there must be no deviation from it. Anyone thinking differently would be met by terrible wrath; punishment would follow and, as the people had been deprived of almost all true knowledge, they believed this.

However, the powers of darkness were not satisfied as the Church still held one aspect that they could not abide and that was the feminine aspect. The Father, Mother and Son idea was adopted early in the Christian era, and then later the Mother aspect was replaced by the 'Holy Spirit' or 'Holy Ghost'. So, the feminine aspect, originally the Sophia, was in due course removed from the greater part of Christianity. Even though, in recent centuries, the 'Virgin Mary' has been elevated to a Mother God level to bring back a feminine aspect for people to worship, it still does not represent the true feminine polarity of the Christ spirit.

Both patriarchal and matriarchal religions give unbalanced influences, for the one tends to accentuate the masculine dominance and the other emphasises the feminine dominance. The Godhead is a balance of masculine and feminine, positive and negative; it is, in its truest sense, a Father/Mother God.

The Feminine Principle

The spirit within Earth, that you call Gaia, is a predominantly female energy. It is because of this, that spirits in human male bodies have desperately sought for dominance, to counteract the fear that, if they did not achieve this, the feminine would overwhelm and neutralise them. We are now reaching a stage of evolution on the planet where it is important that spirits in masculine bodies do not feel that they are superior to those in feminine bodies. At the same time, it is important for spirits in feminine bodies to realise that they need to uplift their whole status and being; but not by trying to be more masculine because this does not actually help. It only creates greater conflict within the polarity.

Underlying all global turmoil today is this lack of balance not only between the masculine and feminine energies, but also between the two aspects within each man and each woman. It is the fear of the outer consequences of balancing the masculine and feminine within yourself that creates the desire to control, the desire to hit out. Instead, each gender needs to respect the strengths of the other.

God does not make man, God makes spirit. And, for spiritual understanding to mature, it is important to appreciate that all spirit is androgynous; it is both masculine and feminine, and it is both light and shadow. When a spirit incarnates, it can incarnate into the body of a female or into the body of a male and will experience each many times throughout its evolutionary cycle. So I repeat, a critical factor in all the world disturbances taking place at this moment is the lack of balance between the masculine and feminine energies on the planet.

The Venusian Influence

There are many expressions of the feminine principle and I would like to emphasise one that connects with a planet you call the Morning or the Evening Star. I speak of the planet Venus. This planet has always played a great role in the evolution of Earth, for many spirits have journeyed from Venus to Earth. But I speak of the guidance around it, the Venusian guidance, and I particularly mean the feminine polarity of that guidance, for all devas have both male and female polarities.

As I have said, it was originally intended that, on Earth, the male and the female should manifest together in balance. But the wave of imbalance that flowed through from another part of the universe disturbed this and as a result we have had, culturally, thousands of years of division, a matriarchal age and then a patriarchal age and all that has transpired from this. Yes, a learning process, and I would suggest that, despite appearances, the feminine has nevertheless always been available to you through Gaia. But now it is time for humanity to restore that balance within itself.

The Venusian archetypal energy connects very much with the feminine. It connects in your mythology with love, with birds, with doves, with flowers, with the opening of hearts. Why do you think that is? Why do you think that your poetry and your drama, your sculpting and your paintings carry the feminine aspect of Venus? It is because this energy has been here helping, assisting; it is the mother, the nurturer, not only for humankind but for Earth itself.

Venus and the highly evolved flower kingdom may seem to be two different vibrations but there was a joining together of the feminine impulse with the Deva of the Flowers. Flowers open a portal to welcome and allow the feminine to be always present upon Earth; and so this energy, that some call 'goddess' energy, always accompanies the flowers at times of human exchange, in every aspect of human relationship and human experience, at times of birth and death, of greeting and leaving.

The Venusian influence is here when there is great fear on the planet, such as in war or following a natural devastation. The flowers will always blossom; even one crack on Earth's surface and they will come through for rich, for poor. And so, Gaia is here as healer, as mother, as the feminine working with the flowers; for the exchange of your flowers between two human beings is a bridge across which forgiveness can flow.

It is important to give you this message because this planet can now move forward in a more balanced way, as home and gentle environment for humankind, animals, birds and plants, through a sensitive understanding, within you, of what it means to feel connected with every other form of life. This planetary imbalance is a state of being that affects not only the human race; and for physical creation to move forward, there has to be something that acts as a collective catalyst to redress this imbalance.

So, I ask each one of you to pause and think for a while on what it means not to have a balance between the masculine and feminine energies within yourself and in your society. While the imbalance remains, whether it be in politics, commerce, religion or on a personal level, it will create disharmony, it will create anger and hatred.

191

Sometimes a spirit will come out of one gender and reincarnate into the other with anger for how it is, and at the karma that surrounds it. In any part of society, in any country throughout the whole planet where there is unfairness between the sexes, there will be discontent, there will be anger, stubbornness and a refusal to see clearly.

A Closer Look at Planet Earth

I would like you now to become aware of what is inside you. You are your physical organs, your lungs as you breathe, your brain, your digestive organs, your beating heart. You are your bones, you are the blood that flows through you, and the water that makes up so much of you as a physical being - and you are your skin. As you think of yourself as an expressive being, you think of your voice which communicates what is in your mind, you are aware of your legs that carry you from place to place, and the energies and emotions that help to make you a whole person living your life to the full. Then you have that spiritual side of yourself, your soul and your Higher Self.

Now, I want you to transfer your thoughts to the planet on which you are incarnate, to that which lies beneath the ground upon which you walk? It is certainly not just oil, or natural gas, or the crystal formations that are turned into gemstones that so interest your commercial world. It is a combination of all things that have come together to make it a physical possibility.

A planet is like a human being. It has a lifespan from when it was first created until it reaches a point where it has discharged what it needs to and physically dies. So, inside there is a lot going on. There are billions and billions of cells and countless different kinds of intelligently motivated and interconnected spirit activity within the many forms and expressions of life that you find there. And when you get right down to the centre of the planet, the innermost part, there is a strong concentration of devic energy that you know as Gaia.

Gaia, is the feminine aspect of the Earth Deva and she incarnated into Earth when it was first created, billions of years ago. She is supported and guided by Mikaal who oversees the planet and everything that is taking place on and around it. Gaia is a collective energy, her essence focussed most potently at the centre of the planet. Around Gaia there is a tremendous fiery heat. In a sense, all that happens on the surface is due to Gaia expressing herself. Now and again, she will get angry and express herself forcefully and maybe there is a volcano erupting, or an earthquake.

Gaia is seeking to evolve by finding new levels of understanding and dimensions of experience. I have often said that every thought, and every action that you make, goes out into the universe for eternity, but it also goes into the planet for eternity. So, each one of you, in your own particular way, is playing a part in the unfoldment of the evolution of planet Earth. And this is why I have so strongly emphasised the need to love and respect the planet, to love and respect Gaia. You wouldn't think of deliberately putting poison on your skin, yet that's what you do to planet Earth. And this affects what Gaia is trying to achieve.

Humankind has never really appreciated how, on an emotional and psychic energy level, everything that you do affects the planet as a whole. It goes right through to Gaia who has to handle it collectively for every form of evolution on the planet, in the same way that the part of your spirit that is in your physical body has to handle everything that takes place in it and to it.

So, let us not think of Gaia as a form of higher energy but as a living spirit, on a comparable journey to yourself, though handling a very much larger body and working to a different timescale. She is experiencing a parallel form of evolution and, within her field of influence, she oversees a retinue of devic and elemental spirits each carrying out particular tasks in specific regions of Earth. She inspires the bands of spirits that are looking after the crystal kingdom, those in charge of the molten lava, the subterranean waters, the gasses held within the earth, as well as those that regulate the big and profound shifts of energy that, if not controlled, could cause devastating earthquakes on your planet. So, when you start to think of it in this way, you realise what a complex structure the planet is, with every part of it interacting with every other part.

It is really important, when you look at what is happening in your lives, what you are planning, what you are trying to achieve, to really think and understand the responsibility that every spirit in a physical body has to a greater reality. Thoughts and actions of hate, violence and chaos will feed the negative influences working in and around the planet; but thoughts of love, harmony and inclusiveness strengthen both Gaia and Mikaal and help to restore balance.

A human being has quite distinct physical incarnations but with Gaia, it is much more that there are phases of evolution that she goes through. Gaia has to face the challenges of the various great solar ages. So, Gaia is about to start a new phase, and is having to adjust to that quite different kind of energy which is the hallmark of the Aquarian nature, just as you are having to adjust, as the trees are, as the animals are.

If you look at it in this way you could liken the early years of this new age to those of a child, and the age that is in the process of being completed is like the very advanced age of a human. What happens with humans as they advance into old age? Some of them lose their memory, some of them become cantankerous. Some find that they have not dealt with the things of their destiny plan that they had intended to deal with and, indeed, today many are trying at the last moment to learn the lessons that they have neglected over the previous two thousand years. And these are quite obvious, for humanity has not learnt how to live in harmony with others, with the animal kingdom, with the bird kingdom, with Earth as a whole. It has lost contact with these and it is now trying to make up ground.

There is much to address, and you might say that humanity has left it a bit late. But, you see, there is a quickening momentum at this time and it is possible for the effects of some misguided attitudes and behaviour to be reversed quite promptly. It is essential that in the phase that follows on, the early years of the new age, Gaia will be able to return to a simplicity, an innocence that resides within her own nature. Then you will experience the waves of harmonious energy emerging from the earth that can heal and transform the complicated ways and structures of humanity, and ray out into the ether, and into the vastness of space, bringing the whole solar system into greater harmony and co-operation.

These new energies are being opposed by those who support the old Piscean structures of power. They are resisting because they feel they have something to lose. Obviously, Gaia wishes to extend her influence strongly throughout the planet, but she is restricted by the rigidity of the spirits incarnated in many of the forms of evolution. It is the fear that they are experiencing, and the control arising out of this, that is preventing Gaia's influence from pervading the entire planet.

I have mentioned before that the animal kingdom and the plant kingdom have attracted to themselves some of the treatment they are experiencing, because of their own imbalance. Let me add that this is not in any way to relieve humanity of its karmic responsibility, but it is not as clear cut as one kingdom being solely responsible and the others, entirely the victims.

Earth is the Planet of Healing and perhaps its most important role is to be the Healer for this solar system. This is, to some degree, why the planet has been going through such a difficult time, because it has been receiving inharmonious energies from elsewhere in space. From this, Earth is learning how to heal on a finer frequency than it has needed to in the past. So, as humanity struggles to understand these things, it is gradually beginning to effect the necessary developments.

Just as you have a responsibility to your nation, to work harmoniously within the structures that society requires for it to function in a cohesive way, exactly the same kind of cohesive development needs to happen within the planet. Gaia is the primary influence, but there is a hive of activity requiring teamwork, with a much needed responsibility being taken by each individual spirit. Many of those spirits within the planet are working to counteract all the things that humankind is doing to it. When pesticides and chemicals are poured onto the soil with the aim to produce something that is cheaper and grows quicker, this is poisoning the planet, creating an illness in Gaia. When you ill-treat the animal kingdoms, whether it is a pig or a lamb or a chicken, and it ends its life in anger, sorrow and fear, then that is affecting your planet as a whole. I don't think this is really understood. And when people are killed in battles, and their blood flows into the soil, something very serious has happened that profoundly affects Gaia.

What you call climate change is reflecting Gaia's concern for the irresponsible way that *homo sapiens* has been treating the planet. And that responsibility starts with yourself. Look on yourself as a planet and then look inside and ask yourself, "Am I taking responsibility for myself. Have I learnt to love myself, to respect myself, to be myself?" These are some of the issues that form a major part of my philosophy and teaching. Two of the most important qualities for all spirits incarnate today are those of harmony and humility, acknowledging that you are an essential part of the whole, acknowledging that love is easier than war.

So, learn to love your planet, and particularly your trees. Many people just cut them down because it is financially convenient to do so; but you are learning to acknowledge the important part they play in the evolution of the planet. Learn to love your favourite tree. Put your arms around it and feel the healing energies within it.

I have tried to give you a picture of Earth as a living being, with feelings, emotions, and the free will to choose between love and fear, light and shadow. It is important to acknowledge that Gaia is neither God nor perfect, but simply an entity on a journey of spiritual evolution, as you are. Sometimes Gaia can make a mistake.

The Shadow of Gaia

Every living being has a shadow aspect. So, if the light and shadow of Mikaal and Lucifer have been reconciled on the higher levels of the fifth plane, how can humankind achieve this reconciliation also? As you aspire to your deepest sensitivity, you are reaching towards the light within yourself, automatically then, the light is attracted towards you. It is a two way process. So, human beings working more spiritually for the light are now registering the harmonious emanations of Mikaal and Lucifer as they direct a more powerful balance into each of the various levels.

One of the great lessons that faces humanity is simply that you are moving into an age in which every spirit in a human body needs to honour and find and accept its own areas of personal responsibility; and then needs to allow all the spirits in every other life form to do the same and, above all, that includes the spirit that is Gaia.

Whenever a woman dies with her creativity unfulfilled, there is a void left in the soul of Gaia, and it is this inability within Gaia to fully assert her femininity in the face of so much masculine control, that shows you the nature of Gaia's shadow. While the male and female principles are seen to be in competition, while man so destructively reacts to the shadow of Gaia, thereby empowering it, this void will remain.

Containment of the Shadow

However, I can say that, over the past decade, the energies of the light have started to contain the shadow of the planet, and that includes the shadow of Gaia. You have seen it in the raised awareness to climate change and in the attempts of people to rise up against repressive regimes. The upshot of this is that it means that the true spirit of the planet can start to move forward. But that containment has meant that those spirits that have for so long supported the Luciferian energy are struggling to get back, they want to regain control, and they are concentrating their efforts where this shadow influence is at its strongest; that is, where spirit is most vulnerable, on the physical plane. To that end, they are attacking in many places simultaneously, ruthlessly supporting the repression of those movements where the people are trying to regain freedoms that have been lost.

The Luciferians are no longer in control, despite what is happening, and I can promise you that if they had been in control, the outcome of what happened on 11th September 2001, and those events that followed, would have been mega disastrous. It would have made the present events pale into insignificance and would really have threatened the future of the world.

Sometimes when you hear certain 'prophets' saying, "The end of the world is nigh", they are seeing a particular potential of the situation. If you want to look at the down side you will see it as a disaster but if you want to look at the up side you will see it as an opportunity. At this moment the pressure is on, and because the Mikaalian influence is starting to contain the Luciferian influence in your world, it certainly doesn't mean that the outcome of the struggle is a foregone conclusion. But it does mean that, once the current round of crises is successfully dealt with, you can look forward to a future that will gradually become less controlling, less fearful, less repressive, less punishing and less judgmental. It means that the heart of humankind, collectively, is starting to open and beginning to understand what is happening on the planet.

The type of information that I am providing, and others like me, is preparing humankind for the next step forward in your evolution, which is to acknowledge the divine within, as distinct from the God without and to find your own personal level of spirituality, rather than becoming part of a sect or a religion that is unable to change. The planet's evolution is moving forward and those religions that are capable of making that step forward will survive; those that are not will eventually crumble, they will destroy themselves. And those individuals and communities and countries that can accept themselves as they truly are, no more, no less, will have reached a point from where they can move forward in love towards even greater enlightenment.

Can Mankind Survive the Ecological Crisis?
The material evolution on this planet is accelerating at a pace which can no longer be controlled. Man is under the mistaken impression that he is the only species of importance on this planet and he tends to forget that he is part of a very delicate balance of nature which, if it continues to be adversely affected, could cause the planet to break down completely in a very short space of time.

During a process of accelerating evolution, humanity has reached a stage where its material and scientific advancements have leapt ahead rather suddenly. Let me make it quite clear that I do not consider achievements of this nature to be wrong, for it is my belief that humankind is here to experience, and any form of experience is appropriate provided that it proceeds in balance. This is most important. Lack of balance is the cause of many of this planet's woes and much of the illness so prevalent today is brought about by a lack of balance in everyday living.

In its attempt to control nature, science is taking on something which it by no means fully understands and is surprised when nature reacts in what it considers to be an undesirable or un-cooperative way. I do not need to elaborate at length on the many harmful results of pollution, for you are already feeling the effects of this.

Toxic gases have been developed which prevent the natural growth of vegetables, plants and trees. The soil is overused, and the trees of the forests have been cut down at an alarming rate, laying great areas to waste and creating dust and unnatural desert land. Living organisms, seen as 'pests', have been sprayed with toxic chemicals, many of which will take decades to lose their effect. Undesirable plastics have been created which, while they appear to be a valuable part of your life today, will create problems for ensuing generations. Materials which do not blend with the natural process of growth and dissolution are out of balance with the rest of nature on this planet. Little has been done to control or recognise this or to cope with some of the by-products of these creations, which are already presenting very tangible problems.

Humankind seems afraid to plan for the future. In living for the present in a quite misguided way, you are plunging yourselves head first into a major catastrophe. You are forcing the physical body to perform in a way that was never intended. Fortunately, nature is adaptable and, in its elasticity, it has accommodated the mutations gallantly; indeed, by and large, most of the forms of evolution on your planet are very patient and very allowing. This is why *homo sapiens* has been able to go ahead in the way it has, but the increasing acceleration is forcing everything to its limits.

If you go back over the last twenty years, and look at the advances in understanding in spiritual concepts, in complementary medicine and in ecology, then I can say to you, quite categorically, that this is nothing compared to what is going to happen over the next ten years.

Balance Between the Sexes
When I speak of equality and balance between the sexes, of course there are certain functions that each gender will perform better. It is the woman who carries the baby and in many cases it is the man who has the physically stronger body. But where areas of leadership and authority are involved, it is important that there is both masculine and feminine energy.

You could have a male first minister who has fully acknowledged his feminine; or a female leader who has fully come to terms with her masculine. This, of course, does not mean that one has to be living out the other aspect of the polarity. It means that the individual concerned has a reasonable balance within, and simply recognises that the masculine and feminine energies are complementary on every level.

There has been much confusion and fear arising out of the events in America with the twin towers, and the loss of life that has gone on and on. It is the masculine run amok. Though it may seem regrettable that the teachings of two great master souls have been misrepresented to such a degree by those purporting to seek justice, if you look at it from a slightly more elevated perspective, you will see that the corruption in the souls of men harboured over the 2,000 years since the death of Jesus has now come fully to the surface. At last it can be released, drawn out by the attraction of the healing energies returning on a higher level. It is not just about the import-ance of global co-operation, it is about global understanding, global forgiveness. It is about acknowledging the different polarities that make up a spirit incarnate in a physical body. It requires self-sacrifice to a degree that is making humanity today quake in its shoes, but it is a sacrifice that is vital.

Return of the Christ
There awaits either the redemption of your planet or its further degradation. The Christ is returning to ask for a third time whether the peoples of this planet wish to accept the love which the forces of the cosmos offer them, or whether they prefer the old ways of denial and darkness. Should the cosmic force, the force of light, be accepted, then all of you will be staggered at the speed with which a golden age will dawn. Humanity will throw off its chains and return to that path which it originally set out upon so many thousands and thousands of years ago. Wars will cease, friction will die away, a new understanding between man, plant and element will surface in the consciousness of the planet - and an age of beauty, arts and music, of spiritual endeavour far beyond your wildest dreams will begin.

Your planet will be welcomed by the peoples of other planets as a long lost friend returning. If you were to see the peoples incarnate on the surface of your planet in, say, two hundred years' time, you would think that many thousands of years must surely have passed, so great will be the changes.

The returning gods, those cosmic forces of light, are already amongst you; the long neglected feminine aspect is manifesting strongly all over your planet. Thoughts which were held by an eccentric few only twenty years ago are now widely accepted. Who today believes it is permissible to carry out irresponsible actions against the natural order? Only those who fear responsibility, who fear change. It is, in actuality, a very small step for humanity to take. Can you not feel the redemptive power waiting to sweep in?

This next 'coming' is something very much more subtle and widespread than the one 2,000 years ago, as pinpoints of light emerge all over the planet. It is coming in on a lower level to begin with, manifesting through small groups, large groups, any groups of people whose motives are unselfish, who have a sincere and genuine desire to bring light to the darkest corners of the planet. Wherever you have a group of people with that motive, then the highest possible help is given; and from those small beginnings will gradually emerge a vibration which will increase in intensity until it is of a frequency suited to the returning manifestation of the Christ energy.

Will there be a new Avatar returning to Earth soon, a new Maitreya, as some are suggesting? Does humankind need another such enlightened presence to show it the way? No, my friends, the dispensation will manifest through you, for now each of you must be your own light, your own saviour.

Chapter 14

COLLECTIVE RESPONSIBILITY

The Ascended Masters
If you could look into the higher reaches of the fifth plane you would
be aware of the great congregation of support that is there for planet
Earth. It could be brought down into manifestation, but it is not yet
being brought down because too few leaders are spiritually inspired,
and too few mediums are able to put aside their ego concerns
sufficiently to reach up to the realms of light. If they could, they
would become channels for the higher teachings, which are always
simple ideas that rest gently within the vast complexity of God's
creation.

The world waits for such elevated teachings that could solve most
of the world's problems, but the dominant planetary ego does not
want unconditional love to manifest on this planet, it does not want to
forgive, and it does not want to respect all living forms. It just wants
the power for itself.

There are a small group of advanced spirits working under the
Christ influence who have come close to the Earth on a very special
mission. They have incarnated on this planet many times and have a
very great affinity with its path; and need now to address the
pressing need of humankind to engender a compassionate understanding of cosmic law. These are all 'ascended masters' who no
longer incarnate in Earth bodies. One such spirit is known as Comte
de St Germaine.

The archetype behind St Germain is a source of sixth plane
energy that has sadly been very abused and misused because it has
been somewhat extreme in its attitude towards unconditional love.
Let me explain: Jesus himself was, in a sense, ahead of his time. The

love that he gave was just too powerful to be accepted in those days. But the Christ energy knew before it over-shadowed Jesus, that it had to prepare the planet for the Aquarian Age, 2,000 years later, and that the energy would inevitably be misused.

Now, the St Germain archetype is not able to bring through that elevation of Christ energy, and is therefore not quite as sensitive to the expression of the higher purpose for this planet, though there is a splendid loving quality there. When, love is expressed towards your planet in a somewhat extreme way, it is easy not to be fully aware of the degree that the power being dispensed is open to abuse. In other words, the level of his love is ahead of its time and so, the shadow aspect of the St Germain archetype has become somewhat accessible to those who wish to use this energy for their own misguided ends, and there are many of them. People with psychic abilities, but with inadequate understanding, have latched onto that energy trying to get access to its power and use it; and they can do this to some degree, because once offered, it cannot then be retracted.

It is the same with all these 'ascended masters' that people are trying to channel in the light, they are actually unlocking powers associated with them that are inappropriate - not only St Germain, but Merlin and Mary Magdalene and all the other titles that they profess to be channelling. Many of them are not. They are actually channelling the shadow. I am sorry to put it so strongly, but they are channelling the shadow of St Germain, they are channelling the shadow of Lady Nada, and the shadow, even, of Jesus – and they are on a very dangerous path. Unconditional love is not about power and self-importance, power is of the shadow.

So, in order to generate the energy to regain its rightful level of understanding, St Germain has the wish to be treated as a sixth plane energy not as an incarnating entity. Certainly he does come close to Earth to help where necessary, but only those people with advanced integrity will be able to make direct contact with the true archetype and receive its inspiration.

All these sixth plane energies have their own archetypal concepts, and approach, and so they are all slightly different in their approach. It is crucial for the workers in this field to make sure that what they have to offer is not abused. St Germain is a beautiful source of wisdom and love and understanding that the planet is not quite ready for in its fullness.

Assistance from Outer Space

When you look into the night sky, you may wonder in how many of those constellations is there life like your own, or experiencing in forms that you could relate to. Not only have spirits from Venus begun incarnating again on your planet, on the inner levels there is much support being offered by visitors from much further afield.

On the cusp of the Aquarian age, the momentum for planet Earth is being stepped up and, to register the force that drives this momentum most significantly, you must look outside this solar system to that star-grouping you know as Sirius. It contains the brightest of stars that sits in the heavens, and the ancients were particularly attracted to the energetic properties of its light, which they imbued with an aura of sacredness.

The early Egyptians were very connected with this Siriun energy and, prior to that, the Atlantean priesthood also, for they recognised its special qualities. They were able to harness the power that lay within that Siriun system and that of Orion, and were able to draw it to Earth. That energy became infused, not only into Atlantis, but into other areas on the planet. Modern telescopes can view, but there are no instruments that can register what exactly is being directed here from outer space for your benefit.

Siriun energy provides one of the most important opportunities for your planet today. There is a great new influence of wisdom emanating from that star system that can awaken within you a profound sense of freedom and a nuanced individual means of spiritual expression. You now have a heightened opportunity to allow your imagination to really flow with new ideas and thoughts and challenges, and this Siriun energy can open you up, stir something within that will help you to value your life, to value what you can be, to honour yourselves, to be yourselves.

Assistance comes, too, from the Pleiades and other constellations. Their role is to help the planet avoid bringing itself to an abrupt and premature end. In other words, if Earth is destroyed, it will upset the balance of the whole solar system, which in turn will affect the evolution of the whole universe. So, a great deal of help is coming in from these sources at the present time, and it is through the main power centres on the planet that this help is most effectively being channelled.

Achieving World Peace

One of your main difficulties on Earth today is enabling world leaders to understand that they will never achieve world peace by threats, by putting down, by punishment; it can only come about by listening, hearing and understanding, and by honouring and respecting your neighbour. It is an interesting time for this to take place because the whole ambience around your planet at the moment is for self-empowerment and the realisation of the individual. On a spiritual level, this means that every individual has access to God, no longer are intermediaries necessary.

Now, this in itself is a threat to the tribal systems on which your planet is based. Look at all the trouble spots on your planet and you will see the resistance to change at work. Throughout history, society has looked on the way to Godliness as being through some form of suffering. The short-cut way to becoming a saint was indeed to be tortured or crucified or hung upside down. And today, hundreds of souls are choosing martyrdom in causes that do them no good. What a reflection on society that is! What a reflection on the needs of society that is! For is not the true need of society to let go, to release all that past patterning that causes so much grief, so much tension, so much fear?

You must understand that the true beliefs of Islam are so gentle that it is very difficult for followers to apprehend and deal with the extreme fundamentalists within their religion. It is very interesting because it was partly this type of issue that destroyed Atlantis. So, it is a repetition, in some senses, of what happened there.

It is totally bounded and held by religious belief. It is truly a confrontation of anger, jealousy, resentment and, above all those emotions, the immense fear that arises out of the clash between opposing spiritual concepts. So, the solution to the Middle East lies beyond religious dogma. It's no use blaming God. It's no use expecting God to perform a miracle, for the miracle lies not within the wishes of God, but within the designs and desires of man.

So, how can one, in a so-called civilised society, persuade people that they do not need to be afraid, and certainly do not need to be afraid of God? For are they not each a creation of the very God which they fear. It is necessary for them to discover that their cause is an empty one, and that the solution lies within.

Spiritual wholeness is what it is about, and the essence of wholeness is achieved by letting go, releasing and giving of your true self, the inner part of you that yearns to give out in service to the planet. For in giving of yourself and accepting your foibles, you become ready to receive understanding, ready to see yourselves as light and shadow, ready to see yourselves as an expression of your own truth.

One interesting feature of the Iraq conflict is that it has aroused the world's concern as people begin to recognise the effects of greed and competition. It has also revealed an understanding that such conflicts, if they are allowed to go unheeded, could create such chaos and havoc that it is beyond the human mind to imagine the consequences. So, in a way, one has to look on those people who live in that area with gratitude for enabling the planet to move forward. They have made a sacrifice to help the world find its levels of spirituality. I believe that humankind needs congratulating on what it is achieving in the sorting out of global conflict, despite the suffering, despite the brutality, despite the stupidity.

So, what we actually need to send to the Middle East and all the other trouble spots, is the gift of letting go, of letting go all those past patterns, of accepting that no one is right and no one is wrong, and that everyone has the right to a point of view, and that everyone is trying to live their lives as best they can. It is not necessary to acquire more land, but to let go of fear. It's that need of fear that makes a person grasp onto the nearest rock, and then another rock and another one, and then yet another one. But those rocks are slippery because they are false rocks. The only real rock is that stillness within, that feeling of oneness, not holiness, but wholeness. That is the rock on which to build your life and your future.

It means that anyone who can accept and understand what I am saying needs to take a lead by facing, acknowledging and moving beyond their own fear. Fear is a part of your makeup. Without it you could not understand love. You cannot have shadow without light, or light without shadow. You cannot have love without fear, or fear without love. It is about bringing the two extremes together and suddenly realising that there is no need for any extreme, no need for anything to be any different from what it is. That is unconditional love.

There are escalating problems with your young people who, in the past, because of their idealism and enthusiasm, have very often been collectively a catalyst for change. But now, many of them are either withdrawing from active participation, glued to their computer screens, or running amok in the streets.

You will solve your crime problems only by understanding why the crime was committed in the first place, and helping those responsible to find a way through their problems and difficulties. It cannot be done by punishment. Punishment will only increase the anger, the resentment, the humiliation within that spirit.

You are also having to face tremendous problems with many of the younger nations of the world, some of which have far more knowledge than wisdom, far more sense of self-importance than evolution. What is going to happen when the mortality rate decreases in these nations? The answer is brutal but frank; you must learn to live within your limitations on Earth. If you do this, there is plenty for everyone for as long as you will need it. But the present reality is that in the countries that are the poorest, by and large, the families are the largest. The many reasons for this are obvious. Maybe they need children to work for them, maybe they do not have the same value of life that you have — or maybe they are here to teach the rest of the world a lesson. However, all of you do need to accept the ecological responsibility of bringing more children into the world.

So far as the future story of this planet is concerned, it is surely not difficult to visualise that, with the way you are heading, you are encouraging certain natural catastrophes to take place. Gaia can take only so much before she is forced to respond. All around your world there are problems, not just the dramatic ones that capture the headlines, but the droughts lasting much longer than before, rivers bursting their banks more frequently than usual. These things are occurring today, but is the cause understood? Oh yes, global warming is happening, but I am talking more about the real causes, the human greed, and that personal and collective irresponsibility born out of selfishness. Are these being addressed by your leaders, your churches, your unions, by you?

Ladies and gentlemen, are you losing your senses? Have you no longer the individual moral courage to take your own stand and to say, "We have enough; more would be superfluous to our needs; more is only making us greedy and dependent". Have you allowed greed to take such a strong hold that it has obscured from you the fact that man has an individual spirit whose subtleties should be encouraged?

I do not wish to come across as too negative, because in the spiritual realms there is an unlimited amount of help available. Some of the power that has been invested into the prayers and meditations of countless good souls over the centuries, is stored in power banks, kept, if you like, for a rainy day. And this is being added to by the new energies flowing in from the higher spheres intended to fuel the transformation into the new Aquarian age. There is so much power that could come in to assist the planet at this time. Some of it is already filtering through; though what it is doing, of course, is drawing to the surface much of the unresolved karma of the past into the waiting human crucibles, to be transformed into positive power for the future.

However, free will does exist, and many people are creating even greater resistance to change, which is blocking further inspiration from the spheres reaching Earth. I don't want to be a prophet of doom, but Gaia has been aroused. All the signs are there and still the prosperous nations are putting off taking action, while some emerging nations are greedily taking an even greater share of the world's resources to fuel their growing lifestyle improvements. Just think of the much greater pollution that this will create. And, of course, the forests, which are the lungs of the planet, are being destroyed at an alarming rate. It cannot go on. Must the lessons meted out by Gaia be even more severe and, even then, will they be heeded?

Whatever the next upheaval that comes to upset your planet, let me make it quite clear: it will affect you, it will affect every person on this planet. I could point out how, for endless ages, man himself has brought about many of the calamities that have happened on this planet but he is so blind and selfish that he cannot see it! It is easy to sit back and say, "I'm all right!", and even the most selfless of persons is inclined to do this. Human nature craves comfort and the structures you create encourage this type of attitude.

Competition or Co-operation

The balance between the planetary Deva and individual spirits incarnating on that planet is very sensitive and subtle and can be easily disturbed. It does not matter which devic spirit is helping you, it is the life forms on the planet that confirm its destiny. If one form of existence on the planet will not co-operate and blend, then the deva cannot direct its influence. If we could take the Luciferian hoards away, what would happen? Would Mikaal just step in? Frankly, I think not.

Man's own greed and selfishness has become so strong, so relentless, that it has gained an impetus that is proving difficult to halt. It has become so prevalent and all embracing that it will need a great deal of light to block the path of this force of, can I use the word, evil? Ignorance is one thing but wilful disregard, when you know the true way, is much more reprehensible. That is particularly so when those who hold positions of power, not only your politicians but your newspaper owners who wilfully choose to flaunt lies and sensationalism in the place of a life-affirming call for a positive and integrated change for humanity. Then there are the banks and multinational conglomerates who make 'profit' the only word in their vocabulary.

However, let me be fair, more and more societies and initiatives geared towards global transformation are springing up all over the place, and although each is merely a tiny pinprick of light in a vast cavern of ever-encroaching darkness, collectively the impetus for change is strong. The monks in Burma, the despair of the starving ones in Africa, and those caught up in conflicts and disasters in many places are cries to the world to listen and to act. They cannot do it alone. Today the pinpricks of light are increasing in number and becoming searchlights as more people become aware of the situation; but the Luciferian force is not going to be lightly pushed aside.

The workings of a planet are indeed fascinating. Think about it and you will realise that they reflect the collective will. What happens next week will be influenced by each one of you, by your thoughts, your ideas, your ideals, your creative impulses, and your actions. All of these are going out into the ether and they are ever-lasting. Every thought you have made in your life is there for all time. No action can be erased. I am not asking you to repent nor to bury your head in the sand. I am trying to help you to realise how important your life is, not only to yourself but to your fellow beings, to enable you to see what a responsibility you have as an individual on this planet. You are a part of the universe; you are a thought of the Godhead; you are experiencing and adding to what already exists, for no two people's experiences are the same.

It is indeed strange that responsibility is something that human-kind shirks. This lack of moral fibre is what the Luciferian forces encourage, for it enables them to tighten their grip. England has missed a number of evolutionary opportunities, for there is a lack of responsibility, not only at the top where business has become the main political force, but amongst so many of the workers.

A Time of Global Initiation
This is the world in which you live, and this is a time when the whole planet and all the energies within and without are coming together and are reaching a peak in their evolutionary experience. I wish to remind you that the future of your planet is not predetermined, not predestined; it is the collective energy in, on and around the planet that determines the way in which it meets this initiation.

One of the main difficulties that the world is experiencing is this dynamic of polarities. When it comes to global morality there is no such thing as right and wrong. There is no right standard other than that of unconditional love which needs to be sent out without reser-vation, and without judgement; and this is not easy to achieve when you are faced with the activities of vested interests, when you see the cruelty that man inflicts on his brother man. The God-given gift of free will allows these things to happen until a collective will inspired by a higher consciousness takes over.

Many acquisitive activities are empowered by fear, the threat of insecurity, the threat of losing whatever you feel you might have gained. The only energy that can move beyond that is unconditional love which never seeks an end result. It is never manipulative. I understand and appreciate the thought-energy put in by all those who would oppose war but, the stronger they become, the more they polarise those who support war and, therefore, in a sense, they are empowering them.

Globalisation
It is so important for all people on the planet to come together in a ground swell of co-operation, for one race or group is not superior to another; and you are already seeing the effects of the coming Aquarian age in your computerisation and internet where communication has never been such as it is today. Everyone needs to be able to access everyone. National barriers are coming down and individuals are putting greater emphasis on sharing and understanding, by honouring local cultures, honouring each other, looking at the shadow in the world and finding ways of dealing with it that avoid the need for more force and more suffering. It needs all the leaders in the world coming together and saying, "Let us work as one, let us see where there is poverty, let us see where there is inequality and see how we can gradually move forward in love".

People are fearful of the misuse of power by influential people who still carry the stigma of the lack of balance of the Piscean age. They are still carrying this image of autocracy. If one is going to look for that divinity within, one can also look for equality within, because that is part of divinity. Equality does not mean that everyone in the world has to share the same customs or have the same beliefs; but it does mean that everyone in the world needs to listen to each other, and respect each other, and share the benefits of each other's ways and means; for every culture has something to offer. The United Nations is your most affirmative attempt at globalisation, and you can see in the issues that are being fought out in that august body the problems that face your planet as a whole.

With this increasing energy of self-empowerment it is very slowly going to make it more and more difficult for these huge corporate bodies to do what they will and for rogue governments to get their way. You have had a wonderful example in your own country over genetically modified foods where quite peacefully, the people said, "We don't want them". And what has happened? There has been the biggest increase of organic foods since artificial fertilisers were introduced. More and more people are becoming interested in having non-chemicalised food and this has been brought about through peaceful means, by people applying their thought in a positive way. But they must now step up their effort.

This shift can happen in every form of industry. Look how complementary therapies are growing, because people are beginning to see that there are other ways in which they can tackle their health and take responsibility for it by encouraging health rather than destroying disease. The problems that are arising due to man's interference with the food chain are only just beginning and, in my opinion, it is becoming one of the areas in which this planet is going to have to decide its way forward.

That old mainstay, herbalism, is going to find it difficult to meet the needs of the future, even if the practitioners are using naturally grown herbs. The types of diseases that are emerging are the result of chemicalisation and the abuse of antibiotics. They have moved into areas of sophistication which will test the capacity of herbs to deal with them effectively.

The new forms of energy healing are getting under the surface of the condition and, in that regard, homeopathy has a tremendous future because the remedies of homeopathy are dependent on the frequency of vibrations. So, some of the moves in homeopathy to use materials which have been activated by vibrational means as distinct from natural means, are very much a move into the future and one which I, personally, would support. If homoeopathy can move beyond the traditions that have surrounded it in the past, then it could be a very powerful form of medicine for the future. But, like any therapy, it is not the total answer. There will never be a herb, drug or therapy that is the total answer because illness is about the imbalance that lies behind a disease allowing it to happen. That balance has to be rebuilt and re-created at physical, mental, emotional and spiritual levels.

The Transference of Power

Spiritual development is all the time moving away from the power being in the hands of the few to power being inherent in the people of the whole planet. It is about the respect of one person for another, of one way of life for another. The more people throughout the world, individually and in groups, who regularly send out thoughts of unconditional love and understanding, the more that balance and harmony will hold sway on Earth.

Yet, I could not say that, if you all do that, everything is going to be fine, for humankind as a whole still has a great deal to learn. I do see that the world is coming to a climax when all the kingdoms on it will need to make their own collective choices whether to move towards enlightenment or towards destruction. The opportunities for it to go either way are most certainly there.

There is a tremendous amount of energy around the planet at the moment, and there are many spirits who have incarnated from evolved levels of understanding that do not want to see Earth destroy itself. They are sending thought forms into the corridors of power that are designed to awaken your leaders to their responsibilities, and into troubled situations to help abort evil acts that are being planned. The future requires you to stop seeing one side as right and the other wrong. It is very easy to blame western imperialism, but it is much deeper than that really, isn't it? It is the polarisation between different forces in the world, and I see the imbalance between the masculine and the feminine as being just as prevalent in America as it is in Iraq, though in a very different way.

One of the most effective ways through is to help people to understand these polarities within themselves - the logical side and the intuitive, imaginative side - because by finding the balance within yourself you are spreading that understanding to others.

Western leaders are caught up in, and only partially understanding, the growing Aquarian energy that is bringing everything to the surface. They need to recognise that they may not always be right. What a terrible word 'right' is, when you think it is better than 'wrong'! Both are equally traps. Aquarian energy is about consensus, not only consensus between a group of people but consensus within you. It is very important to acknowledge your feelings about injustice, but it is equally important that you do not live them out. Release that anger regarding a particular situation, in a safe manner always, and then be prepared to look at it in a deeper way.

Your leaders, whether they be prime ministers or mullahs, are all fallible human beings somehow trying to find what they feel is a set of qualities that is right for them and the people that they represent. The difficulty comes when a spiritual leader or a world leader does not listen; that is the danger, when they only want to control, regardless.

A spirit from the fifth plane who decides to reject God can be a very powerful spirit of evil. You see, the shadow isn't the bottom of the ladder. It is merely the opposite polarity. If you look back over the history of your planet I am sure you can identify more than a few characters who have come from relatively high levels of evolution and have led their nations into quite awful situations; and if you look closely at their lives you will see that extreme fear has motivated their actions.

Today, many of your leaders need to be gently led back into balance through moving beyond the false security of the shadow. And, if out of this a more lenient side of Islamic fundamentalism starts to manifest, then that will help too. When I look at some of the energies at work there I think it is possible for that to happen for there is a growing willingness to listen on all sides.

Spiritual Understanding

I have referred to the need for all spiritual beliefs to be open, because today's truth may not be tomorrow's, truth is as you see it and experience it. The only absolute that I know is unconditional love, which is something that can only be understood in its totality within the highest level of wisdom itself. Everything else is mutable, it is changing all the time and it is really important that spiritual understanding changes and evolves all the time.

The true seeker of the Holy Grail is the person who acknowledges its etherealness, its untouchableness, its unconditional nature. It is something totally beyond physical life, something sublimely delicate, like a little wisp that constantly eludes you; but the honest seeker would be able to say, "I know that it is there. I can sense it. It is like the most delicate fragrance." On the other hand, the wayward shadow energies are very solid, very physical, very sexual; they encourage power over others; they involve the total exploitation of those unable to resist, often in the most bestial and brutal way.

Fear is the shadow at its most active, and collective fear can become an unstoppable force carrying many normally rational people along with it. You can see in Africa today, the most corrupt leaders are attracting many followers to them, drawn to what they think is security within the power of the mob; and then the vicious wildness of the shadow takes over. To them, it is something that is very tangible and very liberating, where they can create their own rules. It is a kind of freedom, to impose your will on others without the need for restraint. But, of course, it is a false freedom.

On a persuasive level, the more restrained national leaders, through the United Nations or other international alliances, need to take this role of mediation; for nations fear, as individuals do, and wayward governments need to be encouraged into a greater understanding of the consequences of their actions.

Surely the same applies to the healing of individuals carried away by their desire to control others. The way to deal with violence and cruelty in others is not by punishment or by ignoring it and pretending that it doesn't exist. It is by facing it, seeing it for what it is and enabling them to see the part that it plays in their own spiritual growth – so that no longer will their hearts want to hurt and take revenge. It has to come through education; it has to come through communication, through listening and by asking such people why they are violent and cruel, and what they are trying to achieve by it. "Was this part of your own background that you are now acting out on others? What are you frightened will happen if you do not behave in this way? How can we help you to deal with that fear?"

Every spirit has choice; but if you just stand there and repeatedly say Yes or No to your impulses, you are stuck. However, by finding the balance between that Yes and No, you can begin to trust in your own process, allowing your spiritual motivation to move you forward in that process. Only then will you start to succeed and evolve in an expansive, loving way.

You cannot step forward without the light and shadow being more precisely balanced, and that means understanding both aspects. It is about acknowledging the shadow within you, facing it, dealing with it; it is about acknowledging the light within you, facing it, dealing with it – only then can you understand the spiritual aspect of your being in an honest, non-egotistical way.

Remember that healing, in its broadest context, is about enabling. It is not about curing, it is not about putting right, it is certainly not about manipulation. It is about helping the spirit within a person, within a situation, to free itself from all the pressures and stresses that seem to tie it into knots. And this person should ask, "Why did it happen to me? How can it help me to move forward?"

It means you have to be disciplined; you can't follow the dictates of your shadow. So, perhaps the hardest lesson for your leaders, and the people who support them, is that the most effective way of dealing with the shadow is to forgive it, to 'turn the other cheek', which means that it is through dealing with the shadow within, that you can deal with the shadow without. This lesson is not one that humankind is fully capable of accepting at this present time but before the end of this century the ability to truly forgive will become more evident and, along with that, I would expect to see totalitarian regimes and rogue governments become a thing of the past. How quickly this is achieved will depend on every man and woman on the planet. It will depend on you.

Chapter 15

THE WAY AHEAD

Releasing the Past

The years ahead up to 2012 are going to be frenetic years, make no mistake about it. I cannot promise you an easy time, but I can reassure you that it is not predestined, it is what you make of it. Never has humankind been so poised to lift itself out of the rut of rigidity and move beyond the fear of new ideas, new tenets, new ideals. But, this can lead to a different kind of stuckness when some people react against the pressure for them to change, and enter into avenues of behaviour that are counter productive.

As a means of escape, many people are no longer prepared to accept natural forms of experience. Instead of a balanced approach to the spiritual realms through the process of learning, understanding and meditating they want instant results with the aid of drugs and artificial stimulants. Whilst the phenomena produced in this way may lend temporary mental entertainment, no true spiritual progress is ever achieved, because spiritual experience can only come with the broadening of understanding and the natural growth and development of the spirit. In seeking lazier forms of entertainment, people are allowing themselves to be channelled into a form of zombie-ism; they are forfeiting their individuality. But let us stop and ask ourselves: "To what? To whom?"

Governments remain in control when the person in the street follows their lead, so their policy is to hide the facts and discourage independent thinking. Fortunately, that is now very difficult to achieve in England where there is a very wide ranging press and television network, and strong investigative journalism. I think it is wonderful that so much is being exposed through the media because it is providing humanity with the opportunity to face it. In the past, people didn't have that choice, they didn't have that confrontation, they weren't able to see what extreme levels of negativity and cruelty can do. They went patriotically to war, without understanding what this meant. They did not see that the ruling powers were plunging the world headlong into catastrophe. This blindness is still present today in many places around your globe, but it is rapidly changing.

I think that the mass communication on this planet is its greatest chance of salvation, but it brings with it a new form of spiritual blindness. Your 'society of acquisition' encourages a relentless grasping for the new that makes it difficult to see beyond the deluge of information and opinion, to discover the simple and everlasting truths that lie behind it.

Over the last decade, the real Aquarian energies have started to be felt. So, the kind of unrest that you've had in the world has changed. Though many who have seized power for themselves have intensified their determination to hold onto it, their grip is weakening. Most of your leaders do not think of the future. They want to continue the control they have over their fellow men, no matter what. It is like an addiction; but for those who are not changing, all around them, the edifices of materialism and self-interest are crumbling, as they must, to make way for the new.

Since the 1920's there has been more and more emphasis on world government. And a dream that I would like to see realised, is that there will be a form of world government established in the next hundred years. Indeed, I would suggest that this move, which has to come from the collective wishes of humanity, is essential if the planet is going to survive. Because of humankind's behaviour and that of all the other kingdoms, the many crises on your planet today are rapidly becoming critical, particularly the escalating environmental issues which need to be dealt with on a global basis. You need to move beyond nationalism.

However, although moving beyond nationalism does not mean the obliteration of national identities, there is a trend towards this happening because of a developing centralisation of global power and responsibility. It is important that, at the other end of the scale, there is greater emphasis on individual responsibility. I do suggest that the expanding European Union needs to take note of this.

It means that the small communities will need to have their areas of autonomy within the whole. It is, as you term it on your planet, consensus management. This has to apply nationally so that in one area a country can operate within itself and yet it is a part of a world economy with understanding and spiritual openness.

Now, that may sound a very simple ideal, but for it to be achieved it means that all countries have to agree to it, and it means that all people have to agree to it. Obviously the agreement can never be total and, indeed, the needs of living in a dualistic world reflect a degree of polarised thinking. But it's about that polarised thinking becoming accepting rather than confrontational. And that is the fundamental quantum leap that society needs to take.

Every decision that is made individually and collectively is shaping the future of your planet. And these decisions relate to all the other kingdoms as well. It is interesting that the major transition that is happening represents the apex, the actual crisis, the precise meeting of the Lucifer and Mikaal energies. And, as I have said, it is not about Mikaal winning over Lucifer, it is not about good beating evil; it is about recognition that both have their place, both are necessary and both can play a part in the progression of the planet into this next age.

Such thinking has not been possible in the past. And it is only now that the planet is ready to contemplate such a huge leap of faith. It is available because the planet has earned it. It is available because the planetary consciousness has moved forward sufficiently in its understanding to be ready to embrace such a step forward.

The Challenges

Many of the challenges that humankind is facing are almost too great to contemplate. The newspapers are full of disaster and foreboding and it is easy to shut your mind off to it. "What can I do?", you say. Well, you can be apathetic, or you can make an effort by bringing kindness, fairness, tolerance and balance into your everyday life? You could push your way forward, but it is not so easy to stand back and let someone else walk before you.

How many of you can honestly admit every mistake you make? How many can really keep an open mind and not blind yourselves to the things that you do not want to see? It is beholden to each individual to do something before it is too late. I urge you to use whatever position you may hold in your life to extend kindness, fair play and tolerance *actively* to your fellow planetary citizens.

Every minute, events are taking place which are dragging the planet closer and closer towards a climax. The pollution that you find in your rivers is beginning to pollute the seas, and even these massive expanses of water could pass the point of no return, as marine life ceases to be sustainable. I wonder how many scientists understand what would happen if, due to man's selfishness, the pollution of the sea really got out of hand, and what would happen if there is a serious shortage of oxygen on this planet; this could certainly happen if humanity is not careful.

At last, people are becoming conscious of the various forms of poison that are being used to pollute the planet and the consequent mutations which they cause. But being aware isn't enough. You are faced with the powerful industrial concerns whose profit margins would be drastically cut if they were obliged to make other arrangements for the disposal of their waste products. So, that is what you are up against, my friends. The prospect of death by pollution is not a pleasant one. And those of you with children must be giving this very special thought. It really is in your hands.

The more you hurt Gaia with your irresponsible attitude towards the planet, the more it will rebound on you, not because of Gaia, but because of your own shadow that you are empowering. That is the main reason. So if, collectively, you do not heed the warnings, you will find that no longer is the soil going to say, "I don't care what pollution or effluent you pour upon me, I will just absorb it as I always have." No, in your world of action and reaction, that type of thinking is now causing a strong reaction from the nature kingdoms. No longer are you able to do what you want with your water, with your trees, for the planet itself is rising up in a loving way, not to create doom, not to create destruction, but to embrace the duality of Mikaal and Gaia.

It is inevitable that eventually a sensitivity is going to emerge, for Mikaal/Gaia is primarily about sensitivity within the natural world. So, the kind of response you are going to increasingly get is one of sensitivity, not violent reactions, not catastrophic intentions. The energies are changing, for Mikaal and Lucifer are now in close alignment. The planet is moving beyond self-destruction, into a new era of understanding and enlightenment. But, as this proceeds, it will continue to draw out of the shadow the old, fixed, ridged, fear of change. That is going to take some handling, and it can only be handled by understanding, not by force.

Certainly, you will survive far beyond 2012, but if you are going to survive harmoniously you must do something about it now, not just with words, those half-hearted promises of change, but with strong, courageous acts. The future of this planet is not rigidly predestined; it follows a certain pattern, but you have the power to shape it either way. If, through a really concerted effort, humankind were to come to its senses, then a lot of the disasters, which could still occur, will be averted. It is not too late.

In contemplating the future, I would take into consideration all of the kingdoms which play a part in the evolution of your planet. When something goes astray in your life, you have to look at what it is within you that has drawn it towards you. It is easy to condemn humanity for all the distortions in the natural order happening today but, what is it within the plant world that has drawn towards it all that negative karma, with the use of chemical pesticides and so on? All the other kingdoms share a responsibility. And looking at it in that way, one realises that there is no one person responsible, no one spirit, but only the entire planet and the billions of spirits that exist as part of physical evolution Earthwise. I think it is very important to understand this.

If we look back to Atlantis again, and at the negative states they created, we will also see that there were tremendous energies coming into that area and, with them, a great opportunity to create a balance so that Earth could move forward. But the ruling elite were locked away in their ivory towers and, by the time they realised what was happening, it was too late.

This is not unlike the problems that you find in Africa today. The world community does not want to see what is happening in its own domain. Looking at all the very challenging situations on your planet today, the biggest are certainly due to the polarisation of power. So it is the people of all nations who must take up the challenge and speak loudly and clearly of the need for collective action to bring respect and renewal into this troubled world. What we want to see, at this time, is a new harmony established that will steady the polarisation and prevent it from becoming more acute. And, when you come through, it will truly be like a global rebirth.

The Population Explosion
At this time there are influences coming from all levels of different galaxies and solar systems within your universe. There are even some energies coming from other universes, because the universes in themselves also need to find a balance between them. Earth is quite an important planet because it has very quickly attracted in energies to fuel the necessary scientific advances; and, because of the speed with which it has happened, many problems and difficulties have arisen due mainly to wisdom not keeping pace with knowledge.

In response to the quickening energies around the planet, many eager young spirits have been drawn to Earth, greatly swelling the numbers - but it is an inappropriate time for them to incarnate. So, you have this situation of wise spirits incarnating to help the planet and many new spirits who aren't really ready.

From the subtle realms, there is much pressure being put on those young spirits to understand and hold back. This will start to have an effect with many women having miscarriages and it will become increasingly difficult for the egg to be fertilised because of falling sperm count. However, we can only go so far from our side. Other measures need to be taken by all those on Earth for the full effect. Your planet needs to find, not a level of discipline so much, but a level of working together in a holistic and responsible way, to address the reasons why so many people are starving. In many cases it is through over-population.

Returning to the Individual
It all comes back to the individual in the end. The need is for you good people of Earth to accept change, and to give unselfishly of your time and good will. You have been called to service in this

momentous period that requires you to face the inevitable challenges as the past increasingly rises up to claim the present as its own. Do what you are able to do, and then a little more, for such is the severity of the situation. On the other hand, remember that to give too much credence to the shadow is to empower it.

Past and future come together in the eternal Now. Spiritual teachings such as this are of no value unless they are made use of on a day to day basis. You could start by refocusing your direction by weaving the three basic tenets of spiritual living - unconditional love, forgiveness and respect - fully and effectively into your life. But you'll need to remember that the past is not a benign thing, it always has the momentum to overpower those who turn away from the light. Indeed, the unbalanced shadow nature seems to have a will of its own when given shelter in a human psyche, although its ability to disrupt disappears in a flash when fully exposed to light. The illusory nature of the shadow breeds fear and dependency, and this needs to be addressed most urgently today, both personally and collectively, because it is contagious.

On the inner levels there are still those who belong, as they see it, to the Luciferian band, who will try to whisper seductive words in your ear. Let them know that you can see them as they really are. Be aware that those people around you, who are unable to let go of their fears, will not be seeing you as you really are when, inevitably, they feel threatened by the light emanating from within you. Expect them to do their very best to drag you down to their level, but do not condemn them, for they are exactly where they need to be.

This present phase of your destiny is a challenge, certainly, but I want you to be reassured that the strength to overcome any obstacle that life puts in your way is always available to you. It has to be. That is one of the immutable laws of this evolving universe. These teachings are intended to give you an added confidence, based on a more subtle understanding of the rays of divine purpose as they stream down to you from the Godhead.

Those ideas, promulgated by your political leaders and your religious leaders, of enemies lurking in the shadows, of sin waiting to overpower you, are born out of fear and sustained by fear, never by the truth. The truth is not their enemy, it is their saviour, and you can help them gradually to understand that. You are not here in this life to do battle with the darkness, for the shadow, if embraced in a balanced way, is an essential part of the richness of your divine nature. It sparks off your creative spirit. It is the reason for your existence as a child of this great universe.

In Conclusion

The advice we give from spirit can help to protect you from going astray, but it cannot protect you from yourself. It is not a time for building the ego. It is a time for becoming conscious that the planet is on the cusp between two great ages, and you have the responsibility of easing it forward in a safe, structured and balanced way.

Despite all the troubles erupting globally due to the acquisitive side of the human character making a 'last ditch stand', on all levels the planet is opening up to change. And even though, in some countries, politics has gone more strongly into opposing positions, and you have seen a tremendous push by the shadow to create more isolation, gradually, painfully, heads of government are beginning to recognise that all countries matter, all communities are part of the whole and, as the planet gets smaller and smaller, everyone has a much greater responsibility for others around them.

A way forward is through giving and forgiving, unconditional forgiving, letting the planet be free from the negative shackles of civilisation. That is what the Aquarian age offers each of you. It is also advisable to look to the seasons to understand how the rhythms of nature are your rhythms - when you let go of the long, hard summer, that period of dryness and drought that exemplifies the short thinking of humankind, and you pass into the softness and the warm mature colours of autumn. Winter encourages inner reflection and preparation for the new awakening that comes with Spring. Each season brings its particular qualities and energies that you can ensoul.

The good news is that, as you all move forward, these tremendous conflicting forces that have brought so much shadow into the unbalanced, authoritarian Piscean era will gradually become less pronounced. Many at the top of the tree will suddenly find the branches beneath them disappearing when they discover that they cannot manage the new consensus way. This transition is offering the integrated Mikaal/Gaia energy the opportunity to once again become resplendent on planet Earth. It will certainly happen, but there isn't going to be a sudden miracle. You won't wake up one morning to find everything has changed. You are entering into a period of gradually increasing opportunity for all those who can think in an Aquarian way, those who have chosen to open up to their wholeness, who wish to embrace unconditional thinking.

It will not be all plain sailing, it will not be a 'Golden Age', for the Aquarian nature has a shadow, too. On its own, the Aquarian concept could be a very empty one, for it is very mind centred; and so, one of the dangers is that people will react against the Piscean influence and suppress the emotional and feeling side of themselves. These qualities are needed, but in a gentle focused way. It is not just about kicking out the Piscean heritage, but about taking the best of it, particularly the warmth of it and the artistic legacy.

It could be looked at from a more holistic astrological perspective, for opposite Aquarius lies the sign of Leo, and the creative, warm-hearted Leo influence should not be forgotten as it provides a balance to the mind-focussed, scientific influence of Aquarius. In combination they draw the mind and the heart into a creative whole that is balanced and productive.

It is your responsibility, because all of you have chosen this life to stand as a beacon for the future, to produce a world that will be noted for self-responsibility, self-empowerment, self-realisation, and a great deal more tolerance. It is about honouring yourself and, through that honouring, being able to give out love and healing to your fellow beings. It is about finding your independence and acknowledging your uniqueness as an individual. And this means moving beyond the need of 'fear'.

It is a time for new ideas, new impulses, new energies, new creativity, a time to speculate, to open up, to reach out and embrace what is. You are but a few short years away from the actual transit into the Aquarian age. They are going to feel restrictive for some. They will be very unsettling, even frightening, as the old certainties are swept away.

Some of you will find yourselves in a state of unfolding magnificence, and it will be so because you have earned it by being yourselves, by understanding the Aquarian concepts of compassion and respect. This is the perfect time to allow yourself to let go and change. Isn't that wonderful? Isn't that great news?

I have spoken about you as natural 'sources of energy' because I want you to see how, in looking after yourselves and finding that balance within your own being, you are doing more to help the planet than by standing on a soap box or by being a politician. Every person on this planet matters and every thought that you think goes out into eternity for all time. So, be in charge of your thoughts, allow yourself to be uniquely creative, allow yourself to establish new levels of communication between that innermost part of yourself and the outermost part of yourself. It all comes back to honouring the divinity within all beings, including yourself.

You are moving steadily towards a climax and you have done well, for you are still here; and the light is spreading and coming into balance with the shadow. Putting it again very simply, your shadow side can only triumph while you hate it. The more you despise your weaknesses, the greater their hold over you. Let them go. Love yourself as a total being, for you are all light and all shadow. Be not afraid! Every time you give in to fear, you are feeding the shadow. Every time you allow hate to take hold, you are feeding the shadow. When you find the balance without denying the negative, then you are strengthening Mikaal and healing Lucifer.

Above all, dear friends, you need to engage the courage of your passion that will move you forward, spreading more light, more forgiveness, and more love, unconditionally and generously into the world, into the universe - and even beyond.

Not nearly The End, only The Beginning!

Other publications by the Eye of Gaza Press:

New Dimensions in Healing
H-A through the mediumship of Tony Neate

The new millennium requires widened concepts and subtler, deeper ways of healing. This book breaks fresh ground, exploring advanced specialist healing modalities. It recommends the rigorous development of both the psychic and spiritual selves. It gives clear advice on many ways of reaching the cause of the illness. Tony was chair of the Holistic Council for cancer, and the College of Healing. He also co-founded the Confederation of Healing Organisations.

IBSN 1 873545 04 5 148 pp   RRP UK £8.99 USA $15.95

Gifts of the Spirit: Trance Channelling
Channelled through Maisie Besant & Greg Branson

Today many people are claiming to be a channel for higher wisdom, but it requires rigorous training. The quality and depth of the transmission is completely dependant on motive, and without a high degree of humility and readiness, distortions can easily occur which are not always easy to pick. The book carefully explains what is going on behind the scenes of trance and it details the various kinds of corruption of the gifts and how they come about. It also explains how to stay focussed on the truth.

ISBN 1 873545 02 9   108 pp   RRP UK £5.99

The Spirit Within
Chan, though the Trance Mediumship of Ivy Northage

For over 50 years Ivy Northage has been a widely respected and much loved deep trance medium and her spirit guide, Chan, has an understanding of the purpose of life that is far beyond our limited human vision. His approach is always practical, sensible and fully comprehensive, and he unfolds it with an uncompromising intellectual rigour that encourages us to take a deep focussed look at our attitudes and motives.

IBSN 1 873545 03 7   148 pp   RRP UK £7.99 USA $14.95

The Guide Book
H-A through the mediumship of Tony Neate

H-A paints an exciting picture of life as it could be on planet Earth and the important role that each of us individually can play at this crucial planetary moment. He speaks directly to us and gives us hope. This book is an introduction to many of the concepts that he explores in much more depth in his other books. It is for anyone, regardless of background or religion, who are interested in exploring spiritual values and their application in daily life.

ISBN 0 946551 35 9   182pp   RRP £6.50

"H-A presents ideas which I personally had not come across before and are well worth pondering. His words have the ring of authority and of truth."

Light Magazine.

"H-A gives guidance, advice and teaching, but it is notable that he never enforces his opinion and always encourages each person to make their own decisions. It is a really creative process of education."

Sir George Trevelyan BT

Serial Consciousness
Johosephat speaking through Greg Branson

Much has been written about re-incarnation but this teaching is quite revolutionary. The guide prompts us to look into what is happening behind the scenes when a past life consciousness begins to influence the present. He will convincingly show that with most people the pattern of incarnations inter-relate in a much more complex way than is usually assumed. Knowing one past life is of limited use if you don't know how that life came to be the way it was. Each one is based in an archetypal flow that is consistent and progressive through all lives no matter which sex body is being inhabited. The guide will also explain how members of a group-soul relate and why there are such conflicts in the world today due to past karma.

ISBN 1 873545 06 1   To be published September 2009

Some useful contacts:

Helios School of Healing, Phone: 0207 713 7120
116 Judd Street, heliosc@dialstart.net
London, WC1H 9NS www.helioshealth.org.uk

School of Channelling, Phone: 01684 311345
PO Box 109, info@schoolofchannelling.co.uk
Worcester WR9 0ZY www.schoolofchannelling.co.uk

College of Healing, Phone & Fax: 01295 26141
PO Box 568 Collegeofhealing@aol.com
Banbury, www.collegeofhealing.org
Oxon, OX16 6AW

Tony Neate Phone: 01684 893697
10 Hatley Court tony-neate@tiscali.co.uk
81 Albert Road South, www.channelling-online.com
Worcs, WR14 3DX

Greg Branson Phone: 0207 713 7159
45c St Augustine's Road, heliosc@dialstart.net
London, NW1 9RL www.heliosenlighten.org

Spirit Release Foundation
Frida Siton Phone: 01684 560725
Myrtles, Como Road, fridamaria@spiritrelease.com
Malvern, WR14 3TH www.spiritrelease.com